Write Beside Them

Praise for Penny Kittle and *Write Beside Them*

Sometimes while reading Write Beside Them *I smiled. Sometimes I nodded. Once, I was so moved by Kittle's story, her student's courage, and our profession, that my eyes filled with tears. Woven through her vivid descriptions and the persuasive explanations of her teaching practice, Kittle draws indelible portraits of her students. They, and the author's wisdom and compelling voice, make this book unforgettable. You'll have new ways to think about teaching and writing. You'll have effective strategies to try out in your classroom.*

—**Tom Romano**
Author of *Zigzag* and *Blending Genre, Altering Style*

Penny Kittle joins the ranks of such wise leaders as Don Graves, Don Murray, and Nancie Atwell with this book, showing us that in an era of standards, one can still create real opportunities to write—and to learn.

—**Jim Burke**
Author of *The English Teacher's Companion*, Third Edition

Write Beside Them

risk, voice, and clarity in high school writing

Penny Kittle

HEINEMANN
Portsmouth, NH

Heinemann
361 Hanover Street
Portsmouth, NH 03801–3912
www.heinemann.com

Offices and agents throughout the world

The author and publisher wish to thank those who have generously given permission to reprint
borrowed material:

"Kristen" by Penny Kittle. From *Voices from the Middle*, March 2008, Volume 15, Issue 3. Copyright ©
2008 by the National Council of Teachers of English. Used with permission.

"Warrant Article #7" (March, 2006) and "What Forty Cents Can Buy You" (October, 2003) by
Penny Kittle. From *The Conway Daily Sun*. Reprinted by permission of *The Conway Daily Sun*.

"Letter to the Editor" (March, 2007) by Logan Dwight. From *The Conway Daily Sun*. Reprinted by
permission of The Conway Daily Sun and Logan Dwight.

Library of Congress Cataloging-in-Publication Data
Kittle, Penny.
   Write beside them : risk, voice, and clarity in high school writing / Penny Kittle.
      p. cm.
   Includes bibliographical references and index.
   ISBN-13: 978-0-325-01097-7 (pbk.)
   ISBN-10: 0-325-01097-8 (pbk.)
   1. English language—Composition and exercises—Study and teaching (Secondary).
2. Creative writing (Secondary education). I. Title.

LB1631.K54 2008
80'.0420712—DC22   2007047357

Editor: Lisa Luedeke
Production: Lynne Costa
Cover design: Shawn Girsberger
Cover photographs: Theresa Sires
Interior design: Joni Doherty
Typesetter: Valerie Levy / Drawing Board Studios
Manufacturing: Steve Bernier

Printed in the United States of America on acid-free paper
17 16 15 14 13 VP 5 6 7 8 9

Gary Millen
1952–2006.

He was devoted to the students
at Kennett High School for three decades.

Gary asked difficult questions,
pestered me for answers,
and made me laugh.
He made me a better teacher
and a better person.
Rest in peace, my friend.

Emma McLeavey-Weeder, Gary Millen, Nicole Veilleux

Contents

PART FOUR: THINKING THROUGH GENRE

Acknowledgments

All my life I have worked with youth.
I have begged for them and fought for them and lived for them and in them.
My story is their story.

—MARY MCLEOD BETHUNE

I've had lots of support in the writing of this book. I want to first thank my students: present and past. Every one of you has brought gifts to my life. Many continue to sustain me. I still marvel at the writing you've done, the honesty and commitment you've shown, and the risks you were willing to take. Thank you for giving me work I can share with others and for showing up each day willing to try. Go and live the lives you've imagined.

My family surrounds me with love and respect. I couldn't write without them. My son, Cam, was a student in my writing class last spring. He let me inside his writing process and inside several remarkable texts. His attention and support in class was a gift I won't forget, and while his intelligence improved my teaching at several points, it was his wit that brightened the room. My daughter, Hannah, is a marvelous, smart writer, and I have learned much about feedback through working with her. She wraps herself around a book; I want to write well enough to be that book. My husband, Pat, is my best friend. He asks important questions and supports my thinking. He brings oatmeal with brown sugar to my desk on Saturday morning and listens as I write out loud on our walks through the neighborhood. Best of all, he says, "I don't want to see you leave this couch all day today; just write," when he knows I'm feeling the pressure of a deadline.

I want to thank all of you who listened to my presentations at conferences and in school districts over the last few years. Your laughter and clear thinking kept me energized. Your tough questions helped me articulate my thinking, and it led to many of the sections in this book. Thank you for asking and for listening as I worked through an answer. I meet such incredible teachers in every state at every grade level, from those just beginning this work to those who have been in it for decades. The teachers I know are rigorous and kind, determined and deliberate in teaching. The teachers I know do not leave children behind. Your fingerprints are on this book. Keep asking the tough questions, and then go and write your own book—I know you have much to teach me.

I would also like to thank:

Don Graves—my friend and my mentor. Your loving friendship is a constant in my life. Thank you for walks in the woods behind your house and deep talk. Thank you for being the generous spirit of twin crafts: teaching and writing. Thank you for the books you place in my hands, the drafts you share of your poetry, the music and photos you offer after every grand excursion. I learn in your shadow, and it is warm here beside you.

Don Murray—for help with the first drafts of my thinking for this book and for your friendship. Your writing was brave and simple and true. Thank you for the spring course, S.O.F.T., and your phone calls. I have only watched one person compose a text in front of me and it was you. I miss you.

Tom Newkirk—for the boys and literacy course at UNH. Thanks for asking such important questions, for encouraging me to find answers to my own, and for asking us all to pay attention to the emotional life of boys in our classrooms. As a mother of a son, I thank you.

Tom Romano—for hurried conversations and funny emails, for your passion and generosity and friendship, for making your writing process transparent and sharing the results. And last, for your work in multigenre, which has given me some of my most precious teaching moments.

Jim Burke—for being the dynamic, where-the-hell-do-you-find-the-time Superteacher that keeps me running just to watch you sprint ahead. Your taunting emails made me howl with laughter. One warning: Someday we shall meet on the tennis court, Jim, and I will take you out.

Kylene Beers—it all goes back to you, baby. I know I've thanked you before, but I have to here because publishing that first piece I wrote, "Writing Giants, Columbine, and the Queen of Route 16" in *Voices from the Middle* made me believe I was writer. And from that belief came this book. You are the smart, funny professional we all strive to be in this work and your vision sustains so many of us. Thank you.

Lois Bridges—I miss you, editor and friend. Your understanding of what I wanted to say and how I might say it helped me see this book before it was. You held my hand as I made those first halting steps as a writer. I find myself still reaching for your guidance.

Heinemann—Angela Dion, Lesa Scott, Vicki Boyd, and Leigh Peake: for being smart, dynamic professionals and for the welcome and enthusiasm for writing and teaching that I feel from each of you.

Kevin Carlson—thank you for all of the time and enthusiasm you brought to filming and editing this project. Your talent with image is remarkable. Thank you for treating my classroom with such care and each of my students with such respect.

Lisa Luedeke—thank you for a million Post-its. My book became stronger because you took the time to dig for what mattered and helped me say what I couldn't quite articulate.

Lynne Costa—for your attention to all the fine details of production. Thank you!

Carrie Costello, Ed Fayle, Ryan Mahan: the writers—Here we are four books later. You can all write circles around me: It's about time the rest of the world found out.

Jack Loynd, Kevin Richard, Steve Woodcock, Neal Moylan, Amy Burnap—You are what it means to care enough to get the work done for every kid, every time. I admire your honesty and compassion more than I say.

Jason Wood—for long conversations about literature and writing and for sharing your passion for this work.

And as always, to my parents, Ted and Barbara Ostrem—You are storytellers and cheerleaders. Thank you for supporting all I do.

Thanks to the New Hampshire Writers' Project out of Southern New Hampshire University. The quick write exercise in Chapter 5 first appeared in *NH Writer*, a publication of the New Hampshire Writers' Project.

Foreword

*I*n this book Penny Kittle speaks of the Durham "Dons" (Murray and Graves) who have inspired her. The two Dons—which makes it sound like some kind of mafia family, which at times it has felt like, with various *capos* and *consiglieres* making their pilgrimages to Mill Pond Road or to the famous corner table at the Bagelry where Don Murray held court. In the summer there would be Tom Romano, such an addict of Newick's seafood that we all think he should be issued a punch card—buy four lobsters, and your fifth one is free. Ralph Fletcher would wander in to talk baseball and writing; Linda Rief could be spotted making an after-school trip to the Durham Market Place (alias "The Dump"), where she might bump into Boston College Writing Director Lad Tobin. (Linda taught most of our kids.) And so on.

In recent years Penny Kittle would join this group, the Queen of Route 16, arriving in her Cooper Mini, a good likelihood that there was a speeding ticket in the glove compartment. A tall woman, she would extract herself from the Cooper with the grace of the athlete she still is, and join us to talk about writing and teaching. We all knew she was working on a BIG book about writing, and we had read her early work, marveling at her storytelling skill. But nothing had prepared us for the book you are now holding. Nothing.

I finished reading it this afternoon, and I am still in its spell. It touches a spot in me that few books of any kind can reach, and I feel at a loss to explain this effect. There is, to be sure, the practical help it will give to high school writing teachers—her careful delineation of a high school curriculum, her use of free writes to help students find topics, her insightful descriptions of her conferences, and most powerfully, the way she uses mentor texts and insights from her own writing process. Many of these practices have been described by others (the Dons, Romano, Nancie Atwell, Lucy Calkins, Carl Anderson, Kim Stafford, Randy Bomer, Katie Wood Ray, and others), and she doesn't cover up her borrowings. But she transforms as she assimilates, a process described by the great essayist Montaigne in an unforgettable metaphor:

Bees ransack flowers here and flowers there; but then they make their own honey, which is entirely theirs and no longer thyme or marjoram. Similarly the boy will transform his borrowing; he will confound their forms so that the end-product is entirely his. . . .

In reading this book, one feels this ransacking quality; Penny is open to the best practice of the past thirty years, melding it all into an approach that is truly her own.

This book will also be an excellent antidote to at least two trends in writing instruction. She shows beyond dispute that effective writing instruction cannot follow any formula, be packaged into any rubric, fit some invariable plan—and, as we all know, these systems and packages are everywhere, seductively promising to take weight off the teacher's back. I think this book also raises questions about the place of a writing class in high school. The course she describes is, keep this in mind, a *senior elective*, shoehorned into the English curriculum. And why shouldn't all students get this rich opportunity? The answer is that writing still remains colonized in literature classes. With the wide world to explain and explore, why should literary analysis dominate high school writing? When will writing get parity with literature?

She has titled her book *Write Beside Them*, and it took me almost to the end of my reading to pick up the double meaning—and that may be the key to the power of this book. She *writes beside* her students, about complex issues in her life, among them a haunting memory of the death of a friend in a car accident (I literally had to stop reading for a while after that piece). In doing so she clearly models techniques but more important, she creates emotional space for students to write about what matters to them. The individual student portraits she creates for the book will inspire—and break your heart.

And she is right beside them, even in the photographs throughout the book, at their side—a listener, advocate, coach, sometimes comedian, sometimes drill sergeant. She is interested in the lives they lead and deeply respectful of the weight adolescents sometimes carry. She shows us how to break through the gridlock, those treaties of nonengagement so common in high schools. She understands that there is no reason for students to engage with school if they see no purpose in what they are taught, no connection to their lives.

I am writing this foreword on a December day, with snow falling, as it did a year ago when Don Murray passed away. My office actually looks out on his former house (like I say, Durham is a small place). The house has been repainted a pastel purple that does not exist in nature. What I wouldn't give for five minutes of Minnie Mae Murray's unvarnished commentary on the color choice. So many conversations that can't happen.

I wish Don could have read this book in its finished form and felt his animating spirit in it. When he read something really great, he often wouldn't say much. He'd just give his giant head a shake of amazement, a seal of approval to indicate it was the real deal, that it had heart and craft. He would have loved this book.

And so will you.

—*Tom Newkirk*
December 2007

PART ONE
FOUNDATIONS

CHAPTER ONE
It's a Wonderful Life

I love writing.
I love the swirl and swing of words as they tangle with human emotions.

—James Michener

I awake before dawn. It's 4:45 A.M. and I won't be returning to sleep. My mind buzzes with plans for the day: a poem by Billy Collins, a sketch in our writer's notebooks, listening to two students read recently completed pieces, time to write. I'm ready before I need to be. I can't wait; and it's March even. It's true that I'm a bit of a caffeine hound, but the bigger truth is that teaching writing is a joyful way to spend my days.

I'm forty-five. If you'd told me in my first year of teaching that I'd feel this way so many years and students and grade levels and states later, I'd have laughed that snorting kind of laugh that people find amusing. But I'm content here in this land of teenagers. I sing on my way to work. I'll be writing with my students today: composing, rehearsing, thinking, crafting. I'll be playing with words in a line, listening to students try to make sense of experience, and I'll be surprised to look up and realize we're out of time.

This book is about teaching writing and the gritty particulars of teaching adolescents. But it is also the planning, the thinking, the writing, the journey: all I've been putting into my teaching for the last two decades. This is the book I wanted when I was first given ninth graders and a list of novels to teach. This is a book of vision and hope and joy, but it is also a book of genre units and minilessons and actual conferences with students.

I've been fascinated by the teaching of writing for years. I've read many books and listened to many brilliant people, but sometimes I feel I've learned only one thing: If you want better writers, all of the power lies within *you*. It's all about teaching. In study after study when researchers took all of the factors that can impact student achievement—from parental income to school resources to parental support to per pupil spending in a school district—the factor that had a greater impact than all of the others *combined* was the effectiveness of the classroom teacher.

By saying that, I do not discount the impact those other factors do have on our classrooms and our students, but simply to remind you that your skills and expertise are more powerful. In my current work as a K–12 literacy coach in the poorest area of our county in New Hampshire, we have real challenges. Some students live in homes with dirt floors. One parent said to me, "Why should she graduate from this place? None of us ever did." We can't fix that attitude, but we also can't despair, throw up our hands, or ever say "There's nothing I can do," because teachers are more powerful than parent pressure, any textbook, workbook, curricula, or central office directive. Teachers are more powerful than The Elementary and Secondary Education Act, otherwise known as No Child Left Behind. Teachers make the difference, not tests. What power—what opportunity—lies in our hands.

> *"Trust the process. If the process is sound, the product improves."*
> —WILLIAM ZINSSER

Because I know this, standardized tests will not rule my world. Politicians will not tell me how to do my job. I've read the research; I know what matters. My teaching of writing rests on the work Don Murray began in the '60s in college classrooms and Don Graves continued in the '70s in elementary classrooms. In the last ten years we've seen a push toward uniformity and product-centered standards, but if we shift back to what the Dons discovered is most important in the teaching of writing, writing improves. We have to focus on the process of writing and help students discover its power to improve their work.

Writing is the "neglected R" according to the National Writing Panel Report (CEEB 2003). Our students are not writing well, not writing enough. I see my colleagues scrambling to get students to write and revise, and frankly, to care. But despair creeps upon teachers like water advances on the sand. Why aren't students motivated? Why won't they revise? How come after all the time I put into commenting on that paper, he just turns to the last page to find the grade?

If you ask them, they'll tell you. We aren't tapping into their passions. Last fall one of my former students, Patrick Haine, went to the University of New Hampshire to major in writing. In his freshman composition class he was asked to write his literacy biography. He wrote about his love affair with books as a child, and then this:

My childhood love of books fizzled when I entered junior high—all of a sudden I was in an environment where I had hours and hours of required reading, so much home-work about boring subjects that I had no time to read what I wanted to read. With this went the writing—we never had "freewrite" time anymore, I always had to try to write what the teacher wanted, the "right" thing, what needed to be done for the grade. Creativity was gone.

This repression of creativity continued until my senior year in high school. I walked into my Essay Writing class expecting more of the same: "That's the *wrong* way to write, write like *this*, we'll be reading what we *have* to read!" I was dead wrong.

Penny Kittle was my tall, goofy, funny teacher who knew what she was talk-ing about. This one had actually written books—a published author! I expected the worst—"She must know the right way to write," I thought in my head. But no. For 10 minutes out of each 90 minute class, we read a book. *Any book.* A comic book, magazine, anything. You could read Aldous Huxley or Roald Dahl or Stephen King or Carl Jung. And when we wrote, it was about what we wanted to write about. "Defend an opinion," not "Explain why Nathaniel Hawthorne yada yada yada . . ." Mrs. Kittle emphasized embracing your *own* literacy; owning what you write, reading what you want. This experience was so new and fresh to me . . . but yet it reminded me . . . of how I'd felt as a kid. I read for fun, I wrote because I wanted to. This class renewed my excitement, my feel for writing and that childlike wonder that I used to feel. It was as if when I entered seventh grade, someone boarded up all my creativity and ideas, dammed up that huge stream of consciousness and personality. When I entered Essay Writing, that dam exploded, and all those ideas and thoughts and observations and my yearning to read and write and experience the world like I once did with that joy of being a kid shot out of my head and into the pages and into my life . . . I felt good again.

When Pat sent this to me one afternoon I had only one thing to say. Goofy?

Actually, I told him how hard it is for teachers to hang on to what they know is right about teaching when criticism comes from every corner and test scores get the most attention in town. Nurturing a creative spirit and unleashing a vibrant mind is every teacher's dream; we just get constrained by government mandates and decisions we can't control. It's not an excuse; it's life in too many of our schools. I'm just too old to take it anymore. I won't be ruled by tests I don't believe in. I won't be told how to teach writing by people who never write.

My students and I are the most powerful forces in my classroom, not the tests. I'm learning every day, every class, with every student. They still drive my teaching, planning, and thinking. I've heard lots of ideas on how to teach writing, seen plenty of curriculum guides and model writing units to transplant to the copy machine, but for all of those experts, I'm still the one who knows my students best. I stand today on the discoveries of Don Murray, Don Graves, Lucy Calkins, Tom Newkirk, Nancie Atwell, Linda Rief, Katie Wood Ray, Randy Bomer, and Tom Romano as well as the hundreds of colleagues I've listened to at conferences and whose writing I've admired from afar. Each day I just try to get a little closer to what my students need.

We wrestle with writing together in a high school writing workshop. Come inside.

CHAPTER TWO
This I Believe

I may not be there yet, but I'm closer than I was yesterday.

—AUTHOR UNKNOWN

Jessica stopped by last week. She's finished her two-year degree in fire safety at a college nearby. She's so much older than I remember. Of course, she was thirteen when I taught her. I couldn't chat: I was late for a meeting. That afternoon when I returned to my office there was a sticky note stuck to my computer asking if I had any of her old writings. What is it she remembers? Something in her process stayed with her, an imprint of pleasure or energy or something.

I remember May Day with her class so distinctly. I brought in carnations in buckets and put them on their tables. The room was filled with that spicy fragrance and color—rich reds, purples, yellows. We wrote flower memories. I thought the students would write about spring, but so many wrote of a time when flowers stood silent at a moment that mattered. Many wrote of funerals; others of family celebrations. They wrote past our allotted time; they wanted to share.

I wrote about Mike getting me roses on my sixteenth birthday. I had fun recalling that memory: how awkward I was that fall as a junior in high school, standing at his locker in my cheerleading uniform, afraid Mike wanted to be more than friends. I saw my students' alert, curious faces as I read my writing, as I talked to them like a human being, not a "teacher."

I looked at what I'd written and thought, how could I make this better?

I didn't know. I really had *no idea*.

I didn't even know where to turn: I suddenly wanted to make the writing represent that moment in my life and I couldn't. I felt a little nauseous as I realized with sudden clarity that what I had been teaching my students for weeks was of no help.

We had been marveling at short stories and novels, but I had focused my students on the topics writers chose to illuminate. I thought finding a magical topic would result in great writing for the class; I didn't consider taking a glimmer like this one, a fragment of interest to me, and showing my students how I might shape it and massage it, trusting the process to lead me to the writing I desired. Of course I couldn't trust the writing process then: I wasn't a writer. I had never waded into that water, believing the sand would hold me.

And so we set aside our free writing and moved on to other English stuff like reading great literature and discussing it. I never went back to those journal pages we shared; I never felt the energy of that day again. There was so much I could have accomplished by building on that moment, if only I was willing to *not* know the answer in front of my students; if only I was willing to model thinking in its raw form.

I'm sorry, Jessica, I wasn't the teacher I could have been for you.

It took another six months and the start of another school year to nudge me closer. Trying to recapture that May Day energy, I wrote every day for a few minutes during our free-writing time. And sometimes I shared it with students. Often it was useless scribblings or venting . . . play time. Now, stay with me: I think that play is good for writers—useful and necessary. It just isn't enough for students or for the teacher. Free-write journals are a beginning, but they don't go deep enough into process to be useful modeling. We have to show how those unformed ideas can be developed to create clarity. The writer's notebook isn't enough—in fact, it's a real waste of time—if all that writing just fills space at the start of class and neither the students nor the teacher ever sees how those entries can be used to find something meaningful to write about.

The only way to make that connection is to show them. For years I had expected my students to go on swimming without me while I barked orders from my chaise lounge. I told myself I had no other choice, for I had too many other things to be doing: important, busy things like managing workshop and conferring with students. I had lots of ideas to share in those conferences, but no idea if they'd really work with writing—or even if they'd help the writer. My teaching was all tell, no show.

I finally dove into the water one afternoon at home. I had no intention of sharing what I was writing with kids, but I found something I needed to say and I decided to write. (This story is told in a piece I wrote for *Voices from the Middle* called "Writing Giants, Columbine, and the Queen of Route 16," Vol. 9 No. 1.) Once I was in, the landscape changed. In bold, important ways, my classroom and my teaching changed.

I now believe you really can't teach writing well unless you write yourself. I wouldn't give my son the keys to our Subaru if I hadn't driven beside him talking through my decisions at each turn and then gripped the dashboard as he tried it, cruising along the back roads of Conway talking through the skills he was learning to use. He needed me to show him first. We don't learn many things well just by following directions. We have to ride together. The apprenticeship with a master in the field is still the best model for learning.

But I've also found out something kind of scary and disheartening about this theory. You can be a writer and a teacher and still not teach much if you aren't tremendously organized. If you aren't as driven to teach and nurture writers as writing demands, then you'll lose kids who need all of the scaffolding that brings the power of writing well within their reach. Organization leads struggling writers to competence. Writing teachers must be writers and they must be master teachers. When the two come together, kids learn fast. That's right, fast. All kids learn with patience, empathy, and good instruction. Kids write remarkably better in a few weeks with good instruction. But the instruction has to come during the process of creating the piece, not in polishing the product, or nothing changes. That's a crucial error I was making for years.

I got up this morning and sat down to write my "fifteen minutes a day," as Donald Murray instructed. I wrote a few ideas in my notebook, an entry on weather and school shootings and teaching, and then I was off to walk my dogs and get on with my day. Today it was all the writing I had. But as I walked my neighborhood listening to woodpeckers in the trees above, admiring the buds that had burst forth with the rain the night before, and feeling spring sun on my scalp, I thought about writing. I continued to play with a response to a school shooting that filled the news. I thought about what I had to say as a teacher of adolescents in a school much like the one all over the news. I was rehearsing, an almost effortless part of my writing process that will lead me further in my writing tomorrow.

I believe that the only way I'm going to be able to teach writing tomorrow is because I did it today. In fact, I believe that reading this book is a waste of your time if you aren't going to write as well: Important things will not change in your classroom until you do. I believe you can't tell kids how to write; you have to show them what writers do. I believe you have to be a writer, no matter how stumbling and unformed that process is for you; it's essential to your work as a teacher of writing. If we don't model smart thinking in writing, our students will write like kids who've read the driver's manual but still hit the curve too fast and just about send us to the hospital. There's no grace in beginning drivers and without a good coach showing them the moves, they don't improve much. Neither do writers.

You are the most important writer in the room. I had read this, but for years and years I didn't write. I had three reasons:

1. *I wasn't a writer.* I read all of those books from Don Murray and Don Graves and I would think, "Sure, fine, you're a writer, of course you write with your students. I can't do it. I'm not a writer."

2. *I couldn't see how it would matter if I wrote with students.* There were dozens of books in my classroom, so students certainly didn't need me when they had Sandra Cisneros and Harper Lee and F. Scott Fitzgerald.

3. *I didn't understand what to model and how.* I had never seen anyone write anything—or talk about how they did it—so I wasn't ready to teach from my writing. There was no one showing me how to do it—just these legends from faraway places like Nancie Atwell in Boothbay Harbor, Maine, or the mighty Tom Newkirk at the University of New Hampshire, or Randy Bomer's years at the Teachers College Writing Project—and I just didn't trust those people to understand my students in my setting.

Perhaps you've felt this way. But I was wrong. I only learned this because I finally tried it. You know how teachers can just shut their doors and teach when they want to try something or just get a little peace? I shut my door and pulled out a draft of an editorial about my nephew who had dropped out of school—a piece I cared a great deal about—and started talking to my eighth graders. And everything changed. Their attention was immediate and full on. They were with me. They wanted to hear this real story from my life, they wanted to see how I was writing it, and they wanted to write their own. I had no idea sharing my process could be that powerful.

As I stumbled along through drafting that commentary, I discovered that all three of my reasons were wrong.

1. I wasn't supposed to *be a writer*—just someone trying to write—like them. In fact, I was a better model because my hesitations and insecurities were just like theirs. It was such a relief to know I didn't have to be good at it; just trying it was enough.

2. All of those authors of books in my room were great models of *product*, but not *process*. That was my job. Since I didn't have to create great products, the pressure was off. As Katie Wood Ray says, "You just have to write a little bit better than they do." I could do that. I finally understood that "model" was a verb. I wasn't creating a model, I *was* the model—which made all the difference.

3. Doing the writing taught me what to teach. It *was* that simple. I knew what my writers needed because I was inside the process of writing the genre we were studying. It actually became much easier to plan for my workshop each day.

And now I can't stop talking about it . . . my great *discovery* of teaching writing that has been documented in the research for the last thirty years. I know I can't take credit for any of this thinking, but I will share my understanding of that theory with you because it makes a difference in my teaching. My students write well. They write with passion. I have eighteen weeks with an eclectic blend of students from our valedictorian to students in the career-technical program or students with no plans for college, and yet they all are remarkably better writers at the end of the semester.

I believe writing with students will keep me teaching. It's joyful work to shape my memories, ideas, and passions into texts I can learn and teach from. It makes me present in my work today; it feeds that creative fire I had as a child. When I took that journal entry on flowers to my writing workshop years later, I sketched a plan on the overhead projector and asked students to help me tell a story of being sixteen and awkward around boys. They were with me; the room lit up with ideas. When I finished my modeling, they were ready to write.

It doesn't get any better than that.

CHAPTER THREE

How Writing Units Work Together
A Scaffold of Writing Instruction

MY HIGH SCHOOL COMMUNITY

I teach in a comprehensive public high school in rural New Hampshire. We have about 950 students in grades nine through twelve, and most come from the eight towns that make up our community in an area known locally as "the valley." Some ride the bus an hour or more each way to come to school. Generations from this area have attended Kennett High School, and it has many rich traditions. We have great economic diversity in the student body, but little ethnic diversity. Students excel in career and technical programs, athletics and academics. Some do not succeed. While I am writing this, our school has the highest drop-out rate in the state. We have all of the problems that most public schools wrestle with. Some students come to the valley after being expelled from other districts; some students live in families without enough to eat, living in campgrounds even in the midst of winter. We also have students with every opportunity and support heading to the most selective colleges. I think we're typical: We struggle with teacher turnover and low salaries. We have a passionate principal who is committed to improvement, and we have great hope for our future.

Our school has always named a valedictorian and salutatorian, ranked students according to academic success, and offered courses at three levels: general, college-prep, and advanced. There are AP courses and students who go on to Dartmouth; there are students who suffer in general classes all day with similarly unmotivated and frustrated peers. In the mix of electives offered to seniors sits our writing course. Most students have just completed American Literature as juniors and some take AP Literature one semester as seniors and writing another. Or they take journalism one semester and writing another. Or they reluctantly take writing only to meet their senior English requirement. We do not level this writing course and encourage all students to feel welcome. We usually have a mix of college-prep and advanced students. Many students have told me it is the first time they've had class together in four years. This creates a particular challenge for our workshop community, but it also allows for an eclectic mix of experiences, values, and abilities. And truthfully, each semester some of the best writers in the room are CP students. There is a romance in our country with perceived challenge in courses; I just don't buy it. I believe every student needs challenge and too many of our lower-level courses are holding cells for the worst behaviors and least academically rigorous experiences. Writing is rigorous. Every student should write every day and continue to improve throughout high school. Too many simply do as little as possible and are allowed to continue. It is rare when a student is ever asked to rewrite a paper. Senior year we take writing development very seriously and devote a semester to it.

We use the writing scaffold of skills (see Figure 3.1) to identify how skills build upon each other to lead students to complex forms for their ideas. We divide our aims into process skills and experiences as well as product expectations.

PROCESS

Writing is a process and by focusing on the process and habits of a writer, writing improves. With the increasing focus on standardized tests in our country, a student can develop habits that do not lead to deep thinking about structure and idea. Even grammar suffers as a student learns all skills on a superficial level, with the product in mind, instead of learning how to use the process to give form to a story, idea, or opinion and then to craft the very structure of a paragraph using a complex understanding of the rules that govern written language to determine how the piece will be read by others.

Throughout the semester of writing I encourage students to find their own writing process for each piece, to use rehearsal and planning within a writer's notebook to find ideas, to talk about their thinking with peers and the teacher, and to revise their writing for increased clarity and effectiveness. I teach students to read like writers, to study model texts, and to experiment with forms in imitation. This is how writers work.

PRODUCTS

We begin with story because it is the most accessible form for writers. It relies on the student's experiences. Throughout high school students write about topics to demonstrate their understanding of something and that understanding is most often incomplete, fractured, recent, unsure. It is hard to write with confidence when the subject is murky. There are countries, events, and conflicts to summarize or analyze in social studies, and they are all a bit distant from the everyday life of a teenager. There are novels set in time periods that seem ancient to kids today—even the Vietnam War is distant history to them—and so writ-

Writing: increasing skills and learning the habits of a writer

Process

what writers need	the writing conference	research	collaboration	self-reflection
conditions of a workshop	asking for feedback	group response	negotiation	identify growth
how writers choose topics	class conferences	study text models	revision	find weaknesses
rereading your writing	revision	multiple drafts	rehearsal	choose best work
	imagine the reader	revision for focus	find form for ideas	
			synchronicity of genres	

Skills

using voice	read like a writer	credible evidence	command of detail	annotate
sensory details	text study & annotation	clarity of claim	skillful, fluid dialogue	proficiency
dialogue	story + 'so what?'	acknowledge other side	voice: narrator	in a wide range
show don't tell	rereading your work	anticipate Q & respond	subtlety with word choice	of skills
a lead that hooks readers	scenes work together	logical, coherent structure	clarity & precision	
sentence structure	controlling time in a story	ethos: credible, smart voice	use of flashbacks	
possessive nouns	zoom in/zoom past	summarizing facts	character development	
slow down time	developing theme	interpretation & elaboration	use of art/sketching/concrete poetry	
			line breaks in poetry	

Product

snapshot moment	narrative	extended narrative	argument	commentary Op-Ed	fiction	multi-genre research	final portfolio

FIGURE 3.1

ing about those books, pulling on a cloak of authority about them, is a stretch. And even in science, students complete a lab to extract DNA in biology, but they are still learning terms and how biology works, so writing well about what they've discovered is unlikely, or at best, a repeat from notes recorded in class. Authority on a topic brings confidence. A confident voice matters in writing. We tell students to "know your topic: write what you know," yet students perform in subjects they barely understand for most of the school day.

When my colleagues and I organized our writing course we decided to begin with story. We wanted authority in a student's voice and confidence on the page first. Our ramp of skills (see Figure 3.1) begins small, with a scene, a moment, and the choice of moments is wide open. I echo Randy Bomer to my students, "You have to select, out of all the possible seconds in your life, some experience that formed you. We are the stories we tell" (Bomer 1995, 156). We ask students to slow down time through sensory details, dialogue, and "show don't tell." We spend most of our energy on setting up our workshop as a happy, productive place (Ray 2004) where writers take risks and rely on each other to produce the best work they can.

We take that understanding and add several skills or techniques to our first unit on story. We teach storyboarding (Roger Essley's tellingboards) as a way to play with an idea before writing it. We teach students how to control time in their story, how to connect several scenes under a theme, or "so what?" (Atwell 2002), of the story. We continue to use study texts to inform our understanding of structure, organization, and idea. Students continue to learn to read like writers and imagine how they can take their understanding of an author's craft and apply it to their own idea. We move the understanding of narrative beyond simple chronology. We encourage revision and celebrate with students who are able to cut a scene or change topics midstream when they discover something that has more energy for them as a writer. This first unit is built on encouragement. Success is a student like Kayla saying, "I never knew I could write like this, Mrs. Kittle!"

The next unit is a repeat of story, but a themed story that has a much larger scope. It is most often much longer than the previous piece, and we ask students to raise the quality of their writing from the former unit: better details, smoother dialogue, precise word choice. Even if not all of our students can make this final leap, all have had the opportunity to practice these fundamental skills in three writing pieces: the snapshot moment, the first narrative (which will include several moments or scenes connected together), then the extended narrative that uses theme and story to explore a bigger idea in the writer's life.

The next step into argument is logical because we are not teaching five-paragraph essays to explain or show understanding of a subject, or to argue a topic the teacher chose. We want students to demonstrate argument the way it is written in newspapers and magazines. The writer says "listen to what happened," and then "this is what I think it means," and finally, "here are the reasons why I think that." We have students develop a claim, back it up with evidence, and explain or expand upon something they're thinking. For example, a student is given detention for being late to school and is angry. To argue effectively, first the student writes a scene from that story to draw the reader into the argument and show that the punishment (now in vivid detail for the reader) does not fit the crime. The scene must be written in a few sentences—to shrink the details to few a key ones—which requires a crafty combination of the skills learned in narrative, but used in a new context. It forces the students to develop their thinking. They study model texts and see how each point is supported by credible evidence. And this is a challenging unit for most; confidence sags. In this two-week study they read and revise and pay attention to the elements of effective argument, but the products are often not as smooth as the prior units.

We continue to study argument in our next unit on commentary, which requires the logical support of an idea, but is more subtle than straightforward argument. Commentary is all over publications from *Sports Illustrated* (Rick Reilly is a real favorite) to *Oprah* to the Internet and the local paper. We flood our classrooms with good and bad examples. When one of our local columnists attacked our high school, and my support of it in particular, my students were quick to identify all of the errors in his argument. Two students wrote articulate replies to the paper. (Logan's letter to the editor is on the DVD. He made the entire faculty of our school smile that day.)

It is important to keep in mind that many students continue to craft these pieces of writing after each unit ends. This is because I allow them to continue to revise all semester and they want to improve their grades, but also because as their skills improve they know how to make their writing better. Every student will have at least five completed pieces at the end of the first quarter in our class.

In order to get students to produce this much writing and be able to provide feedback regularly to drafts and changes, I have to focus on teaching writing only and spend little time on other activities that support the teaching of writing but are not at the center. Vocabulary development and monitoring the reading my students are doing outside of assigned essays do not get as much attention as they would if I had students all year. I've made choices in my work in order to dedicate myself to the improvement of writing. You will have to make choices, too. What is critical is that we examine our practices regularly and look at the growth of the students we work with. Teaching is a creative process. We create new solutions to the changes we see in our student population—we have to.

In the second quarter the students write longer pieces. This quarter allows for student choice: fiction or multigenre or both. Fiction is not just about imagination; it explores an idea, a condition, or a belief anchored in story. Students take their understanding of narrative plus their beliefs about the way the world is and weave the two together. Yes, they enjoy the freedom of fiction, but they also quickly realize its demands on their skills as a writer. We spend three weeks crafting. Student texts average five to twenty pages. Sustaining an idea for this long is new for most students. Our study texts are the best short stories I can find: award-winning, brilliantly written, magical studies of characters and settings moving within a credible plot.

Other students develop a multigenre research project (Romano 2000) of at least five separate writing pieces. Students choose a big idea and then examine it through multiple frames: poetry, commentary, narrative, editorial, letters, obituaries, songs, multivoice poems, mini-movies, and many more. Students present the many ways to see and understand something important to them. This project asks them to raise their writing to one level higher—to bring all of their skills in persuasion and exposition to creative genres, broad thinking, and a cohesive product. Almost all students create something unique and impressive.

And then our semester comes to an end with the final portfolio review and the final exam. Students take all of their work from the semester and annotate it to demonstrate proficiency in thirty-five skills we've taught them (see Figure 3.1 and the final portfolio evaluation, pp. 224–25. They also rank their writing in order of most important, or best, work to least. They review the books they've read this semester, and rate the poetry we've read daily, explaining why five poems are their favorites for the term. Last, they write a letter of introduction to the portfolio that details their growth as a writer.

Our final exam is written in ninety minutes. They may choose to write narrative or argument, but must produce a well-structured essay in one sitting. Students are given parameters the day before the exam and are allowed to bring in one piece of paper on test day that includes notes, a storyboard or outline, or research information that will enhance their piece. They are familiar with the expectations for both forms of writing, but are allowed to choose their strength. The student is in control of topic as well. These exams are graded holistically.

What I can't capture here in this broad overview of the course is the way students begin to understand the complexity Murray wrote of: The writer chooses a form to express an idea. This is my ultimate goal—that students will understand enough about form and the possibilities of products to imagine shaping any idea into a product that will best express their thinking. As I sat beside Amy one morning near the end of the semester, she said, "Mrs. Kittle, I want to write about my mom. I know what I want to say about how we've grown and changed over the last three years, but I'm still thinking of all the ways I might write it." That's power. Every student should know that power, so I work every day to move each one of them closer.

Divorce is supposed to be hell on the kid.
This is just a fact of life; so sayeth the Lord, Amen.
Yet here I was, seven years old, and I didn't feel a thing.

—JOSH BOSSIE

I will end many sections of this book with a student focus, because in the midst of my theory and practices lie the students I teach. Their stories teach me.

He brought his writing that Friday and slipped it in with the others. I remember well finding it on my couch that Sunday evening. I had procrastinated all weekend again, finding excuses for not reading and evaluating student work. To assess those pieces I have to do battle with my own need to make everyone feel good while also giving rigorous feedback. I delay. I watch a mindless video with my husband. I take my daughter shopping or email ridiculous jokes to my parents. Boy, it's been a long time since I made cookies. Suddenly it's 7 P.M. and I force myself onto the couch with a purple pen and no excuses.

I shuffle through looking for short essays that will go fast. The weight of Josh's work stops me. What is this? "Of Time and Rivers." Now that's a title. I quickly glance at nine pages. Double-spaced, yes, but wow. I didn't know he had it in him. It was only the second writing piece of the year, when most of my students still asked, "How long does this have to be?" Josh had listened to my answer, "As long as it needs to be to tell the story well."

I read his opening paragraph and I felt my shoulders relax against the couch cushions. I was in his car driving along Route 16 glancing at the Saco River through the open window as his father prattled on in the passenger seat. As that piece unfolded I watched one remarkable writing decision after another. Josh organized the story back in time through moments, snapshots like we had practiced in class, but he chose those so carefully. He showed his father's inattention through repeated forgetfulness; he showed what he lost as the child of divorce by taking us back to a moment in the car as a toddler watching the colors blur out the window beside him as his mother smiled and glanced his way. It was a piece at once so beautiful and so skillful that I stopped grading and just marveled at what was before me.

The next day I asked him if he'd be willing to share it with the class. There was a hesitation—one I recognize well. It is a lot to ask when a student has written honestly about something painful. Will he now send those words out into a classroom of peers he barely knows? Consider how little time is given in school for sharing a piece of your soul. Kids barely know most of the other students in school, even in a small town like ours. But he said yes.

As with every student who shares work in my room I asked Josh to talk about what he did in his writing. I want all students to see not just story but intention. Josh said first he was interested in how the Saco River had actually been physically connected to every place he'd lived so far, that it seemed to be following him. He started with that notion and began writing. As he wrote he decided to alter the voice in the scenes to more closely resemble the age he was at the time. He discovered that each scene seemed to be about his father and about the divorce that kept surfacing in his quick writes in class. He had avoided that topic. He also said he used an echo ending, where an opening image is repeated at the end to bring a natural feeling of closure to the work.

I wondered why he wasn't the one paid to teach the class.

The applause was long and loud that day. Josh went on through the weeks in that semester to write all things well: argument, research, even a multigenre project on a student subculture called Emo (for emotional) since he'd once been a part of it. But I found his final portfolio evaluation spot on; his most important piece of the semester was "Of Time and Rivers."

This piece poured out of me like a flood. It began as a piece about moving to New Hampshire and focusing on the brook. Then it moved to the playground in Saco, ME and something clicked. The river seemed to be following my life. However, looking back on it, it seems to me I tricked myself and wrote about my father.

I intentionally put this story at the start of my book for two reasons. Josh had big vision, but I believe *all* kids do. The difficulty is to get them all to recognize it and reach for it. It's further than they've ever gone in writing and they can't imagine they can get there, but imagine what'll be gained if they try.

We have to raise the expectations much higher and see who might leap over, and we have to model what it means to leap. It begins with a real writing problem; it begins with a genuine struggle made public. Josh told me that the mentor text that had the biggest influence on his work that unit was my piece, "what remains." I had written fragments of it for years and finally pulled them together into a draft that I shared with students, although it is still a shadow of the piece I want it to be. I am trying to capture a friendship in childhood and make sense of that friend's death at nineteen. As I told my class, the story and all I want to say is so complex that I feel I can't do it. I want to honor who she was; I want to make sense of losing her. The day I shared it I talked to my students about intentional decisions I made as a writer. For one, I tried to paint the scenes from childhood with color and the scenes at her funeral with only black and white. I moved forward and back in time as I tried to present a myriad of pieces to the reader: my memories of our past and my thoughts of her today. Yet, that required complicated transitions as I moved from scene to scene.

I told my students my intent is for the reader to feel what this loss meant to me, but every time I sit down to work on it, I hear, *you're just not that good of a writer; you can't do this.* I keep silencing that voice and working on that draft because I have something to say. I believe that each time I read it and work on it I'll get a little bit closer to what I'm reaching for. I ended my lesson with, "Just try. Try something in writing that you don't quite believe you can do." That day's minilesson gave Josh permission to reach in his writing.

And this brings me to my second reason for telling this story. All writing that soars begins with something to say. It doesn't begin with an assignment. It doesn't begin with a rubric or a grade, but with something the writer feels is important and wants to work out by naming and exploring it in writing. It begins with something you might believe you can't do.

We set kids free when we ask them to leap. In that journey all of the skills and curriculum directives will be accomplished, along with something much more valuable: the confidence that you can write what you never believed possible.

Just imagine what that can do for your writers.

Imagine what that journey could do for you.

 "Of Time and Rivers" is on the DVD. Do yourself a favor and read Josh's work. "What remains" is there as well; it is still a work in progress.

PART TWO
COLLECTING THINKING

CHAPTER FOUR
The Writer's Notebook

I encourage my students to conduct fieldwork on their own cultures and themselves. Together we can take dictation from the world.

—KIM STAFFORD

As Pat and I were out walking our dogs in the neighborhood this morning, he said, "You're not going to like this, but I think writers are like cows." There was a pause before he continued; perhaps he was wondering just how far he could go. We have a firm rule in our house: no comparisons of me to large, bulky creatures. He knew he had my attention; I had stopped walking. I think I was even holding the dog's leash like a whip. He grinned. "You have this thinking building up inside you all the time and you just need to get it out. You need to be milked every day."

I hate to say it, but I think he's right.

One place to collect that thinking is a writer's notebook. There have been a lot of books written about this tool, and I believe any of my favorites—*Living Between the Lines* by Lucy Calkins, *Breathing In, Breathing Out* by Ralph Fletcher, and *The Muses Among Us* by Kim Stafford—can inspire anyone to get started. The notebook is one of the centers of my classroom because it has been so useful in my own writing.

I need ordinary notebooks to do this writing. I have beautiful ones that have been given to me as gifts and I'm afraid to write in them. My thinking is scattered and messy, and these books are so lovely. With the ordinary variety from an office supply store I can write in the margins and tape in notes from

I would have to say it was most useful in the fact that it had me writing almost every day. If it was not for this notebook I most likely only would have written when I needed to for a piece because writing has never really been something I enjoyed until now.

—ZACH

friends. I fill and replace one about every four months. They line a shelf in my study at home: an even stretch of narrow black spines that hold so many things I care about. I think it is one of the few things I would save in a fire.

What's in a writer's notebook? The list below (Figure 4.1) came from opening my writer's notebook one day and taking notes on what I saw there. I give this list to students like a piece of archeology: Here are one writer's wanderings. I want to open up possibility with the writer's notebook, and I want to give them an accessible, messy vision of the work writers do to explore thinking. I expect that most of my students are not keeping writing notebooks, so I start with my personal notebook tour (see DVD of the first day of class) so they get to know me, as well as develop a sense for how writing comes to be.

What's in a writer's notebook?

And by the way, everything in life is writable about if you have the outgoing guts to do it, and the imagination to improvise. The worst enemy to creativity is self doubt.

—SYLVIA PLATH

Life . . . mine
Lists of all kinds of things: stuff I need to buy; people I need to talk to; memories that come to me
Notes to myself
Emotions . . . anger, sadness, excitement, wonder
Memories

Every vivid memory holds some essential truth about your vision of the world.

—KIM STAFFORD

Fragments of life that strike me ("that's weird . . ."; "why did that happen?")
Drawings: especially when I can't write any more about something but I'm still thinking about it
Photographs, postcards, receipts, messages, notes from friends
Questions
Quotations that make me think and respond, "Yes, that's exactly how I feel."

FIGURE 4.1

Song lyrics

Secrets

Doodling and responses to quick writes or other writing exercises (a place where I experiment)

Scratchouts, crossouts, messy writing, notes in the margin of a page, sideways writing

Attempts at poetry; playful language

Writing pieces I abandon because I lose interest or have no confidence in

Writing prompts I create: things I think will help my students write

Story, essay, novel titles

First tries with a genre I'm not comfortable with

Detailed sketches of people and places to practice descriptive writing

Ideas for my classes, my new teachers, my own kids

Things I don't want to forget to do, lesson plans

Things other people say that strike me as important or stupid or that I don't understand

License plates (4U2NV) that make me want to respond

Books I've read and what I thought about them . . . sometimes I stop reading and write, then go back to reading

Visuals: plate, heart, hand . . . with related words for memories or ideas for essays

Poems I love

Sometimes journal-kind-of-entries, but usually not that orderly

Life

The world is busy, but the mind tenacious.
The writing life is all about faith in a fragment.

—Kim Stafford

Figure 4.1 *continued*

The first page of each of my notebooks is a collage. There is a recent one in Figure 4.2.

I tell my students why I chose the pictures, quotes, or ideas that help me write. The first notebook assignment is to create a collage for the inside cover of the notebook. Some students do little with this; it comes back to school with maybe a photo, a few words from a magazine. Many others cover the inside cover front and back and then wrap more words and photos across the outside cover. By the time they're done, they are connected intimately to their notebook.

It was my luck to have a few good teachers in my youth, men and women who came into my dark head and lit a match.

from *Life of Pi*, by Yann Martel

FIGURE 4.2

Even in the first week of school we begin filling our writing notebooks with quick, free writing (ideas for this work in the next chapter) and "now you try it" exercises from minilessons. It's all rehearsal—the prewriting work that will lead us as writers. Using the notebook is a daily expectation in class, and keeping all of our experimental writing in one place is essential for our work. I need to have a storehouse for ideas, raw thinking, wonder and joy, agony and anger, all the rubble of thought that appears out of nowhere and just might shape a piece of writing. The notebook is where we mine the world for story.

The notebook is where we find our voices. The notebook is a place for all of that bad writing that is essential to uncover good writing.

This is how notebook writing works best for me:

1. Quick write. There are so many possibilities with this idea. See Linda Rief's *100 Quickwrites* or *My Quick Writes* (Graves and Kittle 2005) and the next chapter of this book. An example: Write one snapshot memory in as much detail as possible in response to the prompt "I remember . . ." Take five minutes to write.

> *The writing should flow easily. The writing doesn't come easily when you are writing too soon, taking yourself too seriously, or establishing unrealistic standards.*
>
> —Don Murray

I remember trying to stay awake as our car tossed side to side with the curves on Wilson Road, Dad gripping the steering wheel with both hands, me holding the thermos and an open cup of black coffee ready to pass to him when the curves evened out into an un-spill-able stretch of road. The coffee smelled old and bitter and looked like it was scooped from a puddle; it never tempted me. The headlights worked like two searchlights to separate the creepy darkness in the trees by the side of the road from the path we could see ahead. The trick was to have a line in the water as gray morning light began to crawl across the sky. Steelhead bite at dawn. The big ones even earlier.

Soon we were stepping into the river in our boots, careful to make as few ripples as possible. Don't wake the fish: they're smarter than you think, Dad would whisper, a smirk prickling the side of his mouth, his blue eyes dancing as they met mine. I scooped pink salmon eggs out of the jar he handed me and forced the hook inside. Who's hungry? I wondered as I held the line and let the bait swing behind me. I tossed it into the deep water near the opposite bank.

2. Reread the quick write and look for phrases or words where there is more to say. I find:

Dad, coffee, creepy darkness, river, fish

3. Take one idea from step two and put it on a blank page. Write freely.

> *My WN really became helpful with practicing all the different genres because then I could look back on them all and see which I liked better. It gave me a place to hold my ideas and look at them all together at the same time.*
>
> —Crystal

Dad.

When I was home in April we were preparing for a garage sale and their move to a more convenient house. It was time for clearing out and casting off. Dad said he wanted to sell all of his fishing gear. I didn't want to hear it. I knew it was coming: an end to fishing. He stood in the driveway with the now familiar clear tubing wound around one hand. He lives on oxygen now, but I still see us on the water. He tried to sell me—did I want a fly rod? A heavy steelhead rod? Would I like his old vest with something in each pocket? I blinked quickly and looked away. I chewed on the inside of my cheek and watched as he showed me again how to make the line dance when you hold a fly rod. His body relaxed as he held his right hand behind his head, an imaginary rod balanced delicately behind him as he felt for the line floating towards the water. And I tried to learn it this time, to not be distracted by cars rushing by on the street behind us or the sorrow rising in my throat. I still had him standing beside me in the driveway on a lovely afternoon; I could still learn this, before it's too late, but it was his ghost I felt move through me, calling me back across the years to the water.

> "I learned that writing is a great way of expression which I never knew. I used to only write to fill up space. Now I write what my heart feels."
>
> —MATT

By following this series of steps, we get closer to the way writers work with their thinking. There is writing, then rereading and rethinking, then expanding, rereading, and so on. This is the beginning of drafting. I lead my students to this place and let them jump off. I don't know where they're going, but I know they'll be able to follow an idea and find something to say. This is where all writing springs from: something to say. And this is why the notebook matters. My students often say the notebook helps them find their voice. It is free, so they let go and write with confidence. Because they aren't bound up by what the writing is supposed to be, voice appears effortlessly. Controlling voice is the beginning of learning to write well.

 In the video on the DVD there is a notebook tour where I share my current notebook.

> My writing notebook was most helpful in learning the whole writing process. Where before my mind and hand had a few broken connections, staggering my thoughts, they have now at the end of the semester melded together, and writing flows from my brain through my hand like a faucet. I effing love this book; kudos to Mrs. Kittle for making us write in them all the time.
>
> —DAN

This writing notebook helped me to develop voice because I knew I could write whatever I wanted in it and would not be graded down in any way. This helped me to not write like anyone else but myself. When we did our first quick write for "Where I'm From" (Lyon) I got a lot of ideas for things that I would write about in the future like about dance, being onstage and about my brothers. The writing notebook was most useful to me every time we wrote in it because it helped me to get my opinion out and write about things that I've never really been able to say. I really enjoyed this writing notebook because you gave us ideas that we could write about, but never had to write about them. We were always given the option to write about whatever we wanted.

—ALLIE

I try to answer the question: Where do topics come from? How does one writer pursue them? There is also a student writer, Elizabeth, talking about her writer's notebook and what she found there. These might help you imagine how to fill yours. The truth is, though, you have enough collected experiences and creativity to begin your notebook without any guidance at all. Just write. I think with any writing you have to just start. If I could give you one thing that would change your teaching forever it would be a notebook and Kurt Vonnegut Jr.'s belief that, "Anyone can write: all it takes is time."

CHAPTER FIVE

Quick Writes

The daily practice of craft
sharpens the writer's vision and tunes the writer's voice.
Habit makes writing easy.

—DON MURRAY

When class begins, I want every moment to matter. The day feels shorter each year—the classroom period interrupted by too many things I can't control: I want to unplug the intercom, pull down the shades, and lock my door. If you dare interrupt me, it had better be important. Once I have my students before me, everything matters. I believe we have to be urgent about our teaching: urgent to plan, demonstrate, encourage, and then revise our thinking as we listen to what our writers need. I'm developing a community of writers amid the daily drama of high school; I'm not sure there's work much harder than that. So trust me, I couldn't set aside daily time for free writing if I didn't believe in its power.

Quick writing is a no-fail time to write in my room—there are no expectations about what the writing is supposed to be; you can sketch or write or list or line out poetry. I seek diversity, as teacher and writer Linda Rief said. My students know I want a meaningful engagement with writing, and whether the writing becomes something bigger and more important in their writing portfolio really does not matter. For many, that freedom is motivating all on its own. Quick writing is play. This is something most students crave: to write freely, to experiment with their thinking and ideas, to try on voice, or to rant about life. No grades attached: It is a time to speak.

There are only three rules:

1. *Write the entire time.* Stamina is important in writing, so I ask students to stick with quick writing for several minutes. They follow an idea where it leads, and

then follow it deeper, uncovering the layers of thinking that support it. It might be the memory of their grandfather's funeral and then the layers of story that make sense of that loss. I ask students to keep their pens moving and write. It does not have to be an orderly response: one idea and then another and another, some related, others a mystery. I will often say, "Write what you're thinking." The following example was written by a student who arrived late, in the midst of our quick writing. We did three quick writes that day, but he just kept adding to his first thought. I tell my students to break the rules like this: If you find something hot, keep writing what you care about.

All I can say is it's a good thing I don't have ADD. Finding piece and quiet at my house is like finding a needle in a haystack. Before my dad left last year it was the alcohol driven arguments that broke the peace. He left though and leaving in his wake was a bunch of broken stuff and his alcoholic genes for my older brother. I think about him sometimes, is he the same man that brought me to hockey practice before school and turned the backyard into a hockey arena for me? Is that the man that now lives in Chicago hotels running up bar tabs to unknown heights, I'm worried for his health.

Now it's my brother though that insights my mom's insanity and screaming matches. He dropped out of school last year and can't stay out of the police station. He drinks too much at 18 and shows no respect for my mother. They scream, slam doors, and swear at each other for hours on end. Maybe it's the black eye he gave my younger sister, that's good for a call from human services and my possible embarrassment, or he missed a meeting with his public defender, but they are always fighting. Through this though I find ways to get what needs to be done, to get through high school.

When I walk in the door from hockey practice and have homework to do I know it's not the time to accept anything from him that will hinder my thinking.

Then there's my mother. She struggles to keep the family together and tries too hard sometimes. She is emotionally exhausted from worrying about the divorce and my brother's behavior around town. Sometimes I question her sanity. I know every time I mess up it will be magnified in her eyes because I'm the second kid and need to compensate for the trouble my dad and brother have caused her.

It weighs on my mind at times and is the cause of my complacency in class and at times questionable work ethic. Thinking back to a happy family, and now looking at the pain in the eyes of those I love. These memories of being younger and every one being together and happy are even more important now that it's gone. Amidst this, all I can do is swallow a golf-ball sized lump of pride and go to school everyday. I can make things better by setting an example for my two younger impressionable brothers. I'm not looking for sympathy just understanding.

---

2. *Write quickly without letting the critic in your head censor you. If you don't like the way you said something, ignore it and keep going. Too many writers say they are blocked; they say this before they've even given themselves a chance* to write. As Ralph Fletcher said in *Boy Writers*, "Risk taking and fluency are the main structural beams on which you build a strong writing classroom. By fluency I mean velocity: speed. Writing with velocity allows students' hands to keep pace with what's going on in their minds. It also helps them to outrun the censor most of us have in our heads." This won't happen when the paper is due and the student measures every line. Quick writing is supposed to be unformed, messy thinking; and out of this freedom, good writing grows.

3. Relax, have fun, play. In a column in *The Boston Globe*, Don Murray explained how writing seduced him. "Play. The simple fun of making something I did not know I could make. I return to my childhood when a jumble of blocks becomes a tower, collapses, and becomes a castle." Quick writing is play with words. There is not enough play in high school. I'm afraid there is no longer enough play in elementary school even, but I'm certain it is true in high school. Playful writing leads to a comfortable voice that is easy to read. Too often writing assignments in high school ask for a voice the student struggles to find. Students are asked to be an authority on something they know little about. The writer is pinned to the ground by a topic and a voice wrestled out, which of course leads to stilted, awkward writing. In quick writes we seek the writer's confident voice. We quick write—we practice—we discover. My students need to write every day, and expect to write every day, so they can begin to write with the same ease they speak. Later, when a more serious, academic voice is called for, my students will be ready, because they'll have much greater understanding and control over their writing voice.

And that really is all there is to quick writing: You engage with a moment, an idea, or an image and you write freely for a few minutes. Anything can launch this writing. I often lead students along by using poems and model texts in the genre we're studying, and I practice free writing myself to see where it takes me. Here's an example of how I might find a topic.

Now, if I share this with you, you have to promise that you won't go running to a colleague and read this section out loud and laugh at me. I mean it. I just turned on my MP3 player to listen to music on a very long and bumpy flight to Oregon. I selected *Best of Cher* and the song "If I Could Turn Back Time." *I know, I know* . . . it's bad enough that I even have it loaded on my player, let alone that I'd choose that song to mind dance to. It's this little warp in my musical past: the disco-loving, Bee Gee-bopping, platform shoe-wearing part of me that rises to the surface every now and again. Shocking, I know, but something about that song makes me want to dance. So I have my personal Cher concert going and my thoughts drift to what I'd do if I could turn back time.

And just like that, I'm in. I've got a topic. I've got fingers itching to dance across this keyboard and I want to create something—just a snapshot moment that might show you when I was in love in college, fishing the rivers of coastal Oregon with a boy I wanted to marry who, well, didn't think beyond the next fishing trip. I remember steelhead sandwiches, dozing in his car between stops, and the way the sun broke through the clouds to cross the road in blinding white stripes. Life is rich with detail: present and past.

To write about it, I put myself back in time, first person, present tense. I focus on reseeing. This exercise is part memory, part art, and it is fun because no one will likely read what I write but me; there are no expectations I need to meet or worries about what the writing is supposed to be. I would call these the ideal conditions to write. Here's a five-minute draft:

We park his car on the side of the road near a guardrail and I worry about scraping the door as I climb out in my fishing gear. My hip waders make me clumsy. Bob is already waiting by the trunk with a rod in each hand smiling. He's wearing a ski hat pulled low across his forehead, a few bits of blonde stuck out on one side. It's grey and it makes his eyes bluer. My hand is trembling as I reach for the rod. "Where's the river?" I ask. I know this is stupid, but I really don't know. I can't see it and wonder how far we have to walk. The Coast Range rises immediately in front of us and I hope we're not going for a long hike—I'll sweat and my hair's already matted to my head since we left before dawn and I didn't shower.

"Follow me," he says with a white-toothed smile.

Anywhere, I don't say.

We walk through knee-high grass and weeds and I hear the stream to my left, completely camouflaged behind tall trees. Suddenly there's a dirt path and Bob cuts in front of me. I follow.

It's only a few feet down and we're in Wonderland. There is sun and green and water and shade, surrounded by tall trees on both sides. Not a soul in sight.

I forced myself to stop when time was up. I also forced myself not to edit as I wrote, even though I hate the clichés "wonderland" and "not a soul in sight." I know for rough draft writing it is best to just keep going past editing, to keep searching for story. I had to think about what Bob might have said when I asked where the river was, but I didn't pause for long. It would have been just like him to say, "Follow me." This is what I mean by part memory, part art. I remember that moment when we got out of the car near the Necanicum River to go fishing and being led to that hidden river. But I don't know if we had that conversation—it is a likely one, true to who we were at the time—which is essential to my honesty as a writer, but the dialogue is *art* in this memory. Memoir isn't video, but it can't be all invention either. Students understand this distinction because they've listened to family stories for years. The story changes based on who is telling it, and stories change over time. Readers don't test for precision, but they deserve the essential truth. When we quick write in my class we allow

> ## Daily schedule for a block class of 83 minutes:
> 1. Agenda, attendance, book talk—5 minutes
> 2. Silent sustained reading—10 minutes
> 3. Quick writes—15 minutes
> 4. Minilesson—15 minutes
> 5. Writing workshop—35 minutes
> 6. Sharing, homework—3 minutes

ourselves the freedom to retell and invent at the same time: What is important is to free your mind to write quickly. I write beside them to stay in touch with what I'm asking of my students and to practice my craft as their writing teacher.

We spend five to fifteen minutes on quick writing each block class period. If I taught in a sixty-minute period I'd probably spend not more than ten minutes on this. It is priming the pump, not the study of mentor texts or the development of ideas into coherent essays, but it is essential because it develops voice and often leads students to topics. As Molly said in her final portfolio evaluation, "Quick writes have a way of bringing up random topics in your mind, and you write about them because you don't have very much time. I like the idea of writing the first thing that comes to mind, because sometimes your own thoughts surprise you."

Long ago when I first read Graves' *Writing: Teachers and Children at Work*, I said to my fifth graders, "You can write about anything you want," and expected this riotous cheer and furious scribbling. Instead I got the same thing you did, "I have nothing to write about; I don't know what to write; nothing happens in my life." I was confused. I read an interview Tom Newkirk did with Don Graves years later, and Don said, "Unlimited choice is no choice at all." I had missed that part. Choice has to be taught: I needed to learn how to help students discover their topics. Students of any age will

> *Our goal as teachers should not be to fill the world with perfect text, or even acceptable text. Our goal should be to take students to such a place of comfort with writing that they will persist through three pages of random thought to an emerging clarity on page four because they have not one shred of doubt they will get there. After all, only nonwriters fear failure. Writers know clutter and roadblocks and random thinking are all part of the process.*
>
> —Vicki Spandel,
> *The Nine Rights of Every Writer*

> Heidi wrote in her final portfolio evaluation, "In quick writes our goal was to get our thoughts down on paper no matter how incoherent they seemed in our heads. This tool was vital in getting me to write, because I usually have writer's block for long periods, sometimes days. However, with quick writes I was able to write down my thoughts quickly without worrying what other people thought of my ideas or my writing. Most of my writer's block stems from fear: the fear that my essay will not have depth, or will be incoherent. Surprisingly, when I went back to my quick writes I found many solid foundations for the writing pieces that I created. My thoughts were not as incoherent as I had thought before I began to write. Quick writes were the key to improving both the quality and the quantity of my prose this semester."

get discouraged if they just sit and think, trying to uncover an idea that feels big enough to write about. Quick writes get them started. They bridge that gap between student and topic for me, and I couldn't run my workshop without them.

We will quick write a lot when we first explore a genre, much less as they find an idea and move into their own texts. (In the video on the DVD there are several examples of how I use quick writes in my classroom.) I read student notebooks about once every unit, so about once every two weeks.

The expectation that there will be time to write is important. Don Murray wrote about the importance of rehearsal for writers. He said knowing that you will be writing engages your brain on that task in the hours beforehand when you're doing other things. Shania came to class last week and said, "Mrs. Kittle, I know what I want to write today: I was pulling out of my driveway this morning and I saw the porch and the chair my mom always sat in to watch the sunset. I want to write about that." Whether we quick write that day or jump into writing workshop, Shaina's ready to write. That only happens when I make writing a predictable expectation.

TEN QUICK WRITES TO GET YOU STARTED

It is hard for me to separate writing and teaching writing. Most pages in my writing notebook end up in two colors—one the writing, the other the rereading for process thinking that I can share with my students. When a rich writing moment happens for me I try to figure out how I can mimic the conditions in my classroom, always seeking an experience for students that might loose a writer's voice. This fresh experience with the joy of writing is essential in my teaching. I have to play with writing and practice it in order to discover ways I can make writing real for kids. I believe if you aren't willing to quick write yourself, both inside and outside your classroom, you won't have a lot of success with it in your classroom. This can't just be another teacher assignment while you grade papers or take attendance. You're either in the midst of composing with kids, or you're trying to orchestrate from the outside. I can guarantee success with the first, but the second hasn't worked for me for years. Just remember this: You don't have to share anything unless you want to. You can't lose. I trust these words of Ann Lamott: "I know that with writing you start where you are, and you flail around for a while, and if you keep doing it, everyday you get closer to something good." That's all I'm asking for—from you and from me—a little flailing around. Try these and see what happens.

1. *The music in your heart.* This is an idea based on Georgia Heard's heart map from *Awakening the Heart.* I ask students to brainstorm the way music and memories dance together. Draw a large heart on a page in your notebook and fill it with songs that live in your heart. We put the most important songs at the center of the heart—the ones we'll never forget. And then we put those we'd rather forget along the outer edge. Kids giggle and whisper titles across the room—they sing a few lines from the *SpongeBob SquarePants* theme song. There are songs grandparents sang to them, the first one they learned on an instrument, a mother's favorite sang over dishes, or the raps created on a bus ride home after a tennis match.

Figure 5.1 is a sample from my notebook.

<u>Figure 5.1</u>

I've considered bringing that Cher song into my classroom when I tell the writing story behind that quick write. I know it is risky: I can't even pretend to be cool if I listen to Cher, but sometimes I've got to shake off that serious teacher thing and be who I am. Maybe not this time, though. Once we've listed and laughed, I ask them to choose one song and write their memory of the song, the setting, whatever rises to the surface when thinking about the music. They write furiously for five or six minutes; stories want to be told.

2. *Poetry*—thank you Tom Romano, who demonstrated the power of this by reading a poem at the start of every class in a course I took one summer at the University of New Hampshire. The first quick write of the day in my classroom is usually a response to a poem. I read the poem (and yes, I practice beforehand) and then each student might take one line and respond to something that he thought of as the poem was read. I want students to listen to the language of poetry. Most will tell me they hate poetry at the start of the semester; I hope this daily exposure will shift that a little by the end.

> *I really liked responding to poems, because poems can spark so many ideas. From one poem, 100 ideas erupt.*
>
> —CHRIS

I have to work to help some students write their own thinking in response to a poem, not a review or summary of the poem. I teach this by sharing my own responses. I vary my usual collection of Billy Collins, William Stafford, Langston Hughes, Donald Hall, and Gary Soto with slam poetry I find online (like www.taylormali.com) or something a colleague slips to me in the hall.

No one is required to write poetry in my room. I invite; I model; I share; I hope. When students are given a vision for multigenre work, however, they often do write a poem. Some will remain firmly against all things poetry all semester, of course, and I'm sorry for them.

One of my favorite poems is "Days" from *Sailing Around the Room*, by Billy Collins. After reading I tell students, "Imagine if you could go back in time to one day. Which would you choose? Why? What would you hope to do there?"

Dane wrote, "I woke up in the middle of the night from something that I wasn't sure of. I layed there in the dark on my twin bed in my room in the dark of my house. My mind was racing and I couldn't help but think about my mom. Then the hallway light came on and I saw two shadows come down the hall. One went to my brothers' room the other to mine. My eyes opened and I knew. She was gone."

Max wrote:

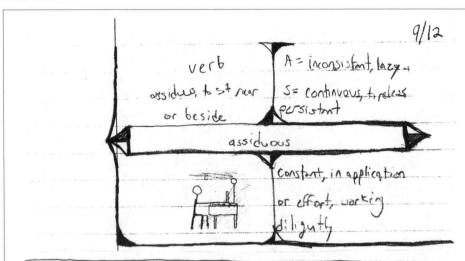

I wish I could go back to the shy age of 10. I wish I could revisit my father and get to understand him better. I wish I could have known him not only as a father, but as a person. I wish I could have brought him with me through time to know of what he'd think about me today. I wish I could have seen his tears of joy when the Red Sox shattered the curse or the Patriots becoming 3-time superbowl champs. I wish I could hear his booming laugh one more time, or see another smile work across his face. I wish I could hear his signature voice echo through the house. I wish I could hear him bring his Harley back to life and see him ride into the horizon. I wish my father was still alive, but I am greatful for the memories I still have.

FIGURE 5.2

Shaina wrote:

9-12-06
Days
A day I would relive would be the day my mom passed away. ~~I would have~~ I would do this because I feel like I never got to say what needed to be said. She passed away while I was at school, a peaceful death with her mother and closest sister in the room. I was young and had never had to deal with someone I love so much dying. It was like I was scared to talk to her, even though she was my best friend. But I never wanted to remember her as being so weak and sick. I wish I could have talked to her one more time and cuddled or slept with her one last time. I really regret the day she died because it seemed as if my sister was more involved with spending the last few hours with her and I just went along with my everyday life and went to school as if she would be alive forever.

FIGURE 5.3

I asked a friend, "How many kids lose parents before college?" hoping for some kind of statistic that would make me less gloomy about these quick writes. She said, "How many in your room this year?" And the answer was six, with one more soon. I have twenty-five students, and six lost a parent before age fifteen. In each case, as I've knelt beside them mid-workshop they have said these words, "This is the first time I've ever written about it."

I shake my head. We're missing something in teaching writing at high school. We assign topics and students respond by going-through-the-motions writing instead of from-the-heart writing that drives them to write well. Emotion is the engine of the intellect; we write more powerfully when it is from the center of who we are. If I ask you to select one moment out of all of those that have filled your experience—and if I convince you that your unique story is worth sharing with the world—you're going to give me something real. At least most of you will. And once those words are on the page, we can work on shaping and forming them into something close to what you experienced. But we have to let go of a primary focus on product, because teaching writing is not as much about what the writer ends up producing as about the process of getting there: solving problems, making decisions, manipulating words, reaching for something greater than what is on the page before them. That engagement is what lasts and that engagement is what will make them strong writers in any setting in their future.

3. *A model text.* We often quick write responses to samples of writing in the genre we're studying. I mix published texts with student texts. I want students to see what is possible from the best writers I can find, but I also want them challenged to write as well as my former students have.

Using model texts for quick writing during our study of a genre allows me to expose my students to many texts in a short period of time. It gives us a variety of anchor experiences to draw on as a class, identifying and discussing the common elements of craft in a genre. It allows students to hear writing read out loud, and it broadens their understanding of topics that work.

Sometimes I organize my quick writes around a theme. One day I might read the essay "Eleven" by Sandra Cisneros, the poem "On Turning Ten" by Billy Collins, and a student narrative about a memorable birthday as our model text. Reading aloud is important because writers need to hear the voice in the text. Three quick writes (five minutes each) is a good mix for my seniors at the beginning of a genre unit. On other days we might have three texts, but we only write to two of them, or we'll write one longer response (ten minutes) after reading all three. I read my class and their energy to make this decision.

4. *Reading blogs.* Independent reading is a cornerstone in my workshop. Each day begins with a book talk, then ten to fifteen minutes of silent reading. Students choose books they want to read, but there is never enough time to talk about what they're reading and share the great finds in content or craft with each other. So about every three weeks or so, we write a reading blog during our quick-write time. Students might write about what they're reading and what they think about the book or the author's writing. This isn't a summary. It is book talk—the way we might chat with a friend or recommend a title. Then we pass our notebooks to someone near by. That student reads what was written and responds. Then we pass again. After two passes, the notebook is returned to the student who can read the thinking of two other students in response to his

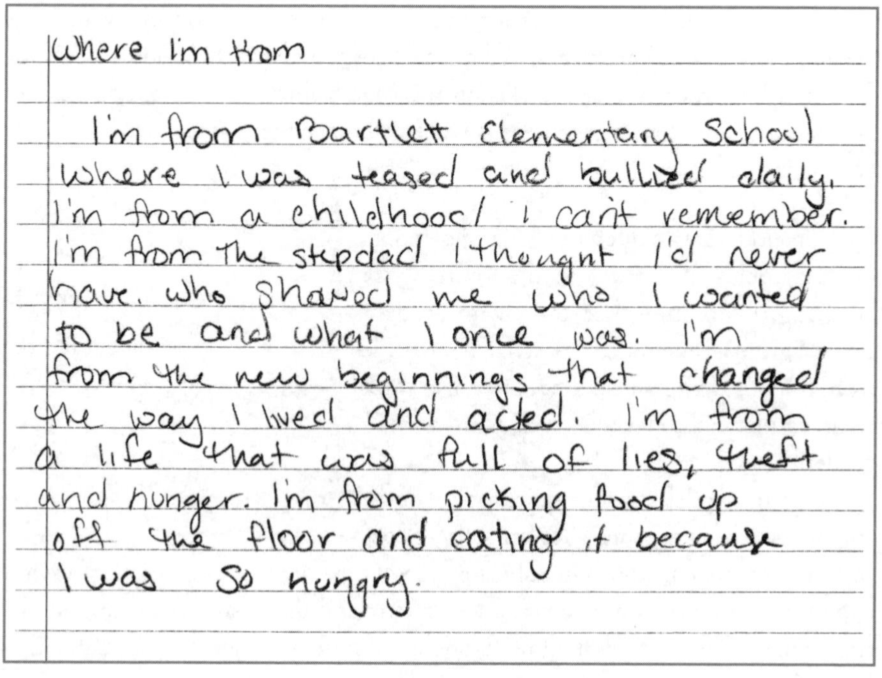

Where I'm from

I'm from Bartlett Elementary School where I was teased and bullied daily. I'm from a childhood I can't remember. I'm from the stepdad I thought I'd never have. who showed me who I wanted to be and what I once was. I'm from the new beginnings that changed the way I lived and acted. I'm from a life that was full of lies, theft and hunger. I'm from picking food up off the floor and eating it because I was so hungry.

FIGURE 5.4

thinking on the book. A lot of titles get shared this way. I enjoy having students write in my notebook.

I don't share other quick-write responses in this manner, though. I've found that no matter how innocent our quick write may seem, it can bring up private moments that students don't want to share. Read Sarah's response (Figure 5.4) to "Where I'm From" by George Ella Lyon, for example.

Or Sam's response (Figure 5.5) after reading a poem about a mother singing her daughter to sleep at night. I asked students to consider fragments of language that have stayed with them.

> Language
>
> Every other word my stepfather says is a swear. Like "That's fucking pisser," or "you fucking retard, you're just like your fucking mother," or "your friends are little faggots." I remember the time he threatened to knife my mother. "You're lucky I don't ram a fucking knife through your eye." when I intervened, he merely said, "This doesn't concern you." when my mother leaves the room, he makes snide comments to himself just like a two-year old does. It would be funny if they weren't so dark.

FIGURE 5.5

These are hard to read. Sometimes I wish I didn't know as much as I do about my students. But I also know that silence is painful; writing can help. I explain—before we begin, of course—that anything written that alarms me will lead me to guidance or administration. Of course that is exactly why some students write what they do. And if this makes you nervous, I understand. I feel the same way. Some students need help, though. Writing may be the safest way they can find to let you know.

5. *Show vs. tell quick write.* Sometimes we experiment with a writing technique in quick writing. When I begin teaching narrative I use this quick write to focus on a skill my students will need in our unit. I ask them to think of something that has happened and summarize it by telling it in a few sentences. Here's a sample I wrote in class:

Tell: Cam cut his forehead open when he was playing on the jungle gym—playing tag!—on the frozen set of bars. He slipped and crashed all the way to the hard pavement, and he had to have stitches in the emergency room. I wished I were home when they called so I would have picked him up in the nurse's office, instead of my neighbor Nancy. Sometimes I was working at the worst moments.

Now, I say, write the same moment frame by frame like a movie. Go back in time and live that moment again in writing, first person, present tense. We focus on physical details. I like what Colorado novelist Pam Houston says about detail: "Writing that centers itself on physical description has at least two things going for it. First, it activates the readers' senses and engages both their minds and their bodies. Second, it helps writers get out of their analytical brains and into their sensory-driven subconscious, the place where the real truths get told."

I model taking the first scene and transforming it with present details:

Show: I drove into the parking lot at the Montessori school scanning for Nancy's car. Where was she? I saw her van sitting by the door and bolted for it, trying to see inside the window on the passenger side. Cam sat with his cheek on his hand and an ugly red line beneath a bandage at the center of his forehead. His cheeks were pink and the minute our eyes met, his eyes filled with tears. I reached for the door handle.

"Cam, are you okay, buddy?" I tried to seem calm, but I was thinking in fast bursts—emergency room—doctors—stitches—scarring. My little boy was hurt.

"I have to get Hannah and then we'll go to the hospital, okay?" I asked. Cam's lower lip quivered and as he blinked a tear fell, running slowing down his cheek. "I'm sorry, sweetie, I'm sorry you're hurt, but we'll take care of it."

Cam didn't say anything but he nodded.

They cut a hole in the cloth so only the cut was visible. The rest of the cloth covered his face. I held one hand and his dad held the other. The doctor worked on stitches, sewing in big loops, then pulling them closed. . . .

6. *Compressing time*. Another quick write that can build writing skill is compressing time. I learned to understand and name this strategy in Rebecca Rule and Susan Wheeler's *True Stories: Guides for Writing from Your Life*, which is such a marvelous, funny, smart collection of writing strategies that I use it as a text in my classroom. (I know I reference a lot of books that have helped me understand how to write, but this one absolutely rocked my world. You must read it.)

Compressing time is a strategy writers use to zoom past weeks, months, or years of time with concrete images. Story is often written like this—a wide panoramic shot of life—and then a close study of one moment or one week in that life. When we compress time, we try to show the wide expanse quickly. This will be used in narrative where I need the reader to move quickly past several years to get to a moment that matters.

For the quick write I share a sample from a piece I'm writing this week. I'm trying to capture my obsession with tennis as an adolescent. I share my example of quick, sensory images to capture moments within a compression of several years at once: *It's the feel of morning—the cool wind brings goose bumps to my legs and arms as I jog in place bouncing a tennis ball on my racquet . . . it's hundreds of mornings waiting in the cold for Cynthia, walking to the empty gray courts, eyeing the early morning joggers and their slobbering dogs. It's a tower of discarded tennis ball cans, so many over the years that we could create a skyscraper in a landfill, and it's hundreds of perfect shots, net serves, blasts over the back fence or the rare corner ace when all the practices come together in a smooth release and follow through to put the ball just out of her reach. In my tennis history I remember one Tuesday in all of those Tuesdays. . . . .*

I explain how I decide what to do next in the writing. And this is some of the most important work I do as a writing teacher. Before I've written—when I'm still thinking about creating a piece—I talk to students about how I might put the ideas together. I am giving them vision for how writing comes to be. And to tell you the truth, this is some of the most fun I have in teaching: It is creation. It's unpredictable and risky and exhilarating. Once I show my thinking, they begin to show each other. Students think aloud, they try out ideas or scenes or plans, and our workshop becomes a rich, vibrant place where writers rock together. (See the DVD where I share my thoughts on this tennis piece while it is still under construction.)

So I say to my students, in the previous example my structure in this is artificial—who knows which day of the week it was—but I'm using it to set the stage for a piece I want to write about lots of things: competition with my friend and how it hurt our friendship—and how I didn't have time to grow out of that and be a better friend because she died at nineteen. How tennis equalized us—or put me on top when I felt I was losing in all of those other areas: clothes, houses, hair—her future looked bright—mine was a scramble. So after I've set the stage with my compression of time—I've shown the readers our history together—I'll zoom in on one scene from playing tennis where beating her led us to arguing and all the childish particulars of friendship. It is this combination of show and tell that moves readers through narrative: compression and expansion of time. I know this is tricky, but readers have been watching this happen in stories for years, so they'll grasp the essential meaning of this quickly. Writing the particulars is harder, so that's why we quick write and experiment before we try to make this strategy work in a draft.

An important lesson in compressing time is to see its opposite: the slow movement of a reader through a key scene in a story. This is the work of quick write #5, earlier, which asks students to show not tell. Too many students write all "tell" pieces that just recount the history of something. No fun to read, no fun to write. By focusing on compressing time, I can remind students of its place in narrative and the need for more than a scatter of details to help readers experience other parts of the story. The writer must help me feel what it was like to hike with their father or take that first ski run down the mountain. Compression bridges gaps in a longer narrative but, when crafted with specific, rich details, can keep the reader in the story.

This quick write asks for a blast through growing up using one vivid, sensory image after another. I ask them to try it: experiment, play, nothing to lose. We will each write a quick review of growing up. Here's what James wrote:

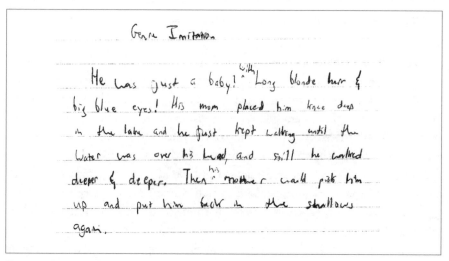

FIGURE 5.6

7. *A place in time.* Remember a place from your childhood that mattered to you and list what you remember about it. Go for the finest details of that place—sensory details—and see what surfaces. I tell my students I'm going to write about my grandparent's house in North Bend, Oregon, and I begin either a sketch or a list in my notebook (Figure 5.7). Many students find it easier to sketch the place because the details come as they sketch. This has worked for me as well. I use this quick write in either the narrative study or when we raise the quality of our narrative writing and try to compose a place narrative.

I think the best thing that I wrote this semester was when I wrote about my old house, because it helped me remember a lot of good times that my family and I used to have there. . . . I also learned that I'm a better writer than I thought I was.

—MITCH

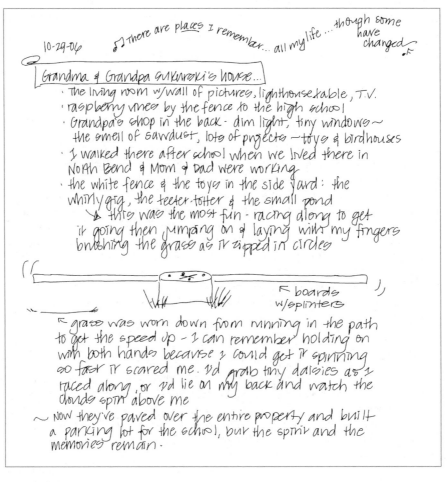

FIGURE 5.7

I have included a student sample of writing narrative focused on place on the DVD. Elizabeth wrote "The House on a Hill" about her grandma's house and the times they spent together from sledding down the hill nearby to snuggling under the covers on Christmas Eve. Elizabeth asks, "Why am I a sixteen-year-old leaving snacks on the coffee table for Santa Claus with my 81-year-old grandmother? Because it means that I still believe: in childhood, in innocence, in the magic of our Christmas Eves, in traditions, in the irrepressible bond that we share. Because it is like being young again, if only in our hearts. I keep her young and she makes me unafraid of growing old."

8. *One moment from elementary school.* I begin by reading "My Indian Education" from *The Lone Ranger and Tonto Fistfight in Heaven* by Sherman Alexie to the class. This is an inspiring piece that leaves everyone itching to write. A fictional character remembers a moment from each year of school, first grade until graduation. In a few short paragraphs we relive each of his school years. I ask students to consider a moment from elementary school and write it with all of the details they can remember: first person, present tense. This is an easy quick write: Everyone has something to say. Pat Haine wrote the following about first grade.

> This was IT.
> This was the big day.
> I wasn't in preschool, I wasn't in kindergarten anymore. I was in first grade. Move over, this was a class that included second grade, so I was surrounded by mean, horrifying, rule-breaking Big Kids.
> A class meeting was in session, but I wasn't listening to the teacher at all; I was incapacitated by fear. I tried not to sit too close to anyone, tried not to accidentally bump or touch anyone, tried even harder to avoid a glance at someone that I wasn't cool enough to look at.
> The teacher finally broke through the wall. "Patrick? I asked you if your lunch is hot or cold today?"
> I didn't remember the temperature of my lunch my mom put in a paper bag for me this morning, I just took it. I didn't even know what it was!
> I hazarded a guess.
> "Hot?"
> "Okay, can I have your lunch money please?"
> OH MY GOD! What have I done? Thoughts flew through my head, my eyes darted toward the exit. I didn't have any money! What was I supposed to do?
> "Uhhh . . . Mrs. Glady, I have to go to the bathroom!" I shouted, running to the small restroom with the orange light switch.
> I locked the door.

FIGURE 5.8

Many students use these moments to anchor longer pieces.

9. *Interest journals.* I first heard about these from Louise Wrobleski at the University of New Hampshire.

This fall I took thirty journals and wrote a topic on twenty-five of them. Five were labeled "free." Topics included driving, sports, parents, friendship, movies, video games, cartoons, and snow. About once every two weeks, students choose an interest journal from the pile on a desk. They read or skim the prior entries and then on the next blank page write for about five minutes. They can add a thread to an ongoing conversation or create a new train of thought. Their writing can be loosely related to the theme of notebook and they do not have to sign their entries. Interest journals are truly entertaining. (See "Notebook Work" on the DVD.)

There are two samples from Hair (Figures 5.9 and 5.10), which was a favorite topic this year.

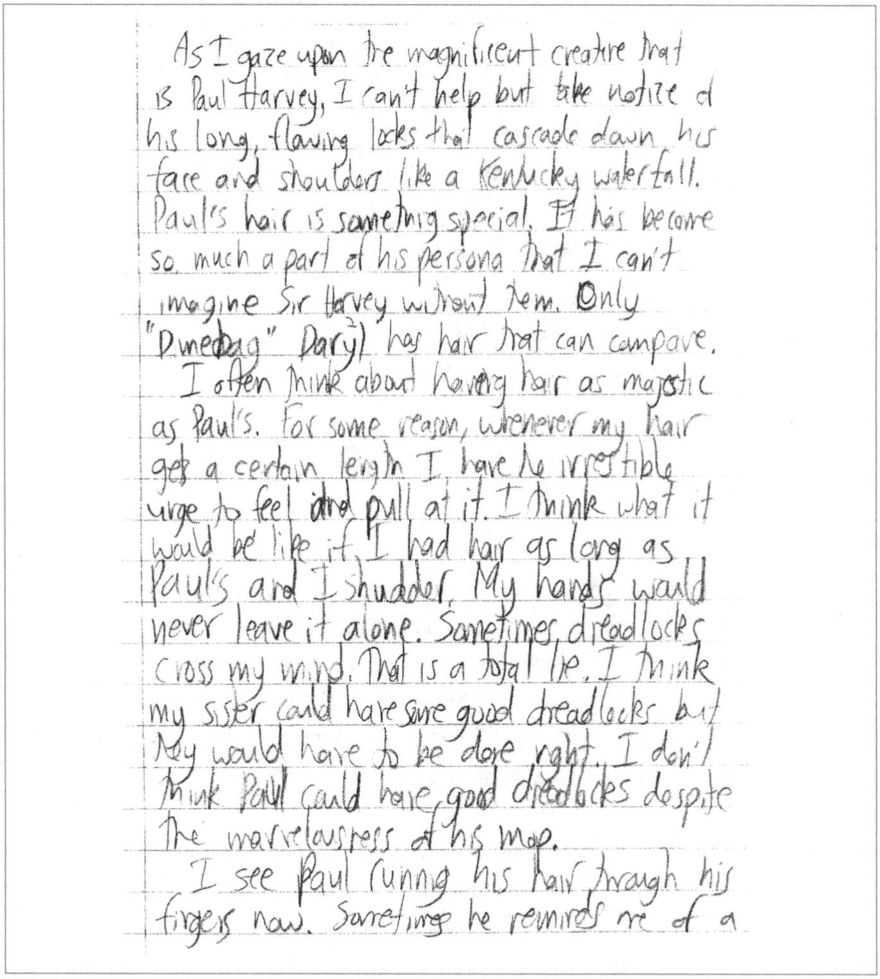

As I gaze upon the magnificent creature that is Paul Harvey, I can't help but take notice of his long, flowing locks that cascade down his face and shoulders like a Kentucky waterfall. Paul's hair is something special. It has become so much a part of his persona that I can't imagine Sir Harvey without them. Only "Dawg" Daryl has hair that can compare.

I often think about having hair as majestic as Paul's. For some reason, whenever my hair gets a certain length I have the irresistible urge to feel and pull at it. I think what it would be like if I had hair as long as Paul's and I shudder. My hands would never leave it alone. Sometimes, dreadlocks cross my mind. That is a total lie. I think my sister could have some good dreadlocks but they would have to be done right. I don't think Paul could have good dreadlocks despite the marvelousness of his mop.

I see Paul running his hair through his fingers now. Sometimes he reminds me of a

FIGURE 5.9

lion. Just the mane part. He doesn't have any other resemblence to a beast of that caliber—however unbelivable his hair is.

Paul forced me to take a break in my writing to talk about post-secondary education. There is a piece of lint in Paul's hair. I can see that while typing and it isn't making me very happy. I just removed it. Paul just told me he'd like a sample of his hair to be inserted into the book. I think I will do this. I need to go get some tape. In the words of Arnold Schwarzeneger playing the terminator (in T2: Judgement Day??? I believe—PLEASE CORRECT ME IF I'M WRONG—it was) "I'll be back." And then he comes smashing in with a truck and that lady doesn't even know what hit her and such and such.

Here is Paul's hair. I got up to get a stapler but it wasn't necessary, I had to salvage a piece of tape from my binder. Enjoy.

FIGURE 5.9 *continued*

I recently added riskier topics to the mix: sexual harassment, alcoholism, death. I've also considered funny stories or jokes, ghost stories, and candy. I've had to cover over "marriage" and "love" after they remained empty.

One favorite interest journal in my class this year was snowmen. I pasted into the front cover of this journal photocopies of the Calvin and Hobbes cartoons that show snowmen doing all kinds of wacky things. Students have added their own drawings, many with creative and interesting details.

10. *Argue writes.* When we begin to study argument and editorial writing, I change the focus of quick writing. Each day I bring in an article from the newspaper that provokes a response. "Prison officials cut calories to save money," "Passing on wealth a matter of priorities," and "First grader shoots playmate" can lead to rich discussions of cruel and unusual punishment, inherited wealth,

> **Bad Hair day!** (How I fix it!)
>
> Some days you wake up and your hair is just a MESS! So you wash it and try to tame down the frizzy mess. So now its soaked, Now what!? you brush it, yanking through the knots, now its slick to your head. Now its time for the blow dryer, once your done w/ that your hair lots of volume, (or for me it does) so I put my <u>extra</u> hot Chi hairstrightener to it. The hair that is still damp sizzles as I run the strightener through it. After a good 20 minutes of doing this, it looks somewhat decent and there goes 40 minutes of your morning! All that to make your hair look somewhat decent. I just LOVE being a girl!!

FIGURE 5.10

and gun control. But first, we write. I read a news story or an editorial out loud and then students write for five minutes. Many write letters to the editor, since letters are a predictable, familiar structure for argument. We share these and discuss the issues that bother them. Students quickly see the connection between the confident voice of the writer and the quality of evidence presented. They begin to hear weak arguments, but they still struggle with topic choice. My students need help finding issues they care enough to argue well.

Voice before these quick writes was spoken and now I know how to make my strong voice heard on paper.

—MATT

This semester I found an article from the *L.A. Times* about administrators eliminating cupcakes and other sweet treats from classrooms in order to combat childhood obesity. In the article they mentioned that the Texas Legislature had created a "cupcake amendment" to preserve them in their schools. My students listened to the facts and then were asked to argue one side or the other in the "cupcake wars." Elizabeth's argument appears in Figure 5.11.

"Please, leave cupcake clashes to classrooms . . ." brought high fives in my room. There is nothing like just the right phrase to inspire writers to reach. Elizabeth was not interested in further work on this topic, but in playing with the sound of argument, she developed a strong sense of this genre. She wrote on

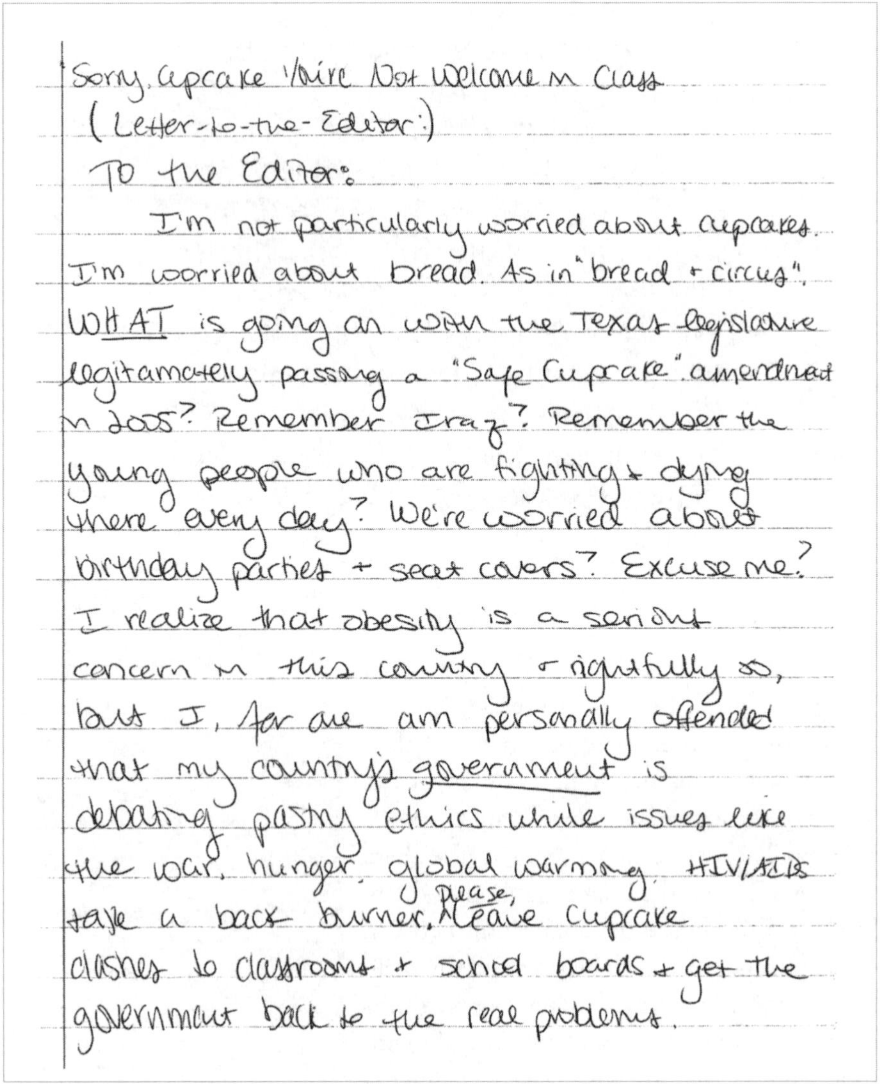

> Sorry, Cupcake You're Not Welcome in Class
> (Letter-to-the-Editor:)
> To the Editor:
>   I'm not particularly worried about cupcakes. I'm worried about bread. As in "bread + circus". WHAT is going on with the Texas legislature legitamately passing a "Safe Cupcake" amendment in 2005? Remember Iraq? Remember the young people who are fighting + dying there every day? We're worried about birthday parties + seat covers? Excuse me? I realize that obesity is a serious concern in this country + rightfully so, but I, for one am personally offended that my country's government is debating pastry ethics while issues like the war, hunger, global warming, HIV/AIDS take a back burner. Please, Leave cupcake clashes to classrooms + school boards + get the government back to the real problems.

FIGURE 5.11

the cost of the Project Graduation party for seniors and argued her position effectively, even though it was contrary to the wishes of the rest of the class. ("Blank Check and Party Hats: Unworthy Charity" is on the DVD and pp. 135–36)

Argue writes help students respond with their first thoughts on an issue. Before they are able to censor themselves or judge their ideas as ineffective, they write. Over several days of argue writes they discover which topics they have firm opinions on and which they have enough interest in to begin collecting evidence.

REREADING QUICK WRITES: DISCOVERING WHAT IS THERE

Kids mimic what we do. They copy our engagement in work, they copy our moves in revision, they copy our joy for living. When they arrive in class they read our energy; they read our passion for what we teach. Is this worth learning? Then when they go to write, they watch how we write. It is precisely why we have to take our roughest first draft and put it on the overhead, reread it out loud to them, and talk about what belongs and what is a rabbit trail that should be cut.

I complete a quick write on a transparency and then reread it in front of my students: Rereading is an essential and often overlooked part of teaching writing. I look for moments of insight or interest. I look for places where I have more to say. I talk aloud as I think through the entry. Then I ask students to do the same work with their entries.

Figures 5.12 and 5.13 are two samples of the rereading I have done in front of students.

This is how I talk about this quick write with students:

I started this quick write just thinking about photographs that came to mind. I have been struggling with my teenage daughter, so I think that's why the first picture I thought of was Hannah on horseback on our vacation one summer. She looks so happy and I cherish that moment. Then I thought of my husband Pat in a frame that sits on my desk, then a picture of my son, Cam, and daughter, Hannah, talking, and then my grandparents' wedding photo. I listed choices at the top of the page before I started writing. I know that sometimes it helps me to have choices to think through before I start writing. (With other quick writes, sometimes I just start writing because I instantly know a story I want to tell.)

Once I wrote "grandparents," I just started writing because I love the photo and want to know the story behind it. The funny thing about this quick write was the way the whole tone of the writing turned instantly when I wrote "knee-length wedding dress" because the long-buried frustration over my own

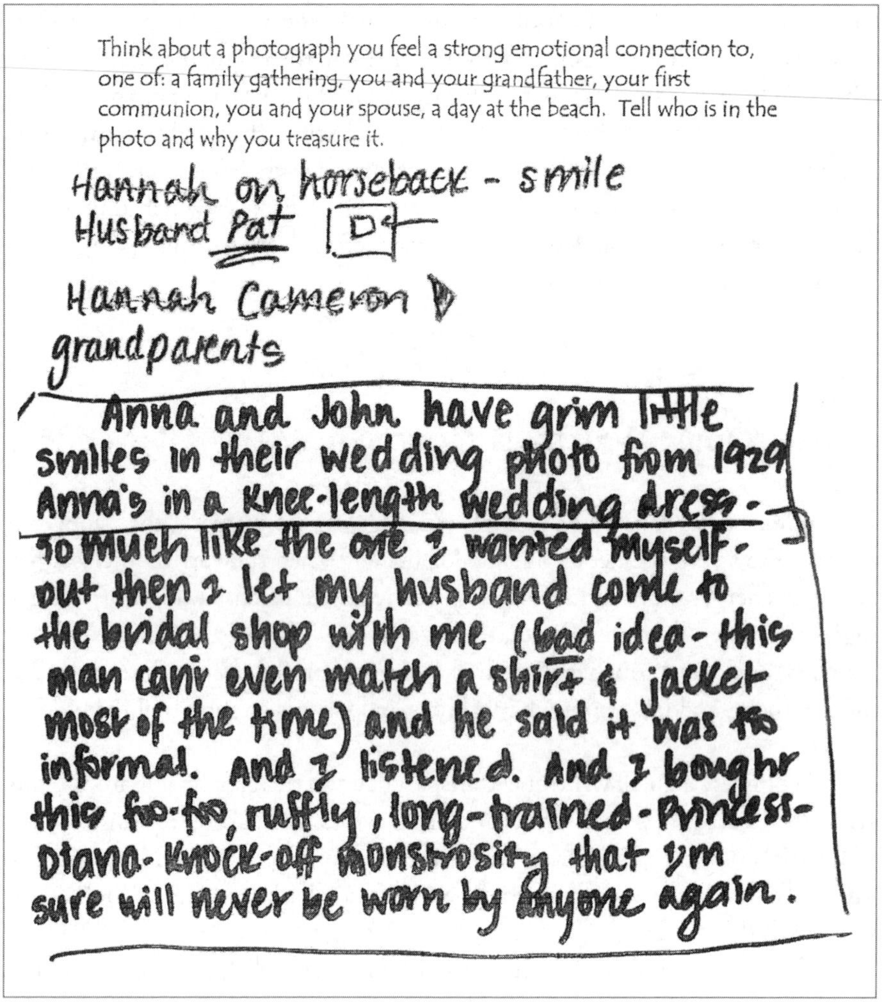

Think about a photograph you feel a strong emotional connection to, one of: a family gathering, you and your grandfather, your first communion, you and your spouse, a day at the beach. Tell who is in the photo and why you treasure it.

Hannah on horseback - smile
Husband Pat [D]

Hannah Cameron ▷
grandparents

Anna and John have grim little smiles in their wedding photo from 1929. Anna's in a knee-length wedding dress - so much like the one I wanted myself - but then I let my husband come to the bridal shop with me (bad idea - this man can't even match a shirt & jacket most of the time) and he said it was to informal. And I listened. And I bought this fo-fo, ruffly, long-trained-Princess-Diana-Knock-off monstrosity that I'm sure will never be worn by anyone again.

FIGURE 5.12

wedding dress burst to the surface with that phrase. (I draw boxes to separate these stories on the overhead as I talk.)

I put boxes around the two different stories that could be written from here. The second box is more interesting to me because I've written a lot about how close my husband and I are, but not a lot about how frustrating stupid things are in relationships. I also would like to write about our wedding because one disaster after another happened all night long (lost wedding ring, bodice of the dress unraveled, and so on), and I'd like to write that story. I haven't thought of it for years, but I really want to write about it.

It isn't unusual in my quick writing that I begin wanting to write about one thing, but find something better just by being engaged with pen and paper.

When I was ten years old (or any age)...

age 6 or 7   hand me down trolls

present tense...

I'm sitting on my floor in my bedroom with my big box of troll furniture in front of me. I'm setting up house for the trolls — which means: choosing their felt clothes, braiding their hair, deciding who's the mother, who's the father and who's the baby. I always make the older sister wear ugly clothes and I don't fix her hair; I even name her Linda. ha!

, and   ;   Do they have to follow the rules?

scene -

dialogue detail

June. Early morning.

FIGURE 5.13

I really believe the act of writing uncovers topics for us and they float into our consciousness, begging to be written.

The drawing/sketching helps me figure out a topic sometimes. I tell my students that adding detail to a drawing can help a writer find story details. In this case I drew a picture of myself at six or seven in my school picture wearing a hand-me-down jumper, then drew my favorite toy of the time: a troll doll.

I pictured myself playing with the trolls as I wrote. "I always make the older sister wear ugly clothes and I don't fix her hair; I even name her Linda," made me laugh. I know I want to use that line in a writing piece sometime to show my younger-sister rage at my smart older sister.

When I reread this quick write, I focused on punctuation. I often write quick writes with dashes to represent breaks in thought, then go back and add more graceful punctuation later. I used this opportunity to give students a mini-lesson on how you can punctuate using the colon to say "which means." We have to show how writers *think* with punctuation. The quick write can be the perfect vehicle for those reminders.

I get energized when the act of writing brings back a moment from child-hood that I had forgotten. I can say with confidence to my students that the same thing will happen to them: They'll rediscover moments long forgotten.

I ask students to reread their entries and do the same: Circle words or phrases that invite you to write more or consider other topics that are hiding within your writing. Add to what you've written or underline things you want to come back to. Rereading helps my students focus on how the notebook can be useful in their extended writing. Your goal is not a great quick write; it is seeking your voice to capture your experiences and ideas.

You'll notice on the DVD that I had students do this on the very first day of class. I had them respond to "Where I'm From" by George Ella Lyon and then reread their entry and add to it or identify phrases or ideas where they had more to say. I want student to realize this is our work as writers: We write and then we reread and look for more to say or a place to focus just as we reread to understand when faced with really challenging texts. After we find a place where there is more to say, we write just from that idea for another few minutes.

But as seriously as I take free writing in notebooks, I take just as seriously the need to move beyond it. Collecting a lot of rough draft, first-thinking entries are not in and of themselves going to improve writing, or not enough anyway. As Lucy Calkins said, "Children will never write well if they are accustomed to writing briefly. Elaboration is one of the very first and most foundational quali-ties of good writing." We must take our notebook entries and reread them for crafting opportunities—read for deeper connections and possibilities, reread many entries at once looking for themes in our thinking. Although rough drafts/journal writing can build stamina and voice, it is the crafting of those quick writes into full-length drafts that improves a writer's ability to make deci-sions to improve the clarity of a piece. That is why I believe quick writes are often a part of rehearsal, not drafting. But once the writer has found the theme or the story, the notebook might be set aside and further composition happen primarily at the computer.

At the start of a unit I might ask students to reread their notebooks with a highlighter, looking for topics that reoccur and might be useful to consider. Those are usually hot ones. (You can watch students search for multigenre topics in notebooks on the DVD.) Other students have stayed away from topics that reoccur. Some students do not want to work through the complicated emotions that accompany a difficult writing choice in a classroom filled with their peers. I will say, "You know, you may want to write about this later, when you're ready, even if that is years from now; it may help you to write about it. For now, I think you want to choose something else."

How Quick Writes Fit in My Plan for the Week

You'll notice in Figure 5.14 that quick writing is a small part of the work planned each day in workshop. I allow a little time for sharing. I might say, "Who found something to say well? Who would like to share something they wrote?" (There are examples of this on the DVD.) Students might respond with a best line, or a few might read entries or comment on their thinking, but I'm cautious about giving over too much time to quick writing when students need time to shape ideas into essays. Sometimes I find pairs of students sharing notebook writing during our workshop. I most often find students referring to their notebooks as they begin to write longer drafts.

Final Thoughts

The energy from work in writing notebooks is contagious. Some students venture out to risk and share in the first few weeks, and then others spring forward in the next. The room changes in such remarkable ways when we look at our lives and figure out how to put our ideas and experiences into words.

I believe what was said in the foreword to the 2007 *Writing Next* report, "Around the world, from the cave paintings in Lascaux, France, which may be 25,000 years old, to the images left behind by the lost Pueblo cultures of the American Southwest, to the ancient aboriginal art of Australia, the most common pictograph found in rock paintings is the human hand. Coupled with pictures of animals, with human forms, with a starry night sky or other images that today we can only identify as abstract, we look at these men's and women's hands, along with smaller prints that perhaps belong to children, and cannot help but be deeply moved by the urge of our ancestors to leave some permanent imprint of themselves behind."

We help students craft their lives to save forever: to teach their grandchildren—to teach themselves. Teachers tell me they just don't have time for all of

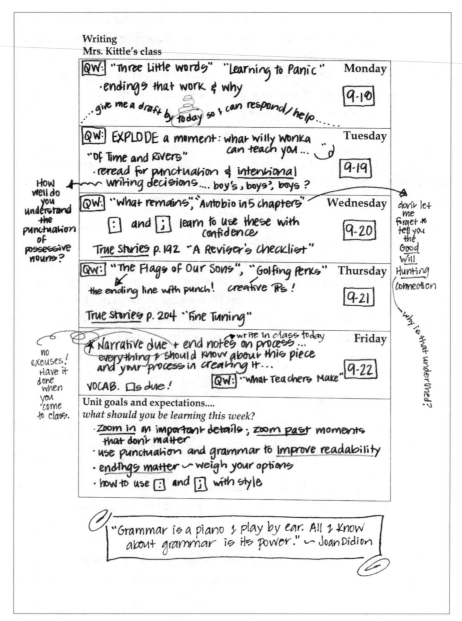

Writing
Mrs. Kittle's class

Monday 9-10
QW: "Three Little Words" "Learning to Panic"
· endings that work & why
give me a draft by today so I can respond/help

Tuesday 9-19
QW: EXPLODE a moment: what willy wonka can teach you ...
"Of Time and Rivers"
· reread for punctuation & intentional writing decisions.... boy's, boys', boys?

How well do you understand the punctuation of possessive nouns?

Wednesday 9-20
QW: "what remains", "Autobio in 5 chapters"
: and ; learn to use these with confidence
True Stories p. 192 "A Reviser's Checklist"

don't let me forget to tell you the Good Will Hunting connection

Thursday 9-21
QW: "The Flags of Our Sons", "Golfing Perks"
the ending line with punch! creative Ps!
True Stories p. 204 "Fine Tuning"

why is that underlined?

Friday 9-22
write in class today
Narrative due + end notes on process ... everything I should know about this piece and your process in creating it...
VOCAB. □s due!   QW: "what Teachers Make"

no excuses! Have it done when you come to class.

Unit goals and expectations....
what should you be learning this week?
· Zoom in on important details ; zoom past moments that don't matter
· use punctuation and grammar to improve readability
· endings matter ~ weigh your options
· how to use : and ; with style

"Grammar is a piano I play by ear. All I know about grammar is its power." ~ Joan Didion

FIGURE 5.14

this personal writing anymore. I say, this isn't about genre. I'm talking about immersing students in thinking and crafting writing vs. playing the game of school. How do we *not* have time for it? Forcing students through a process to mimic a structure they are reproducing with little understanding is not the responsible teaching of writing. It has to be about more. Students have to be given the time and vision to choose a structure for their ideas. Once students see writing as communicating something valuable to them, our work can begin. And yes, I believe that leading students to immerse themselves in craft leads to better writing in all genres, even those papers they must complete just for school. We teach them how to write well about their lives and their immersion in the process of making meaning improves all of their writing skills: their thinking about structure changes, their flexibility in writing—what *Writing Next* says we value most in this age—the ability to write about anything and find a form to do it well. Their understanding of how writing can work—how to move readers—their language for assisting others, and getting to the heart of what matters changes. It all just shifts in the most important, lasting way.

This is what I want for every one of my students: Nicole visited our school when she was home on break from college, and I asked her as I ask all my students, "Were you prepared? Tell me about the writing they've asked you to do in all of your courses and how well you were able to complete it."

She said, "No problem, Mrs. Kittle. I know what good writing is and how to get there."

Rick

Always give sorrow words.
Grief that does not speak whispers to the over-fraught heart and bids it to break.
—William Shakespeare

Rick has long ago lost his writing notebook. He has a fat red marker in one hand and a piece of scrap paper on the desk in front of him. After I read aloud an editorial I say, "Write what you're thinking. . . ." and it's June: My students know what this means. Still John says, "Write what?"

I say, "You might write about this author's struggle to negotiate his personal values and beliefs as he sends his son off to a war he doesn't believe in."

Rick interrupts, "I have no values and beliefs, so I can't write." On the white scrap before him he writes *1. No.* John glances at him, amused, then begins to write.

And I don't have the energy today—not this morning—not for this battle. You know the last week or two of classes with seniors? Yes, every age unravels a bit as the sun illuminates dust in the room and bakes us from open windows, but it is worse with seniors about to be released from their twelve-year prison sentence. As the year crawls to a finish and only some follow the rules we all agreed to early in the year, teachers unravel as well. The same battles with the same kids suddenly seem intolerable. Coffee doesn't help. There's no singing on the way to work, just the dark brooding of bad heavy metal. I need a little reggae in my life. So I watch Rick and do nothing. *You win; I'm too tired to fight today.*

But I look at his hunched shoulders. I notice the way his wavy brown hair falls in front of his face or creeps beneath a hat pulled low over his eyes and I remember the way he stares at the computer thinking when everyone else is writing. It isn't easy being Rick. He's all "I don't care about anything" in my room, but it's a disguise. There's always a reason. I don't need to make it worse today.

The rest of the class is writing. It's true that the two boys sitting near Rick write less than they did a month ago. Perhaps they're influenced by him, but they're all set after graduation: Williams College for one, the honors program at the University of New Hampshire for the other. The future's so bright, they've gotta wear shades. Rick says he's "taking a year off to save money . . ." when I ask.

So what do I do when a student won't take the writing notebook seriously? Sometimes I wait. And I wonder if it's the right thing to do . . . but I wait.

I believe the human spirit seeks creation; expression is irresistible. Most students will find something to say. Some I won't reach, but I'll keep trying. I'm hired for 180 days—every one of those. So I say to Rick as he leaves that morning, "I know quick writing was a joke to you today. You can't take it seriously with scrap paper and a marker, but I also know you have things to say. I'm just asking you to try." And you know, when you take away accusations and assumptions (*you don't care!*) and look a kid in the eyes and say, "I know you can do better and I'm waiting for you to show me," it's hard for them to keep resisting. Some still manage to, but often there's a turn . . . and all is revealed.

Two days later Rick arrives with his multigenre project. Here's his dear reader letter:

Dear Reader,

Here we are. The project is two days late and I have been stumped by what to do it on. I have never been a perfect student model and I have always procrastinated but I have always loved writing and could usually get writing based assignments in on time. I have never been through that much bad in my life. My psychology teacher gave us an assignment to write about troubles that shaped us. He assured me that, even though I didn't have to overcome very many obstacles thus far, nobody gets through life without a crisis . . . or two. He did not mention that the two crises would be so close together and could make every day seem like a strange nightmare.

I have been listening to the same James Taylor record for about a month straight. Sometimes it would blast all day and into the night and further into 3 or 4 a.m. I used to not mind Mr. Taylor's hokey beats but that LP in my mother's hands is a recipe for chaos. From the other end of the house I can feel the bass pound on my door. It's part of my fresh-out-of-Berlin-Mental-Hospital-mom's new plan to make either me or my dad snap. I am Mr. 2.0 according to her, citing my less than satisfactory grades. My dad is also responsible for killing my grandmother in her twisted mind. Together my dad and I are the "Batter Brothers" because we took so much pleasure in beating her up one morning when she tried to run half clothed down the road saying she had been poisoned and we had no choice but to restrain her while the ambulance came. This began right after my grandma died and I haven't had a chance to even begin grieving for her because of everything my mom has put our family through. Although I should've expected no less from some one who disallows pictures of our family on the fridge.

There is so much more that I want to rant on about but that is not what this writing project is about. That would be weak. I needed to put it there so it is off my chest because I don't have anywhere else to put it and I'm not about to swallow it so it can arise in 15 years 10-fold and put me in the same place she was. That's what's been on my mind and it's not the easiest thing focusing on school. I firmly believe the only way through something is not to forget who you truly are, and to find sanctuary in fond memories and humor. My multi-genre will not be about Mother. It will be about me, my memories, and maybe some humor.

Sincerely,
Rick

I wish I could rewind the semester and see Rick from the start. I wish I had known this was what he was living with; I would have been kinder, more patient, more willing to listen. But we don't know. Too often we'll never know. It's groping in the dark so much of the time—trying to understand these complex kids before us. I promise to remember that in the fall when my next group of silent, reluctant, angry, or apathetic teenagers slide into their seats and barely look my way. What are these kids carrying? How can I help and teach writing at the same time?

I pick up my writing notebook and wonder.

PART THREE
WRITER'S WORKSHOP

CHAPTER SIX
The Opportunities in a Writer's Workshop

We rarely ask our students: tell us what has to happen around here in order for you to be willing to study hard, think deeply, and take real pride in your work?

—Robert L. Fried

I'm at my desk trying to write, but the orchestra music on a Navy ROTC video repeating in the lobby just feet from my office door is taunting me. These are my students; we are a country at war. I want the recruiters to stay away from my school; five of my former students are already in Iraq. How can I work on this writing when I should be organizing a protest?

I look around, trying to focus. I've reached a point in the school year when clutter outweighs purpose on my desk. This is not the time to be writing; I should be organizing. But Don told me "never a day without a line." I need fifteen minutes to write. And it is always like this. I mean really. I find those stolen silent moments in my house before dawn like everyone else, but unless I book a year-long retreat deep in the Icelandic tundra, there won't be enough moments to get any writing done. I'm going to have to write through distraction; I will have to write and revise amid the chaos of living.

There's a reason I'm telling you this. I know what is going on with me this month: I am terrified of writing this book. Fear creeps through me, creating all of these interesting, time-wasting tentacles: I am anxious, so instead of drafting, I think up excuses I'll give my editor when things are late. I feel inadequate, so I keep thumbing through books by other authors, noticing how superior they are to anything I might have to say. I am seeking some kind of stability in the face of this giant project, so I have just gone through and changed every document in this folder to Perpetua, a most serious and deliberate font. I tell myself that opening each piece and having it look the same matters right now. My students live in every one of those examples: I see them fiddling, distracting, and procrastinating during workshop, and I have to remember it is process at work. The writing process reminds me of watching my daughter learn to drive a standard shift—leap forward, screech to a halt, stall, roar to life. There is a deep connection between Art and Fear (and a great book of the same title about this), so my writing classroom hums with productivity some days and lurches along with what feels like little success on others.

When writing workshop is at its finest, it spins the way Meagan wrote in a quick write one morning, "The computers are humming and the air vent buzzing. The various keyboards are click clicking away with the gentle tapping of students' fingers typing out argument papers. Soft voices blend together speaking the way a stream would, babbling continuously over the little stones that block their writing pattern, and the leftover dispute of the day's sample argument paper. The soft keyboards are persistent in their voice, as I am persistent in writing the rhythm of Mrs. Kittle's first block writing class." Ah, just like a Disney movie!

It sounds so simple; if you peeked in the door on a productive day you might think it was just a good class of well-behaved students instead of the series of decisions I make each day to tune instruction to the needs of a particular group of personalities and keep all moving forward in their work. Some days writing workshop even sounds like Meagan wrote, but not always. I'm still working on that.

The foundation of my writing workshop is seven interdependent principles:

1. I expect everyone to write well; I believe every student will. Some students will need more time and support than others, and I will give it to them. I structure independent writing time for all students so I can be available for re-teaching some.

> *One who learns from one who is learning drinks from a running stream.*
>
> —SILETZ PROVERB

2. Collaboration is at the heart of our work. It isn't a community unless I'm a part of it: working, thinking, learning.

3. Studying the elements of craft that make writing effective will help all of us write better.

4. All students will listen to their own writing if I teach them how. As they listen, they'll hear the rhythm of precise, effective sentence structure and learn how to craft it.

5. I learn from watching and listening to students. I respect the myriad ways student writers think and organize their ideas, as well as the multiple ways all writers work through their own process on a piece.

6. Writing is flexible; for every story and idea there are many forms that might lend it light. Formulas (like the five-paragraph essay) limit the development of thinking and confuse the priorities of a writer. Writing will always be about the idea first, then a form that gives it shape.

7. Every student will write with more skill and grace by the end of the semester. It is my responsibility to make that happen.

Organizing my workshop is as simple as having a three-hole punch in a predictable place so I don't waste time locating one for a student, and as complicated as redirecting a student who is firmly resistant and confrontational. I organize my work to make writing workshop productive, supportive, and challenging for all students every day.

THE FIRST DAY

The DVD includes a clip from the first day of class one semester. I knew the students would be nervous and so would I. We did a quick write, we looked for writing qualities in the course outline, and we tried to get this thing we call writing workshop off the ground. As you watch, consider the thinking I am beginning to develop with students. Figure 6.1 shows a summary of my thinking about teaching in a workshop that I pass out on the first day. I ask students to read for voice—and to underline it when they find it.

Writers need

CHOICE

TOOLS

RESPONSE

You'll have **choice** in each genre we study . . .

I'll provide the **tools** you need to write well . . .

I'll respond **often** and quickly so that you can continue to craft
and learn . . .

Our first unit will be narrative.

You'll write two narratives, due two weeks apart. We'll study ten different
things that make narratives work, but they are **tools** you'll use in all kinds

FIGURE 6.1

of writing. Narrative is often the foundation for a college admissions essay, so it can end up helping you find that focus as well. We will follow narrative with a unit on writing the college admissions essay, so it will mesh nicely together.

You will decide what you want to write about because I respect you enough to believe you will choose wisely. Making **choices** about what to write is some of the hardest work for writers. Part of the purpose of quick writes is to help you find topics you care about and are interested in pursuing in longer pieces of writing.

One of the **tools** I will use to teach you is my own process of creating writing. Here's why I teach this way. I believe that writers are told what to write (assignments) and given due dates, rubrics, and so on, but are not often shown what the actual writing of writing looks like. In other words, you're all alone out there. You bang out a draft and reread it (maybe) and hope for the best. In fact, you even hope that the teacher won't have time to read it. And you turn it in, along with sixty-five other kids that day and the teacher is buried under papers. You won't see that paper for weeks most of the time. When you get it back with a letter grade and a few comments it hardly feels like fair payment for all you put into it, or even fair justification for the letter grade you received and there's no time to fix it if you don't like the grade . . . and who would want to go back to that piece a month later anyway? So you move on to that next piece of writing and it isn't any better—in fact, you have even less faith in your writing because you seem to be trying to figure out what this teacher "wants" instead of what good writing is. Maybe you write six papers all year like that . . . and you're not sure you're much better at the end of another year. How frustrating. No wonder most kids tell me they hate writing.

However . . . this semester all is turned upside down.

First of all, we will study writing as a subject all by itself.

This isn't also a literature class requiring the analysis and study of great books from the last 200 years; in fact, the study of reading as a subset of writing will be entirely different than you've known for the last few years. We will read for fun . . . books you are interested in and choose to open each day. We will read to figure out what other authors are up to in their writing (actually studying the moves writers make), and we will read to respond. We are going to explore what we think about things by writing about things we read.

FIGURE 6.1 *continued*

Second, I write. I will quick write with you. I will always be working on whatever genre we are studying together so that my understandings of what writers need to work in that genre are fresh and helpful. I do not share my writing with you because I think I am the best model of writing—not at all. I read far too much to ever believe that: I know how good those other writers are. However, those other writers show you only the finished products. It looks like magic. Or divine inspiration. Or just plain gift. I can never figure out how those writers managed to come up with the stuff they write! But my writing is in the midst of process: I'll show you the rabbit trails and incomplete thoughts and mixed-up messes that are trying to be coherent in order to lead you through your own messy, mixed-up process. We muck around together in this class. That means you'll be sharing drafts with partners, small groups, and even the class altogether—and we'll be telling you what we see and what we don't understand.

You'll be on display in here: Writers usually write about things that matter to them, stories that they remember well many years later, or just ideas that they believe in strongly. This means I take the respect and trust themes I mentioned in my Information Guide really, really seriously. If someone has the guts to write about their parents' divorce or their grandparent's death or being humiliated on the soccer field, you'll not only respect their courage in saying it, you'll listen hard. And if they ask you not to repeat it, you won't. Writers need a community of readers in order to thrive. You are that community for each other and for me. We need to have a code of honor here. I need to trust you and you need to trust each other.

Last, you'll write a lot. We won't be watching any videos or doing any busywork. I mean that. If you don't understand why you should be doing what I've asked you to do, ask me. I sometimes skip ahead to the doing without enough explaining, and you may think I'm just filling time. Never. I think very carefully about what I want you to do in order to become more proficient writers. None of us have time to waste. But it also means that writing and reading and listening and responding and writing some more is pretty much what we're doing day after day. You'll say, "Mrs. Kittle, can we walk down to Chinook for coffee? Can we go outside? Can we watch a movie?" and I'll say, "No, no, no," and you'll think I'm absolutely no fun at all. Sorry. It's true. I'm far more determined that you'll leave here writing well than that you think I'm the coolest.

FIGURE 6.1 *continued from previous page*

And on that note . . . I really do expect you to work all period. I'm just not that sympathetic when it comes to staying up late and being tired in my class. I understand you have other classes, but only like three of them . . . and mine is the most important anyway—(joke)—and I know there will be times when you won't "feel" like writing. It happens to all of us. I really do get that. But I also know that when you're at college next fall or sitting at your desk in an office of a big corporation and someone gives you an assignment to write something, no one will care if you don't feel like getting the work done. You'll just do it. You know it is true. So when you come to class, settle in and get the work done. It isn't about me catching you talking and assigning you a lunch detention or keeping you after school or calling your parents to say, "Who raised this kid?" It is about your commitment to your own growth in writing. I can't do it for you. I'll give you every possible tool to help you along the way, but in the end it is you in front of the screen or the page writing. If you don't put in the time with your writing, it won't get that much better. And you'll look back in January at all of those wasted days and say, "What was I thinking? I could have been learning!" Okay, maybe you won't . . . but you have the chance this semester to give your writing everything you've got and produce pieces you never thought were possible.

Let's do it.

FIGURE 6.1 *continued*

AN INFORMATION GUIDE FOR STUDENTS AND PARENTS

On that first day of class I also pass out the information guide shown in Figure 6.2. I want to be sure my thinking and expectations are clear from the start.

Writing
Information Guide 2007–2008

I love teaching writing; it is one of the central joys of my life. I look forward to learning from you, and with you, as we aim to improve our skills as writers. It is hard work, but your writing will improve through regular feedback and revision. **I can *always* find time to provide extra help when you need it this semester**; we can read and discuss your writing together or

FIGURE 6.2

think of ways to approach an essay. **Don't be shy; come and see me for help.** We can plan for a time that works in your schedule, either before or after school, or even during your lunch block. Bring cookies.

We will be sharing drafts of writing we care about, which requires trust and respect. I expect all students I teach to respect each other. I will enforce all Kennett policies in my classroom, particularly the ban on food or drink because of the expensive equipment in this room. I will work diligently to create a community of learners and teach you how to support and encourage each other as developing writers. I do not tolerate harassment of any kind in my classroom. Don't push me on this.

I expect all students to arrive on time to class with the materials needed and to have completed homework. **During class I expect all of my students to work.** If you are frequently disruptive or missing work, I will keep you after school or have you join me for lunch. I also nag a bit and get testy when students won't cooperate. We are here to learn; it's an opportunity for all of us to improve as writers by working together and working **hard**. My job is to show you how to write well; your job is to seize each opportunity.

Gary Paulson says, "Read like a wolf eats." Writing and reading are intimately connected. **Readers are better writers.** Sustained reading of twenty minutes or more is expected Monday through Thursday at home. Choose your books well. Read books you love, but also challenge yourself to read widely in all genres and grow as a reader. Reading absolutely impacts vocabulary development and writing, so it is an essential element of this course. I will provide you with dozens of essays to read in class. You'll learn to mark them up as you study the craft of others.

Nancie Atwell says, "There's nothing better for you—not broccoli, not an apple a day, not aerobic exercise. In terms of the whole rest of your life, in terms of making you smart in all ways, there's nothing better. Top-ranking scientists and mathematicians are people who read a lot. Top-ranking historians and researchers are people who read a lot. **It's like money in the bank in terms of the rest of your life**, but it also helps you escape from the rest of your life and live experiences you can only dream of. Most importantly, along with writing, it's the best way I know to find out who you are, what you care about, and what kind of person you want to become." Think about that. **Stop your whining about not having time to read**; I've heard it before and I know it isn't true. Make different choices. Give up something for half an hour a night.

Just
do
it.

FIGURE 6.2 *continued from previous page*

Grades will be determined each quarter based on these guidelines:

- Reading homework and responses to books, 15%
- Essays*, 70%
- Class participation and your writer's notebook entries, 15%

*I will provide you with feedback on your writing regularly, in fact most often within a few days of when you turn it in. However, I will not **grade** individual drafts during the quarter. Writers need more feedback than evaluation. You'll get more suggestions and coaching than you will letter grades. It will make you a better writer. The reason is this: As you learn to write well **you need to take risks** with words, with structure, with organization, punctuation and ideas. You are less likely to take risks if a grade is on the line. I will grade essays at the end of each unit, once you have had many opportunities to perfect your work. However, **all drafts are due on time**. Email your work to me if you are sick or have a friend put it in my mailbox.

Essays even one day late lose 10%.

Always deliver a clean, neat copy that shows you've worked on the piece. Save drafts. You will have a list of qualities of effective writing to guide your understanding of good writing, and I can help you see where your individual essays sing and where they fall short. You will work toward a portfolio of writing that represents the best that you can do.

Read often, write hard, complete your class work on time, and show up. You'll do well.

You will need two things for my class: a **writer's notebook** (school issue or your own, whichever you prefer), and **a three-ring binder** (with a clear plastic pocket in the cover) to use for a portfolio of written work. It would be helpful if you brought a **computer disk or flash drive** to save work we do on the computers in class, so you can continue to work at home. We will also use **colored pencils** most days (just three or four colors), so if you'd prefer to have your own set, bring them in.

I look forward to the challenges of working together to improve our writing. I know we'll have a great semester.

Penny Kittle
Email: p_kittle@sau9.org

Final note: Please share the contents of this letter with your parents. They are busy people, so be prepared to paraphrase, without missing anything essential. Please make sure they start their **parent homework** as we talked about in class. Imagine the possibilities!

As writers we are always exploring what happens, what comes next, turning it over, finding words to sit in like chairs . . . because words shape the strange sorrows we are living in, help us connect.

Naomi Shihab Nye

FIGURE 6.2 *continued*

Here's a template for our daily schedule. Like all lesson plans it is subject to variation, interruption, and teachable moments. What is predictable is time to read and write in a supportive, structured environment to improve. I will explain the particulars of each part later in this chapter.

1. **Introduce daily agenda:** the big idea of what we're learning and how it connects to our current study (2 minutes)

2. **Silent sustained reading:** book talk (3 minutes) and free reading (10 minutes)

3. **Quick writes and notebook work:** experiments with writing (15 minutes)

4. **Minilessons:** (15 minutes on one of the following)
   a. **Studying mentor texts**
   b. **My process in the genre we're studying**
   c. **Rehearsal, revision, and rereading**
   d. **Grammar and sentence structure work** (see Chapter 15)

5. **Writing workshop:** independent work time (30–35 minutes)

6. **Closing:** sharing best lines (3 minutes)

1. INTRODUCE AGENDA FOR THE DAY

I post an agenda each day on the whiteboard and list the model texts we'll look at and the skills we'll focus on. I review this road map as class begins. I give the big-picture version: "Today we're looking at dialogue in narrative. We'll read 'Like a Person' and watch how one writer shows what is said and what is *not* said. As you know, dialogue is an essential element in story." I explicitly connect today's learning to our current genre unit. (You can see these agendas of each day we filmed on the DVD.)

2. READING

Students choose their books and keep track of their progress (in pages read) each week. I expect all student to read 100–150 pages each week, adding together pages read in class and those read at home. Most students can complete this with two hours of reading each week outside of class.

Most days begin with a book talk. I introduce a book or a student reviews one. On the DVD I lead three book talks: *Looking for Alaska, Ultra-marathon*

Man, and *Sailing Around the Room*. Here's what is important to me in a book talk of two to three minutes:

- I've read the book and I recommend it because it is a great book, not just a good one. I review all genres. I review classics as well as the newest books in our library.

- I summarize the essential elements of the book—who tells the story, a skeleton of the plot, why I enjoyed it, or why I think they would enjoy it.

- I read a short passage so they get a feel for the writer's voice.

Parent Book Talks

I encourage parents to visit class and talk about a book they've read and loved. It is a great way to bring parents into school: a nonthreatening, casual conversation with students about what they are reading. I want students to know that adults they know value reading.

This fall a stepfather of one of my seniors emailed me a long letter thanking me for focusing so much on reading for pleasure. He wrote about his history with books and his passion for reading. He is one of the most successful businessmen in town and I seized the opportunity. When Steve came to present his favorite books that morning in his business suit, my students listened. He had seven books in a shopping bag, from *A People's History of the United States* by Howard Zinn, to *Band of Brothers* by Stephen Ambrose. He told my students that he never did well in college and left before he finished, but he always loved to read. He reached in the bag for that last book and said, "This was my favorite of the year," and out came *Harry Potter and the Deathly Hallows*. These are the moments you can't script in teaching, but what power they have to influence teenagers.

I read along with students most of the time. I do attendance first almost every day and then sign passes for students who need to get a new book from our school library. Sometimes I make a point of noticing what students are reading and do a brief, whispered talk with them about this as I see kids settling in. But it is essential that reading is just silent some of the time. Long ago at a conference I was reminded that the teacher may be the only adult the student has ever seen reading. Think about that. If at home the TV is always on and there aren't any books nearby, this is possible. Be that one adult who reads. Immerse yourself in the literature you love.

During reading I send around a clipboard. It is a space for students to record the page they're on each day (because they are expected to read twenty minutes each night) and the title of their book. This clipboard helps me stay in touch with what students are choosing to read and if they are reading at all. This is all self-monitored. A scan of the room will quickly reveal students who don't have books or aren't engaged in one. I watch for a few days and then ask questions. I insist that only reading happens during reading time and they do comply. (Watch Matt's interview on the DVD for a student's perspective on the importance of this time.)

Yes, I allow magazines. We read a lot of articles from magazines or newspapers during mentor text study, so it would be inconsistent to ban them during class time, but I also ask students to search for books so they have the pleasure and challenge of sustaining interest in one subject or story over time. (I think there is a conflict between what reading looks like for this generation and what it looked like for mine. Students read websites rapidly, skimming for information, stopping to read a bit, then moving on. I don't allow this kind of Internet surfing during our reading time, even though it is one of the ways students read at home, simply because I'm not sure I understand it well enough. I know that students acquire information in all kinds of ways and I try to be respectful of that. But I also know there is a value in a sustained focus—on reading deeply.) I seek the reading zone (Atwell 2007) for every student.

Now, in case you feel like silent sustained reading (SSR) is a place you can shave off a few minutes and save time, listen to a few of the students I've quoted below.

Amy wrote in her final portfolio, "SSR is valuable to my writing and my everyday life. I always used Cliff Notes and hated having to read until I got the opportunity to read what I want. First semester I watched kids who I knew never read rave about the book they were reading. The books I read helped me write stories because I can see the way they structure scenes and their word choice. Reading books helps me to improve my vocabulary because I am reading words that I don't hear in everyday conversation. I personally look forward to reading my book everyday during SSR time. For example, I was bummed today when Mrs. Kittle said that we had to read papers on the computer before we could read our books. This shows how important SSR is to me. I have learned to love reading in this writing class."

Alex said, "I think that SSR time is very valuable. It gets me into my books so that when I go home I want to keep going with it. If there was no SSR time, there is no way I would know what book I was even supposed to be reading because I would never bother to open it. I am not an avid reader, but SSR time has led me to be interested in reading and actually like it. I went home the other day and got into my pajamas, got under the blankets and read, just because. I have never done that until this year. SSR time has definitely influenced that and I value the time. When I start reading it seems as though mostly every time when we are supposed to stop, I never want to because I am enjoying the book."

And Erin said, "From when I was a young child, I always advanced in reading and even got sent into a grade above to read with them. This was one area that I was very strong in, but as my schooling proceeded and I read less and less I began to become awful at reading. I could read the assigned reading for thirty minutes a night and have no clue what was happening in the book. I began to get frustrated, and I found myself with a new best friend and it was Spark Notes. Until Mrs. Kittle's class I honestly think I had not read a whole book on my own since junior high."

Jess said, "Some kids do not feel they get a lot done in the short ten minutes we have to read, but I do. It gets my interest. For example, last Friday I started reading *The Truth About Forever* during SSR and ended up finishing it on Saturday. I don't think that would have happened if I didn't start it on Friday because I wouldn't have had the interest to start it on Saturday."

And last, Tiffanie said, "Many students don't read outside school. They dread the occasional assigned book and quickly jump online to use quick notes. Some never read and when they come to class and are required to read for ten minutes they become engulfed in books and want to continue reading. Forcing them to read really makes them likely to do it more. I know I didn't read a single book all first semester, and now that I have to read in class I get interested in books and go on to finish them at home. Reading is also an important part of writing; it allows you to observe techniques for getting your point across and also allows you to get ideas of what to write about. Without reading along with instruction I'm sure my writing wouldn't continue to improve. Reading shows you different ways to write and also can help to improve vocabulary, and draw a student into writing at the beginning of class."

3. QUICK WRITES (SEE CHAPTER 5)

4. MINILESSONS

I call them layers in my writing workshop: There is the study of great products (other writers' work) and the study of process—mine. Another layer is the students' experiments in each genre through quick writing in a notebook. During our daily minilessons we explore craft by looking at published work and looking at work under construction as well as looking at the way punctuation determines how writing will be read. Here are a few samples of each.

Reading and Thinking Like Writers

It's essential that I search long and hard for smart, funny writing as well as thoughtful, poignant writing and everything in between, hoping to spark something in my teenagers each day at the start of class. Good writing makes writers want to write. The idea of reading like writers came to me from the work of Katie Wood Ray. I have learned so much from this little southern gal I can hardly trace where I was before I read *Wondrous Words*. As I've read and reread her books I've learned to really notice what writers are doing and show my students what I see. How do I choose mentor texts? I look for the best writing in the genre we're studying while we're studying it. That way I find fresh work I can read with students for the first time discovering a writer's craft. Most model texts used again and again begin to dull for me, so I'm always seeking the surprise of new ideas. In Figure 6.3 are questions that drive our thinking. We do not try to answer all of these questions for each text or answer them in any particular order. We talk about the writing, circling ideas about structure and writing decisions as we highlight what really works for us in the piece.

Students read the mentor text with colored pencils in hand to find examples of sensory detail, the effective use of dialogue, the theme or "so what?" of the piece, or other qualities of writing we are studying in that genre. I read the piece aloud while students annotate these qualities. We discuss what we found in class or in small groups and then add what we notice to a class list of our understandings about the genre (see Figure 6.6 for an example of the class

Read Like a Writer

What do you notice about how this text was written?

Underline repeating phrases or repeating ideas or images.

Notice how examples that support ideas are written. Underline evidence to support a position.

Where does the writer show not tell?

Why do you think the author chose to organize the piece this way?

Why did the piece open the way it did? How would you define the lead?

What do you think the writer left out of this piece—or cut in revision?

What did you notice that you might try in your writing?

FIGURE 6.3

study of one author's work). All kinds of "in the moment" lessons arise out of this reading. One day we might look at paragraphs or sentences that break the rules they've been learning, and we talk about why those sentences work. It is refreshing to students because they understand that the way people communicate is much more complex than the grammar book says. Writing sounds like talk much of the time, but the talk of a smart, reasoned writer. In conversation you might stumble around trying to spit out what you're trying to say, but in writing you keep tuning your words until the piece hums. I show them how writers make it happen.

Here's an example of work with a mentor text. Last fall Tom Romano sent me a link to an essay he wrote for WMUB in Oxford, Ohio. It was called "My Father's Voice," and Tom wrote it for Father's Day. (This essay is part of *Zigzag: A Life of Reading and Writing, Teaching and Learning*, Romano 2008.) After we read and noticed repeating lines and images as a class, I stole some of Tom's lines and imitated his structure using my mother's voice as a topic. I shared the draft in Figure 6.4.

I remember my mother calling my name as twilight descended on Yamhill Street where I stood with Julie practicing foul shots. I knew her call was coming, my urgency to get a few more shots in began as soon as the streetlight came on above the hoop. Each night she interrupted our play with a call to dinner, her voice rising above the drumming of the ball on the pavement and the distant sound of traffic on the street nearby. Just one call and I responded; I may have groaned, but I always complied.

My mother's voice. It had so many tones: the trill of laughter as she chatted on the phone with a friend, the dancing notes as she sang along with dinner-making, the shrill tone of anger or the silence of hurt feelings, all wrapped around our home like the airy sugar of cotton candy. Mom was in the air around me, her spirit in every corner of our house and in the yard outside.

My mother's voice is crumbling a little at 71, after a stroke paralyzed her vocal chords briefly and took away her ability to sing. She speaks more slowly now: my mother's old voice, I call it, not the voice I knew as a child.

FIGURE 6.4

My mother's voice on the phone, calling to celebrate my first book . . . we're so proud of you, Penny, we could just bust our britches. She, the storyteller, the keeper of family history, the writer of a million words she'll never put on paper, cheering on a daughter who does what she could not. She, who wanted to be an English teacher, but quit college and became a mother instead. She, who wanted to return, but nursed a husband through alcoholism and despair instead. She, who went to work full time while her daughter was in middle school to establish a working history, so that we might qualify for college loans, insisting that her youngest, at least, finish college. It is her voice I hear as I'm introduced at a conference or rise to meet my students as they come to my classroom door on the first day of school: *don't forget how lucky you are to be here.*

My mother's voice rising into the night sky, carrying over mountains and rivers and railroads from the Willamette Valley to the mid-western plains to roll across the Great Lakes and north to the mountains of New Hampshire where I listen hard, waiting for her counsel. My mother's voice at twilight on a summer evening in the shadow of Mt. Tabor Park in Portland, Oregon. My mother's voice calling me home.

FIGURE 6.4 *continued*

After I shared Tom's piece and my own, my students wrote a quick write on someone's voice they know well. I like to have students experiment with the technique we're noticing. We then discussed the repeating lines, the different qualities of voice that can be revealed by showing a moment, the details that keep our attention. Several students shared quick writes that day. One student, Hattie, turned her quick write into a narrative on her relationship with her mother and how her mother's voice had changed during different periods in Hattie's life. (Hattie's piece is on the DVD.) Although Hattie wasn't ready to share her work in class, she wanted it included in work for future students to learn from. I try to convey the possibility to all of my students that they might create study texts for future units in my classroom—that they all can write powerfully and use an understanding of how writing works to develop their craft: that all can raise the quality of their writing to be a model for others.

My Process in the Genre We're Studying

I also teach through the thinking I'm doing in the genre we're studying: providing vision for how to get the work done and teaching students how to respond to each other through whole-class writing conferences. Once or twice during the unit, I'll plan a lesson showing students how I am working. I might brainstorm and begin a draft in front of them. I might list three things I'm thinking about and then show how I draft a scene from one of my choices. I don't write more than a few sentences as they watch, and I keep this process model to about fifteen minutes altogether. On another day I talk through how I might write a full narrative essay on the whiteboard in front of them including the options for scenes, the questions I have about the ending, all my "I don't know's" modeled to give them permission to work in this manner (see Figure 6.5). Although I may refer to my piece often in individual conferences with kids, I use this model of my thinking for only one lesson out of the five that week. The other lessons are based on other model texts.

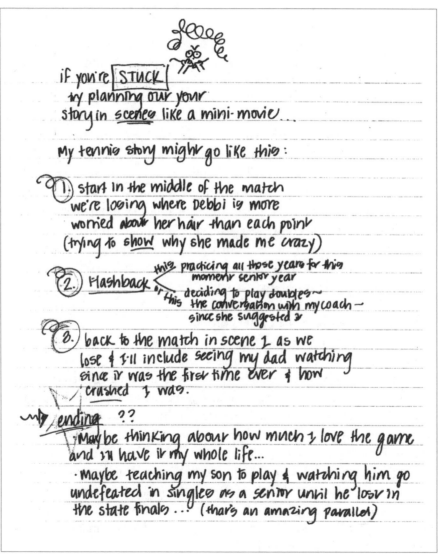

if you're STUCK
try planning our your
story in scenes like a mini-movie...

My tennis story might go like this:

1.) start in the middle of the match
   we're losing where Debbi is more
   worried about her hair than each point
   (trying to show why she made me crazy)

2.) Flashback ← this practicing all those years for this
                     moment senior year
            or this deciding to play doubles ~
                 the conversation with my coach —
                 since she suggested it

3.) back to the match in scene 1 as we
   lose & I'll include seeing my dad watching
   since it was the first time ever & how
   crushed I was.

ending ??
   ·Maybe thinking about how much I love the game
   and I'll have it my whole life...
   ·Maybe teaching my son to play & watching him go
   undefeated in singles as a senior until he lost in
   the state finals... (that's an amazing parallel)

FIGURE 6.5

Later during the unit, I will bring in a draft of the piece I talked through with them in class. I put it on the overhead and I reread it in front of them, talking through what I want to do with the piece and what I'm struggling with, marking up the text as I revise my thinking and add notes or cut parts to make it flow better. Students love to participate; they comment on what I'm doing and suggest phrases. I use this opportunity to talk about peer-conferring techniques. I point out which feedback helps and which doesn't. Sometimes I do this as a "fishbowl" conference with one student offering help and feedback and the others listening in, able to comment at the end. The key here is the model of re-reading a text under construction. I have found students don't reread their own work well—they don't hear the text, they "bark" at it, sounding out the words, but not listening for the impact of their text on a reader. Strong writers learn to listen to their writing. I use an authentic "under construction" draft of mine as I verbalize the questions and thinking I bring to my own listening to my text.

It is important that I maintain control of my writing. Student "help" can take over a story, just like teacher help can, and then I lose the drive to write.

I don't often share the final draft with the class because my work as a model with the piece is done. I finish many of the pieces I start with students and use what I learn in polishing a draft in my conferences with students—"I decided to go with the second ending I talked about in class because as I wrote it, I discovered that . . ." but I don't read the entire piece again. One advantage we have in our writing lab is that those pieces are often available in our shared network folder. This folder holds only pieces students are willing to share with others in the class. Students who are interested can go there and read a finished piece of mine, but most don't. My goal is to model thinking, not to create a model or mentor text in the genre.

Rehearsal, Rereading, and Revision

This is how I define rehearsal: It's the beginning nudge to write . . . the moment when you think about a topic and make a connection that feels like it could be something. It's a commitment of heart, not words; it's a writer's sense for story. It can be a word like *marshmallow* that puts me beside a campfire again. It can be a glance at a photograph that takes me back to childhood and urges me to craft an experience I remember. It is a hope to create from the raw materials of life. Rehearsal begins with thinking and play.

I believe it is just because she is fifteen, but my daughter and I are struggling to find common ground these days. I often find myself revisiting things from the past, wondering if I could have been a better mother. I know I've been good to her, but I've made so many mistakes. I wonder how many of them she remembers. So I ask her one night.

"Do you remember learning how to ride your bike?"

"Sort of."

"What do you remember?"

"How you and Dad got really mad at me."

There it is. It's the piece I've been thinking about writing, just because I wish I could rewrite that time: I remember getting mad and hating myself for it. I remember feeling like I was blowing what could have been a wonderful experience by being frustrated. I remember trying to be patient and failing. I remember saying things like, "We should just take this bike back if you aren't going to try." I shudder inside. This piece is about more than motherhood: It is about teaching. Why was I such a poor teacher of my most precious little girl?

So for days I've been rehearsing a writing piece on this. I've been thinking and wondering and looking at old photographs. I found one of her with a beaming smile, braces gleaming, sunlight on her helmeted head as she leaned down to pet the head of our golden retriever. She looks happy. I cut it out and glued it into my writer's notebook. Then I wrote "teaching Hannah to ride" on one page and left two blank pages in the middle of the notebook: This is what I show my students in class. I need a place to hold my thinking—to write or not to. It may remain blank for months, or I may be looking for a distraction during a boring budget meeting and decide to brainstorm there instead. This writing won't be for anyone, that's for sure. I imagine I'm going to remember more poorly chosen words, confirmation of my bad mother image . . . and that's not something I want to share. I just want to know. I am writing only for me, but with as much energy and dedication as I'm putting into this book.

Rehearsal should be failure-free writing and thinking. I think through beginnings and toss them aside as I put my groceries on the belt and scan tabloid headlines. I haven't invested anything except free time in that move and so it is painless. No words crossed out or worried over, only to be discarded. Writing can be such hard work, but rehearsal is much more likely to be play and likely to be in my head, not on the page.

I can talk about rehearsal for past pieces, but it is more vivid to use a current piece, and it tends to maintain my students' interest in our unit as they watch my piece move through the stages of process.

You see, the rehearsal for the column I wrote this week for *Voices from the Middle* about a former student, Kristen, was quite different than the work on the piece about my daughter. I knew I was going to write about Kristen. I had this big jumble of moments from our year together that I knew might work to tell a bigger story of her, but I hadn't put any time into selecting what to write. I kept remembering moments of dialog in odd moments. One day I just put her name in my journal and started by describing her. I started present tense, as if she was walking toward me at that moment. The writing poured out and I knew I had found an opening scene for the piece. I think the drafting went easily because

I knew I was going to write the piece for some time and had considered and discarded several openings already. I was also sure of my audience, and the confidence in the voice led the piece to tumble out quickly. Rehearsal helps with a rough draft, and it can also help with crafting other sections of the piece. I share both examples with students because it shows different ways rehearsal can work.

Rereading

Christine tells me she tried to reread her research paper, but she got bored and quit. She ran the spell-checker. "It's a modern age; let technology find the errors," she says smugly. She's in my office to complain about the B– she got on the paper; I'm the department chair this year, so she thinks I should "fix it."

"Yeah, well," I say, "what you've written here doesn't make sense. Did you listen to what you said here?" She looks a little guilty and a little incredulous. Of course she didn't. She doesn't even know what I'm talking about: How do you listen to your own writing?

Rereading was this mysterious thing to me for years, an activity meant to catch the *there*, *their*, *there*'s and the misplaced semicolon: I confused rereading with editing. I knew most kids weren't doing it, but I thought they should be. I preached about revising their

> *Right away . . . or when you have time, read what you have written aloud.* <u>*Aloud.*</u>
>
> *There is a line in a 15th-century monastic rule that specifies: "No one shall read while others are trying to sleep." Reading then was always done aloud, for literature is musical thought.*
>
> —Kim Stafford, *The Muses Among Us*

work, rereading for meaning and rereading for editing, as if sounding out the words several times in order would polish the grit and leave nothing but shine behind. Most kids didn't buy this, but dang, I told them to. How come they weren't listening?

I wasn't teaching; I was preaching. Now I know.

Here's what I'd show my class about rereading after working for a couple of hours this morning: I went after my introduction with a machete, hacking up words and phrases and moving whole paragraphs to get to what I was really trying to say. I didn't plan to do this work. I wanted to reread just to hear the story and move on to my next piece, but I couldn't get past my first sentence. I was in a heap of trouble two paragraphs in. I had to stop, go back and start again. I played reader and was lost.

Now, what my students need to know is that chopping, slicing, and dicing really improves writing. I keep track of changes I'm making so I can show them what I did, and then when the writing finally comes together and the piece starts to sing, I hear it. And so do they. I'm sitting up straighter; I'm pouring another cup of coffee; damn, I can write!

Writing well is such an energizer.

Not many of our students know this.

And they should, because if they did, they'd do it all the time.

Revision

Teaching revision is about providing vision and a few strategies—tools—that might work in the piece they're crafting and might not. I don't waste time on assignments like "change three verbs and circle and correct them on your draft." Revision is simpler and more complex than this: I read and think about what I'm trying to say, then I try to say it more clearly. Of course I will show students what verbs do when chosen with care, but I teach this with vision in mind. My lessons are showing a way, not testing students on their ability to use each tool I provide. Besides, I don't want to waste my time grading those three verbs exercises when I have drafts to read and respond to.

For me, writing is never linear, though I do believe quite ardently in revision. I think of revision as a kind of archeology, a deep exploration of the text to discover what's still hidden and bring it to the surface.

—Kim Edwards

I don't provide "answers" in class, I provide possibilities. Just in that one word the pressure is off. I don't have to be right or to defend my territory. Perhaps changing three verbs in a particular essay a student has written really won't improve it. I'm just showing a strategy that might work and ask them all to reconsider the choices they have made in their current work in writing. Because the truth is, sometimes a student writes a piece in one draft that knocks my socks off and they should probably leave it alone. I don't want them to go through false exercises to revise it if the draft doesn't need it. The next piece they write may need tons of work, but that isn't predictable.

Lessons on structure and craft can come from student texts under construction; in fact, the best ones do. Student rough drafts bind us as a learning community because students share so much of themselves in their work, and their hesitations, when shared, help other students develop the confidence they need to plow through their own rough ideas toward clarity and good writing. Student texts also provide the fresh, vibrant work that keeps all of us from slipping into complacency. There's a different feel to a lesson that begins, "Yesterday in class Jake tried to . . ." I know it keeps me on my toes as a writer and a teacher; this is the creative work of unpredictable teaching. What can help this writer? As I consider possibilities, a student offers something I didn't see.

Grammar and Sentence Structure (see Chapter 11)

5. WORKSHOP TIME

Writers need work time. We need to understand what work time looks like: time to think, sketch, write, read, reread, scratch out, delete, cut and paste, stand up and walk around, ask a friend, get frustrated, and just get space from the writing piece. But this time cannot all be tossed into "homework." We know what most teenagers' lives look like outside of school: Many of my students do not have, or will not take, thirty minutes of quiet time at night to consider topics. In a classroom, this time allows students to fumble around a bit considering choices. It was just like Atwell said about reading, if we don't make time for it during the school day, then it won't happen for many of our students. If we value something enough, we'll make time for it.

Like all of us, my students will procrastinate and produce nothing some days and waste time. I recognize it because that's what I do when I'm feeling like I can't write. (You would be amazed at all of the shoes I've bought trying to avoid working on this book!) I try to give student writers space, as long as they are not disturbing other writers. I respect their need to read another fifteen minutes before writing one day or sketch in their writer's notebook about something unrelated to their topic on another. My workshop has to be respectful of writers and responsive to what I understand about good conditions for writers. As I confer throughout the classroom I watch what they're doing. I provide gentle pressure and deadlines. I don't let kids put off work when it is due because teaching them to work under pressure is important. Not everyone writes with furious engagement every day, and I notice and nudge harder on the next. (And let's be honest here: You will see students mostly attentive on the video clips included with this text and those you view at conferences because there were cameras and an extra three or four adults in the room on filming days. Plus, we can edit all those other things out! Video children aren't real children: In my regular everyday workshop, there are giggles and notes passed and students zipping between prom dresses on a website and then back to their writing as I cruise by. This multitasking generation doesn't always work in a way that I celebrate. I am part nag, part teacher. We teach adolescents not automatons, I remind administrators who slink into my room on a rough day.)

If writer's workshop is going to remain a "happy, productive place" as Katie Wood Ray suggests, then I can't disturb it with an insistent background beat of "Get back to work! Stop talking!" I know this, but it isn't easy. It doesn't mean I give myself over to students' laziness and inattention, but rather, I address it when I see it in a consistently *kind* tone. I get it. High school for me was mostly about these four things in order of importance: boys, hair, cheerleading, and cutting class. (What a horrible little combination that is, and if you ever bring it up, we're not friends.) I wouldn't go back to the Penny of 1979, but I do remember her. In the agonizing process of coming to be, young adults will disappoint and frustrate us. They will amaze us with their depth and dedication one day, and then waste an entire class period obsessing over the school dress code the next. This is who we teach.

Here's my cure for any teacher who is consistently, unapologetically annoyed and impatient with teenagers. Go into your basement and find your high school yearbook. Turn to all of those pictures of you and study the fine details: the self-conscious smile, the slouched shoulders, the begging-this-acne-will-end wrinkles across the forehead. Now sit down with your journal and write in the voice of that teenager. Write for twenty minutes or more. Write and remember.

Oh yeah, *that's* who we teach. No wonder we have to repeat everything.

Promise me you won't trust any expert who tells you that teaching the complexities of thinking through an idea in writing to teenagers will be easy and follow a perfectly controlled structure. I've never met those teenagers. Watch your writing process and learn from it, listen to your students, and study writing: It's all you really need to launch an authentic workshop that will nurture, support, challenge, and unfold writers.

Room Setup

We did all of our filming in our writing lab, but I don't live there every day I teach. I haven't had my own classroom in seven years. Our school is overcrowded and just about everyone moves. So, when I'm assigned elsewhere, I keep a few things constant. Students know they need to bring their writer's notebook and their SSR book to class, plus their portfolios of collected pieces we are studying. I prefer tables to rows of desks, but sometimes it doesn't matter. During the mini-lesson or text study, they can sit individually, then scoot desks together for discussing what they notice with a partner. I will have students write in notebooks instead of computers if we're bounced out of the lab for several days in a row so that progress on their drafts can continue. None of this is perfect, but it is the way schools work too much of the time. We have to share space. My workshop works far better when I'm in the lab every day and students have easy access to the technology they depend on. Here's my bumper sticker: Someday schools will have all the technology they need and students will realize its power.

So, in my ideal room there are four computers to a pod. I have them set apart with space to move easily from student to student during conferring. You'll notice on the DVD that sometimes I have to crouch down on my knees and at other times I can bring my stool with me. This will change when we move to our new school with portable laptop labs. I set up my room so I can get to every student and manage all of my students by moving all over the room all the time. We know it is just good teaching to be able to teach from different areas of the classroom.

At the front of my classroom is the whiteboard that holds the day's agenda and the posters from our units of study. Each poster (see Figure 6.6)

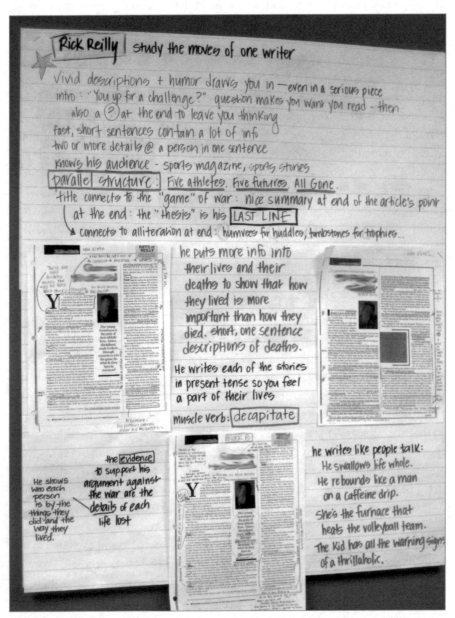

FIGURE 6.6

holds the thinking from a study in a genre. The poster is a list of the qualities students notice in our mentor texts. It is a reference for students throughout the unit and a reference for me. As I review the list mid-unit, I ask myself, "What is essential that this class has not noticed yet?" If something is missing, I make a study text decision based on that, hoping to nudge all of my students to discover what is effective in a genre. This is one way I plan carefully for the time I have. This year I started putting the name of the mentor text we were studying when we made the particular discovery on the poster as well, as a tool to assist those absent. Posters don't replicate the rich discussion in a writing workshop in real time, but it is an accommodation for sports dismissals, field trips, illnesses, and family vacations.

Also at the front of the class is a large table with basic supplies: stapler, hole punch, scissors, colored pencils, and so on. We have shelves to store portfolios by class and copies of the class text, *True Stories*, plus hundreds of donated books that make up our classroom library. Those are the essentials.

Conferring

Writing workshop is time for students to draft and for me to confer with individuals or small groups of writers. Giving feedback during the process of the piece has been shown (Rief, Graves, Murray, Atwell) as *necessary* to growth in writing, but it takes some mighty fine juggling to make it happen. I confer as quickly and efficiently as I can (see several conferences on the DVD), and I ask students to turn in rough drafts throughout each unit. I appreciated Carol Jago's practical advice in *Papers, Papers, Papers* where she said she gives up the less important tasks so that she can focus more on writing. I make whatever trades are necessary to spend more time with drafts. The result is not only a much easier time with final drafts, but students who invest more throughout the process. Their motivation feeds mine.

Writers grow with regular response to their work and to the work of other writers. Students need time to respond to each other about ideas. Writing requires this talk about the models and about the approximations writers make in imitation. Response might be teaching one on one with a student using an anchor text from our minilesson to make a point with that student. (Watch this on the DVD with Zach's grammar conference and Amy's "big idea" conference. In both cases I refer to the class study text that day.)

> *I must create a climate in the writing conference in which students can hear what they have to say so they can learn to listen to their own writing.*
>
> —Donald Murray

Students need response to their choices. They need encouragement to follow passions and hauntings and how they might write about them. That can happen by responding to a writer's notebook outside of class or having short writing conferences as students are considering topics. Students want to hear what other students are writing about and will listen in, doubling or tripling the value of that writing conference. Writing depends on talk. (See Chapter 7 where I detail what these conferences on topics looked like in one class period.)

Conditions

When writing time begins I'm on the move from one student to the next, holding short conferences where I try to stick to an "architecture" of a writing conference I learned from the work of Lucy Calkins (2006). I listen to the student first. My students learn that I'll begin with, "How can I help?" or "How's it going?" (from Carl Anderson's brilliant book on helping first-grade writers). Students speak first. They need to tell me what they're struggling with and how they think I can help them work with their writing. Second, I decide as I'm listening what is best to teach this writer. I focus on one thing. I teach it, then I encourage them to keep working by noticing and commenting on all of the smart decisions they're making as a writer. I don't stick to this order, and I don't always stick to only one thing in the conference, but I work hard to listen, encourage, and direct my teaching toward something that will help this writer at this moment in time.

I expect all of my students to work while I'm conferring. I move around the room quickly and from writer to writer, trying not to get trapped into conferring with the same kids each day. Some students will need a lot of encouragement and I check in often, but I also keep track on my clipboard of who I've talked to during each unit so that I can be sure to get to everyone. I've been caught too many times by a student who seemed to be working, but then I discover late in the unit that he hasn't even started. I plan on completing five to eight conferences in the thirty minutes I leave for writing time each block. I can reach the entire class in a week and see each student twice before the unit is complete, but I have to work quickly. There are a dozen conferences on the DVD, and you'll see a range of issues there. There are also two ways to watch them: First, you are an observer listening in; second, you can click on commentary and I'll tell you about the student and the decisions I'm making during the conference and why, based on what I know and understand about the writer. I don't always have the answers, but I try to talk through issues with students and then understand the kinds of minilessons that will help the class best at this point. If I listen well to my students, I know what to teach next.

Watch how this happens through one unit with one writer in the following example.

Sample Writer's Conference

Step 1: Thinking about topic and structure

Kayla has decided to write about her grandmother dying. When I stop by to briefly confer with her on topic choice, she tells me she'll use a snapshot technique similar to the one Sherman Alexie uses in "My Indian Education" where he tells a different scene from each year of school. Her grandma's dying took three days, and Kayla wants to write this as morning, noon, and night for each day. This is not a bad thought for a first draft—although I can see the inherent problems she'll face in adopting a structure as rigid as this to write the piece. I don't dissuade her in the discovery draft stage. I listen. I don't revise *plans* very often. I let the kids run with ideas. I believe writing that first draft is, as gross as it sounds, a vomit draft. Empty it out. Get the whole story out in front of you so we can sift through what you find.

Now, this approach rests on my *hope* that Kayla will revise. Not my demand that she will—my hope. Kayla may spend our two week time frame for this writing piece just spitting out those three days. And the piece may be pretty awful to read. If that happens, I'll nudge harder for revision in our next writing conference and remind her of all the possibilities, but I won't force her to rewrite anything she isn't committed to working on. It just isn't worth the aggravation because the learning in those situations is seldom lasting. Adolescent resistance is more powerful than I am.

Step 2: Notes on her first draft

Kayla writes the entire draft that night in her journal. Pages and pages. This happens more often than I expect when I give students real choice in what they'll write about: They work harder and produce more. She tells me she likes some of it and wonders if I'll read it and tell her where I like it. By listening to her question I know Kayla has a sense that some of her writing isn't working. There's an opening for me to offer help. I read it and make notes in the margins, returning it the following day. I congratulate Kayla on the great lines I find—moments that really work in the piece—and I nudge in several places for cuts. I ask questions. She reads my notes and begins typing that day in class.

Step 3: A quick check-in during workshop

I stop by to see if she understands my notes. She nods. She doesn't want help now.

Step 4: Notes on a second draft

She hands in her draft with the rest of the class later in the week and it reads like she hasn't changed a single thing from what I read in her journal. I bet that sounds familiar to you. She has typed draft one, that's the change. What do I write? I set her piece aside and decide to discuss it with her in class.

Step 5: A conference in class—short and honest.

I do not make notes on her typed draft: She already has my feedback. I hand Kayla's draft back and tell her I think she's being held hostage to her frame for the story—the one she established with morning, noon, and night for three days—and that she feels like she has to stick to it. She doesn't really have something Important and Significant to say in each of those scenes; she's filling space.

Perhaps you sense the quiet that descends in this corner of the classroom when I say this. Heads turn and I know it has become a small group conference; it is important to do well, so I'm careful. I say, "Kayla, this is an important story. You told me you feel strongly about losing your Nana. Your readers, however, don't know what's important. They're trying to follow your clues and getting confused. Like here—the first scene in any piece of writing says 'Pay attention! Look at this! This matters,' because it is first. In this piece the first scene is you and your sister getting up in the morning, having breakfast, getting in the car, driving to the hospital. None of that matters." She nods. I can tell she's with me. I know her piece and have thought seriously about it. That was *my* homework. It gives me permission to speak so frankly with her. I have also established that this piece matters to her and deserves work, which honors her as a writer. I believe this is why she is listening. I have to earn this attention anew with each student and each piece, it seems, at least for a while at the start of each semester.

Since she is still listening hard, I continue, "Here, where you walk in the room and Grandma—sorry, Nana—is gurgling, pale . . . there's an intensity to this scene that clearly shows it matters. If you want your readers to understand what this moment meant to you you've got to spend your sentences carefully. Respect your reader's time. Cut anything that doesn't serve to tell *that* story well." She's nodding and I can see she gets it, so I keep going.

In order to honor all the work she put into that first draft I end our conference with, "No one cares that you brushed your teeth before you went to the hospital—not even you—but you had to write all of that in your first draft in order to immerse yourself in memory and get to the stuff that *does* matter. It's essential work in the process and never a waste of time. But now you need to be merciless and make big cuts to get to what lies beneath. I know you can do this."

Our conference was not more than five minutes, but five times the ten other kids listening is time well spent. I was careful as I left that conference to give Kayla a possible place to start—with the scene of walking into Nana's room.

Step 6: Kayla responds with revision

Kayla turns in draft two the following week, and she nails it. Four pages became two, and it was remarkably better. I can't wait to get to class the next day.

Step 7: Use Kayla's work to teach my class

I need to reinforce what Kayla accomplished and provide vision for my other writers. This "what's possible" from the mouth of a peer will be heard, as you know, far more clearly than anything I say. So Kayla goes on my schedule to present her process in class that week. She's our minilesson. I'll get to hear what she learned and what she was thinking as she made changes . . . and so will my other writers.

Writing Conferences That Don't Work

It's a busy Friday and I've been zipping about the room conferring, from the farthest corners of the room and back again. Steven isn't working today. He is curled around a novel he's reading, draft untouched before him. I sit.

Steven was proud of his piece yesterday. Why isn't he working? He looks up and I say, "Are you pleased with the revisions you're making on your story?"

He puts his book down and looks at the screen. I read along as he does. I have to stop myself from butting into the silence and telling him what I think. This listening thing is a problem for my impatient, active self. Listening takes time; I'm restless. I feel I need to be everywhere at once. I can't linger at his desk too long, but he can't work at my pace. I try to remember Don Murray's suggestions: Student speaks first. Student maintains control of the piece. Student determines revisions. I wonder briefly if Don's ever had a student like Steven. But I know. We all have Stevens.

"Well," he looks away. "I guess."

"Not really though, huh?" I nod.

"I wanted . . ." he stops for several seconds and I scan the room to see if everyone else is working.

"I wanted . . ." he pauses again. "I wanted for you to like it better," he says, "so yeah, I'm happy if you like it."

Uh-oh.

"This isn't for me, Steven," I try, but I know I can't go back and redo the conference the day before. Somehow I did too much and now the writing is for me, not him.

I get trapped sometimes. I teach the writing, not the writer. My ideas bubble to the surface as I'm reading and I want to help, but if I just "fix everything," then the writer learns little. Writing becomes an exercise. This writing won't be any more valuable to Steven than sentence combining or punctuation practice if he isn't driven to improve it. My job is to instill confidence in writers, not to make them dependent on my revisions. I curse these mistakes and try to learn from them.

Because I'm waiting in silence, expecting Steven to talk, he continues. "I think I still have a problem with words—like, there are too many—and that's why I didn't get more positive feedback from the class."

And here's my opening—my chance for redemption.

"Tell me what you mean," I say, looking at his blue eyes and dark curls across his forehead until he looks away.

I wait.

This time I'll really listen.

Response Groups

Early in a unit I assign students to a group of three, what we then call a "response group" to look at a mentor text. I mix abilities and interests. I keep one group of students together for several weeks and usually at least two full units so that students become comfortable with each other and begin to learn from each other. Response groups are asked to complete specific tasks at first (consider the effectiveness of dialogue in this scene, for example). Later I'll ask them to meet to talk through their process or drafts. I am always seeking bridges between students in my room so that they can learn to depend on each other for response. Writers need lots of readers; it broadens perspective. Plus, I just can't read and reread each student's work as much as they need me to. If I don't create a group of good responders, students will learn less.

I manage groups tightly. I circle, I listen, I intervene when necessary. Sharing writing, sharing drafts, and working through ideas can turn into "what are you wearing to the dance?" and "I heard Michelle and Kyle broke up last night!" if time drags on too long. My students are just not evolved enough yet to always make appropriate decisions, so I'm on the move ready to redirect them.

6. Closing Each Class Period

I like to end each class period with the sound of language, usually a student essay or a poem of the day. I try to time my work so that at a minimum, I can share a few lines from student work. I believe that closure of our workshop matters—it sends students into the halls hanging on to the beauty of writing; it can continue to play in their heads as they stand in line in the cafeteria or toss their books into the trunk of their car.

There are two common ways I close class: the Quaker Share or the Symphony Share.

End or begin a workshop by filling the room with lines of student language. Hear language, see language, say language, feel language, in order to help students write with voice, authority, and passion.

—Karen Ernst

Quaker Share

At the NCTE conference in Nashville in 2006 I had the privilege of presenting with Karen Hartman, Director of the Colorado Writing Project, and Meg Peterson, Director of the New Hampshire Writing Project. They are both smart women and beautiful writers. Karen ended our work that day with a Quaker Share, and I have borrowed her idea to close many workshops since. First I ask students to look over their writing and find a few lines they like that they would be willing to read aloud to the class. This is less intimidating than sharing a whole draft, and many more students share when I limit it to a few lines.

A writer stands and shares a line or two. When finished, the next writer stands and reads. There is a simple formality to this that makes everyone listen hard. My students usually lobby against the standing part, but they will read. It is important for students to reflect on where their writing is strong, and it is lovely to have a few lines of carefully crafted student writing to carry us on with the day.

Symphony Share

I learned this term from Sue Ann Martin, a fabulous elementary teacher in Concord, New Hampshire. As I confer with students during workshop, I take notice of lines I love. I say to the student, "Would you be willing to read these lines at the close of class today?" I choose three or four students to highlight and then stop class with a few minutes left. I stand at the front as the symphony conductor and point to students to read. What I like best about this strategy is I can highlight students who would never share on their own. By giving them a few minutes warning, they can practice saying the lines and deliver a smoother performance than if called on to read without warning. It is a safer. Students rarely resist, but if they do, I accept that they aren't ready for others to hear their writing. (You can watch a brief Symphony Share on the DVD.)

FINAL THOUGHTS

It's like I have a mafia boss lurking over my shoulder: *today you write, tomorrow, forgetaboutit.* Sometimes the rough draft first thinking flies onto the page. As I bounce into the kitchen to refill my jumbo coffee mug I say to my husband, "I'm afraid I'll jinx it by saying this, but the writing is going really well this morning." And in those moments—shhhhh, don't tell anyone—sometimes I don't revise it at all.

We know about those other days: one baaaad sentence after another. One stupid, pretentious lie of a sentence followed by a forced perky paragraph of lies. Whose voice is this? What the hell am I trying to say? Delete it all! Delete it so no one can ever find it, not even my super-techno-savvy brother-in-law Todd. Don't ask me to save all of my work in these moments; I need to zap it from my own memory bank and leave no trace behind.

Now jump to my writing classroom and watch similar moments with teenagers. Watch how ineffectively I could respond. First, I could pressure students to reread and revise everything. Instead of trusting their own voices, students begin to believe all work is revised, always. This belief might force them through a process that doesn't fit the writing they are working on. They just might take a smooth paragraph and turn it inside out trying to meet my expectation.

Thanks, Mrs. Kittle, that really helps. Second, I could ask students to save all of their drafts. I did this for years, but I have to wonder who is served by this paper trail—the writer or the teacher. I feel successful when counting a dozen or so fitful starts to a piece as I scan a student's final paper: *What a masterful motivator I am for revision and rethinking.* But what if collecting evidence of bad starts to a writing piece bruises a writer's confidence? Sometimes bad writing needs to find the trash bin. Alex attached a little ziplock baggy with the ashes of a draft to his final piece. I like to think of him sitting at his desk watching that draft go up in flames: what power.

You see, I want order in my teaching and expectations, but it isn't always the right move with writer's workshop. I believe that the teaching of writing is not a linear, easily replicated plan each day. Each writer has his own process, and each writing piece has a process that fits that piece and likely will not fit another. I know, it's a hard truth: It is a lot of uncertainty to digest. But here's what it means to me: There is no paint-by-number approach that serves writers. No revise on Tuesday and edit on Wednesday and polish on Thursday and begin again on Monday. It looks neat in the plan book, but writers do not grow under these conditions. "Writer's workshop" becomes a busywork model that moves students through a process—but not one that will teach them how to solve problems on their own with the next misbehaving, disorderly, bedlam of ideas trying to convert itself into a draft. A writer's workshop must serve writers, not a teacher's need for order.

So how do we figure out what to do? Well, we watch our own process as writers and the process of the writers in our room. We share our methods and learn from each other, collecting strategies like stones. Each idea or way we figured out how to write a particular piece is individual and, however small or incomplete, adds to the collective understanding of the writing process we share as a class, just as a collection of stones speaks of hidden trails and hikes through shady woods.

I know the essentials my students need in order to write argument well, so I teach about credible evidence and ethos in writing every semester, but those are all parts of the skeleton: the stable center, the hard structure of my work. Teaching adolescents requires more. The flesh and form of my workshop comes from the eclectic mix of students who walk through the door. I have twenty-six students assigned to Block A and another twenty-four to Block B in September, and I don't know who they are and what they'll teach me, but I'll be able to tell you by October because they will live at the center of my workshop. I know structured, prewritten writing curriculum is popular these days: Take this unit, transplant it to your class. But that can't work for me. I like the writing of Rick Reilly, but I choose which of his articles are most likely to appeal to the students in a particular class, and I'm constantly on the lookout for current writing that might move the students I'm coming to know. The match of student to mentor text is too important to be predetermined by me or someone outside my classroom.

A match between a unique group of adolescents and my content is an essential element of teaching; I need every advantage. My students get on buses at 6 A.M. or throw themselves into cars before 7. That runs against everything we know about their biological needs at their age, but my school board is too stubborn to change, or simply too afraid of the powerful sports lobby to start school later and move practice time. So my students arrive cranky and jacked on caffeine. It takes work every morning to entice them to study a text I've chosen; it takes an authentic purpose to persuade them to risk writing their truths. If I don't know the kids before me, I don't have a chance. If I don't match my content to their particular interests, I'm not likely to hold their interest for long.

I don't have a lot of patience for teachers who stand behind their twenty-year-old lesson plans with the admonition that "I'm giving them good teaching, but if they don't take advantage of it and learn, that's not my problem." Teachers have to adjust their work to meet the needs of kids. If the kids aren't learning, the first place to look is at the teacher and the curriculum. All kids can write well; I just don't accept anything else to be true. I will work every day (weekends, too) to make it happen for whoever walks through that door. That's professionalism. That's responsibility. I won't pretend this work is about anything less.

And knowing students well is also where the good stuff is! Teenagers are fascinating. They have so much before them—and so much that calls to them from their past. They are perfectly positioned to write well. When we align curriculum with their personal interests, put the skills within their reach, and give good feedback, they write with power. I wouldn't miss it.

Writing workshop has been misunderstood in the years since Murray and Graves proposed it as a model for teaching writing. I've misunderstood it myself at times. I remember being afraid to move a student away from poetry (even dull, lifeless poetry) because the student was so absorbed by writing it; I misunderstood choice. I can remember thinking I had to fix everything in a writing conference; I misunderstood who was supposed to do most of the talking. I can remember reading Atwell's *In the Middle* and figuring my classroom would never look like hers, so some weeks I didn't try. It was easier to organize instruction around activity (read this short story, answer these questions) rather than thinking.

But I kept reaching. I had to find my own way. My students were pleasant enough, but I knew my classroom was just a distraction from the vibrant lives they lived outside of it, an orange traffic cone to maneuver around on their way to what really mattered. I didn't want to be that traffic cone anymore. I wanted an investment from students and became determined to get it. As I've struggled to master the planning of my time with writers, I've returned again and again to educators with vision. There is a better way to teach writing. It takes courage, it takes commitment and deep thinking, but the reward is student engagement. Each class leads me to places I've never been, showing me the sights and sounds of experiences I've never had through clear, vivid writing. Each June I'm full of questions and plans for the next, but deeply satisfied; I love my work. Writing workshop is more than just a model for teaching, it's an exhilarating opportunity.

Student Focus
Kelsey

So I've carefully constructed a community of writers—the planning and thinking and wondering and sharing—and these layers are creating a tower of experiences. My students are learning how the voice of the writer is in the details and the organization of a story determines what the reader will see as the central idea. And I see this smart, tight construction of classroom time and experience leading twenty of my students forward.

Just don't ask about the other four.

Four are just never there.

Of course, there's a story, but whatever the reason for dozens of absences each, I just can't re-create all they have missed.

Kelsey misses at least a day each week from the start, then three or four days in a week, then more than two weeks at once. And I collect all the model texts and give her a super-abbreviated review of what we're learning, but there's no substitute for the collected experiences of a writing community. There's no way to get her on the same page, but there's also no reason to give up on her. I'm tempted, of course. My evil twin who loves to complain wants Kelsey to suffer somehow: She should pay for cutting my class. Because that's the truth here: There are excuses turned into the office, but I've seen her some days in the afternoon on campus. She's sleeping in, not sick; it is not at all the same thing. And I'm sorry, but my ego is taking a beating here. I'm a good teacher. Can't she tell that on the days she is here? Shouldn't she be charmed by my pedagogical mastery and rush to get up with the alarm the next morning? Apparently not.

So here she is. "Mrs. Kittle, what did I miss?" as I take attendance and put the agenda on the board.

"Well, we finished argument last week and have started commentary."

"What's that?"

"Well," I will myself to be patient and point to the poster that holds the collective understandings of the last unit and the start of this one as I smile at other students arriving. "This is going to be hard to explain. Can you stay after class for break?"

And in the pause that follows I keep my mouth closed. Teenagers don't realize their break is ours as well, a chance to make copies or answer email, and I'm offering to trade that time to myself to re-teach her when I know she missed the first opportunity just to sleep in. But these daily sacrifices are required: We're the adults after all. It isn't like I can choose when to teach and be done with it—sorry, lesson over. You missed your chance to dance, sweetheart. Kelsey gets another chance because she does. It's the right thing to do. And that means without any attitude, either.

"Okay, but I can't be late to Spanish," she says.

"Okay," I snicker to myself. Of course you can't be late to *Spanish*.

When she's here, Kelsey works. She contributes to group conferences and writes up a storm. It is easy to direct her. She's a good writer and willing to be led. But her relationship with the class is trickier. She's been pushing the limits of our school attendance policy for the last two years—and the students have noticed all the days she wasn't there when they were—so when she shares plans for an essay on how the policy is unfair because it is preventing her from graduating with her class, her classmates turn on her. This issue is compounded by her missed classes the unit before. Two students argued against the policy in drafts we workshopped together. She missed it. They interviewed the assistant principal, and we dissected the particulars of evidence. When Kelsey tries to share her ideas for an argument on the same topic she is countered from every corner of the room. They're annoyed to be repeating what was already covered and are not willing to give her the time to work through her thinking. Her voice breaks as she says, "You don't know what it's like to find out that everything you've worked for for the last twelve years is worth nothing." And I hear whispers across the room; I see impatient sneers. When I read notebooks later that week more than one student comments that they have no sympathy for someone who so rarely comes to school.

I have to be the model of second chances.

And third.

So I take her seriously and treat her with respect and make time to sit beside her in conference that day. I encourage Kelsey to write this piece for herself. She can't graduate with her class, and she has to own some of it, but she can also argue that her multiple surgeries after a dirt bike accident contributed. And as I sit beside her to listen I see how fragile she is. Teenagers act impulsively; *let's just drive past school and out for breakfast,* she writes in her notebook. Or *I just don't feel like going to school, can't be one of those A-students who always has homework done, but I can't tolerate being treated like I'm stupid when I don't understand what everyone else learned yesterday.* I see her frustration and she's a firecracker, quick to spark: Watch her ignite.

So it is hard for me the next week when she walks in on time, but in shorts far shorter than our handbook policy. "Kelsey, those are not mid-thigh," I say. And I wish I could just look the other way, but I agreed to follow the rules when I signed my contract and that really does mean every day with every kid, so I grit my teeth as she turns to face me.

"Huh-uh! They're fine. Mr. Woodcock said so." (Our assistant principal is of course, the ultimate authority.)

"Well, then you need a note from him to get in my class because I sent Sara out yesterday and I can't play favorites."

She tries again, big smile, "He just said so in the hall!"

"Then I'm sure he'll write you a note," I counter. She's exasperated and she's lying. Minutes later she flames through our door to collect her things and loudly jangle her car keys, but we keep reading. The drive home and back will take most of our class and I curse yet another absence, curse the way all these factors converge to make our time together relentlessly difficult.

She does write that piece and she admits a few of her own mistakes, but she's anxious as May arrives with talk of graduation practice. She is finishing her diploma at a night school nearby, but she needs her credits in my class as well as courses there to finish an adult diploma program. And what's even crazier is because the night school is outside our district's boundary, she'll be recorded as a dropout in our records for the state. Some things in education make absolutely no sense at all. More than some. But Kelsey endures and keeps coming to school most days of the week.

Kelsey's disconnect from school has deeper roots than I know. When we begin a study of multigenre writing, students are asked to review five projects written by former students and then respond with their thinking in their notebooks. Here's Kelsey's:

Multi-genre based on the novel Speak.

I suppose I could sit here and tell you, Mrs. Kittle, that I learned a lot from this piece, yet I can say that I would be lying because I already know. When I was 14, yup, it happened to me too and I can say it was definitely something that caused me great pain. I did not tell anyone for almost three years until my mind and body just could not take it anymore.

I broke down. I felt like it was my own fault and I should have to deal with it. Rape is not an easy thing to talk about, so many people feel as if they come forth they will be accused a liar, plus it is the most uncomfortable thing to talk about.

I really enjoyed the book Speak and I'm glad I was able to read it. I have been debating for days on whether or not to include this in my "Life" multi-genre project, but now I realize that it is not something I should be ashamed of. It is just something I had to deal with as a young teen. It has made me ten times the person I am today, but if I could take it back I would. I had to deal with a lot as a younger teen. A year before I was raped I was sexually assaulted by one of my dad's friends (well, they obviously aren't friends now). This is the reason I did not say anything. I felt that because if I told them (my parents) about the assault they may of thought I was crying wolf about the rape. Boy was I wrong. My parents cried more than I did when they found out. I know now that I should have told them earlier, but rape is such a touchy subject and it shouldn't be. Girls should not be afraid to step up. (Easier said than done.)

Kelsey seemed to relax a bit after this confession in her journal. She ended the semester with her portfolio organized and her writing an impressive collection of stories and arguments, all reflecting her fire. She left me a note with her final exam:

Thank you for all of the great advice and helping me open up as a writer. You saw potential in me when not many people did and if it weren't for you, Mrs. Kittle, I may have dropped out of school; you made me strongest when I thought I was at the weakest point in my life. I could never thank you enough for the great year of senior writing you have given me. I will never forget you!

Sincerely,
SR Sullivan, Kelsey
(^that means Seaman Recruit!!!)

This note is taped in my journal.

I don't want to forget that Kelsey needed to be welcomed into my workshop every day, no matter how disruptive it was. Kelsey needed me to see what was possible, to search and listen to her and ignore my instinct to nag and lecture. I did good work with Kelsey, and in return, she blessed me with her tough honesty and personal integrity. Because there's always the blessing, you know? Kelsey was hard to work with one moment, but kind and filled with light in the next. She was generous and respectful; Kelsey was still willing to trust people. Students who've been broken are sometimes the most likely to rise when it matters and stand up to speak for someone who can't. I see her giving orders on the deck of a ship somewhere, a firecracker illuminating a dark sky over a country I've never seen. She'll be helping someone.

PART FOUR
THINKING THROUGH GENRE

CHAPTER SEVEN
The Art of Story

There is only one story of our lives and we tell it over and over again,
in a thousand different disguises, whether we know it or not.

—Pam Houston

I tell people who've never visited my home state: There's Oregon green, and then there's everything else. I tell writing teachers a similar truth: There's story, and then there's all of that other writing. There's a power—a Superman flying power—in creating stories and listening to the messy particulars of living revealed on the page, and then there's technical, analytical, and persuasive writing. All have value, but story binds us as human beings.

Why narrative? We are a people of story. From the cavemen to families gathered around the fire at night, we've told stories. We embellish; we craft dialogue; we invent details; we create the story each time we retell it. It is the writing process in oral form. It is the most natural writing for our students, and I always try to lead the semester—our limited time together—with success. My goal in the first weeks is to infuse confidence in my class. I want them to realize they can write well—to believe it. But I don't believe crafting story is easy. What is true about narrative is the student is the authority on the topic. Authority empowers voice. Students feel at first surprised, and then confident when they can hear their voice on the page and learn how to tune their voice to connect deeply with readers. By presenting a combination of truly remarkable published texts with my own struggling steps through this creative process, my students become willing to try to shape something of their own. They see the flexibility in writing story, and as they watch their classmates try to shape experience, interest begins to percolate in all the corners of the room.

You know this: The single most efficient path toward success as a teacher lies in knowing your students in *important* ways. Not if they complete their homework, but how and why they do. Not if they arrive to class on time, but what they're thinking as they move through the halls. Not if they have a sister, but the relationship between them. I will need to have honest conversations with each of my students about their writing or their behavior or their plans for college; I need to know them in order to do that well. I need them to trust me, so we can get to the important work of learning. Trusting relationships are at the heart of keeping adolescent learners engaged at school (Deci and Ryan 1995). Story is the window into my students, and it is a genre I passionately embrace in my own writing. I can't imagine starting the year with anything else.

I begin by trusting my students. I write stories from my past and expect them to respect me and listen with compassion. I write about school and growing up—universal themes that they can connect to. I write what I know and remember. I write about things that wake me in the night. I show my students why I write. I'm not just writing to create something as a model in the genre; I'm writing for me. There is a palpable difference.

School's a jail for the most part, and we just clang our tin cups against the bars and nobody listens, nobody hears, or cares to hear what we have to say.

—MIA
TUNED IN AND FIRED UP?

I haven't written much about sports in the past, but I plan to this semester because so many of my current students compete in skiing, track, and golf. They can probably understand my singular drive to be the best. I dreamed of playing at Wimbledon as I held a twenty-dollar racquet in my hands, bouncing the ball on a court in a public park. Memories of my passion drive me to write that story. My students understand that moment when you realize you're not even close to the best and won't be—when you have to let go of child-hood dreams of athletic domination. It may be that I'll write about how success in sports is too often related to the money and thus the opportunities available to young kids are few—a lasting bitterness from my own experience—or I may stay focused on my naivete in thinking I really could compete with the big dogs because I could beat everyone in my neighborhood. However I approach it, I will open a door for some to tell their own version of that story. The most important thing is that I *want* to write this. I can see myself studying my opponent across the court and smell a new tennis ball in my left hand. I want to live that moment again in writing. Motivation comes from a writer's desire to answer his own questions. I want my students seeking as I am, not doing assignments.

I'll learn a lot about a student's proficiency in writing by reading a draft, but I'll also often learn about more than writing. Some students will reveal little and others will spill a story I can't imagine I could have ever told a teacher. I say, "Se-lect one moment from your life that has formed you," and Sarah writes of being assaulted by an older boy in the neighborhood. Chris writes about his brother's attempted suicide. Ryan writes of being raised by his grandparents, longing for his mother. Courtney writes of her brother's dive off a pier that broke his neck and left him paralyzed. And Kelley writes of having her pants pulled down on the soccer field while her coach laughed.

Growing up isn't always a great and fun thing. You can often leave a lot of yourself behind.

—NICK

I respond with compassion and interest in my notes on their drafts, and stop by during workshop to look in their eyes and commend their bravery in writing the truth. But I watch as some share drafts with a few others nearby. Students listen and respect the individual stories of their peers. What work is more important than this in the life of a teacher?

There are definitely stories that I'd rather not know. Some of my students have written those stories. I'd rather believe all went home to a pot of stew on the stove and parents gathered around the table, interested in how their children's lives were unfolding, but we know some of our students are barely surviving the chaos of living. Some are raising themselves. I ask students to reach for an emotionally charged place because that's where the energy to write well comes from. That place can be joyful or heartbreaking, but it leads to real writing. (See "Last Will and Testament" on the DVD.)

In quick writes sometimes my students stumble upon areas of their lives that they don't want to write about. Kate did several quick write entries on her mother's alcoholism, and then she set it aside. She told me she was tired of living that topic and she didn't want to write about it too. I think we were both relieved.

When you put it on paper and regurgitate what you once felt, the feeling comes back and the words flow because it is just you, a pen, and paper; the words won't judge you and tell you that you're stupid.

—BRANDON

But across the room from her Shaina wrote about losing her mother in a journal entry from the first week of class and never let that topic go. It was part of the final piece she shared with all of us on the last day of class; it was the subject of her multigenre scrapbook; it was the center of her college admissions essay. I believe Shaina has a lot more writing to do about that topic. But our classrooms should be big enough for both: the student who zips from one topic to another looking for passion, and one who finds it immediately and doesn't want to let go.

HOW TO BEGIN: THE FIRST WEEK OF CLASS

We begin our study of story with the elements of narrative scene. Students are asked to write a snapshot moment in our first week together. I start small in order to practice a few essential elements: dialogue, sensory detail, and voice. This entire snapshot rests on "show don't tell," where the writer zooms in on details that matter and zooms past those that don't. I tell my students to think of a scene from a movie: that's a snapshot moment. Figures 7.1 and 7.2 show student examples of this.

"Now here's an accurate map with good lines and color . . ." my mind trails to the toasted cinnamon raisin bread with peanut butter I had for breakfast. It was straight up delicious, no joke. The example Silk Road map Mr. Bailey parades around in front of us like a blue ribbon poodle obviously belongs to a girl from last year with nothing better to do. I'm being judgmental. Why are we wasting time looking at it? We need class time to "work" on our masterpieces, Bails. Patches needs to tell me about yesterday's impromptu meeting between his ski boot and Seth Bartlett's face. I hear much blood was shed. I sense the oppressively warm, odiferous scent of time, effort, and detail seeping from the map. It sickens me. I don't have the artistic skills necessary to pull off something as good. More importantly, I don't have that kind of time. What a pointless project. "This is what your maps should look like—notice the legend in the lower right hand . . ." this exhibition needs to end.

"That girl has no life," I say a little too loudly to nobody in particular, but directed at Mr. Bailey. Maybe it'll garner a rise out of my cronies, who are undoubtedly aboard the same train of thought. The boys at my table who are paying attention give an obligatory smile, the girls, as if listening for an approaching predator, stop quietly exchanging words at their tables. The dudes at the back table, perpetually oblivious to Mr. Bailey, continue to go nuts over something which is probably atrociously stupid, and Mr. Bailey smiles. "This is Regina's," he says. My stomach drops as my shoe shoves its way into my mouth. I don't even know her at all, but she's right behind me. I'm an idiot. "Maybe we could show a little more respect for our classmates?"

FIGURE 7.1

I glance nervously around the Little White Church in Eaton, while the evening light strains to make its way through the dusty windows. Mom, Dad, Teacher. They are all staring back at me, nodding encouragingly, as if to say, "Anytime now." I breathe unsteadily as my friend's bow pulls across the strings of her old violin, releasing the first lonely notes into the stale air between us. One, two, three. One, two three. I count silently. I clasp my hands tightly, not sure what to do with them as the solo continues. Should I be looking at her, rocking to the music, preparing myself for my entrance? I tick off the time with my fingertips touching the pads of each one like a human metronome. Wishing to have anything but their attention: the flu, a flood, anything. I feel my body shake as each measure brings me closer to the end. And yet, I haven't even started. I bury my thoughts in my hands, willing them, urging them to move to the keys, sticky with the heat of the night.

FIGURE 7.2

My first chord resonates deep and lulling under the weight of my fingers, cradling the delicate shape of the Ashokan Farewell, building a strong and able base for the violin. Stay with it. We melt into one another, the music and I. We waltz into a comfort so unlike that of the stuffy church. The last note draws out of the Steinway and I lean away; the dampness of my forehead suddenly significant and noticeable. We break apart, the silence pulsating through the pews. I brush against the keys one last time, feeling the vibrations, the energy left behind, and I bow out.

FIGURE 7.2 continued.

> *You don't write your whole life, but the vivid parts that have stayed with you.*
>
> —KIM STAFFORD,
> *THE MUSES AMONG US*

Later my students will learn to connect these scenes or moments to create a narrative. Moments are chosen carefully in story to show something experienced and what the writer thinks or wonders about that experience. So students first write a snapshot moment, then a longer narrative (usually two or three pages, although there is no limit). Following that, we spend two more weeks centered on a "place narrative" or a narrative that connects moments around a theme. That means in my eighteen-week course we spend five weeks focused on story. I am also teaching other things about writing during those first five weeks: elements of grammar and punctuation that I see are necessary as I study their drafts; how to read like writers; and how to work together in a supportive, structured environment.

WHY TWO FULL UNITS ON STORY?

Once students have written that first narrative, while lessons are still fresh in their minds, we go after this same genre again in hopes of raising the quality of narrative writing. We stand on what we learned in the unit before, for example, story is built on scene, but scenes connect in complex ways. And this re-teaching matters to most students; they're more likely to really know at the end of the two units together how all of the elements of story work and be ready to move forward in other genres with a solid foundation in the structure of story. Or perhaps they were "playing school" in the first unit and now want to write something deeper. As Isaak said when I collected the first writing pieces, "Can we do this again? I didn't really take this one seriously until I saw what other people were writing."

This second unit on narrative builds on voice, true, necessary detail, the subtleties in dialogue, and expands on theme. This time the topic is chosen particular to theme; in other words, choose something that is big in your life—a place you've revisited over time and how you've changed in that time as the place has remained mostly the same. Place is only an option for them, however. I frame the unit on a concrete example of theme—a setting—in order to lead students to consider how an image or idea repeats in a complex narrative. A story anchored in a place helps even my weakest writers understand this construction, while stretching the minds and possibilities for developing larger ideas with my sophisticated and skillful writers. (During the "Storyboard" minilesson on the DVD, Logan speaks of turning the whole idea of place upside down by focusing instead on moments that matter to Marc. Logan doesn't need a theme predetermined by setting because he sees writing in a more sophisticated way.) No collection of writers is the same, so I try to provide vision that extends the thinking for many while scaffolding understandings for those who need a clearer, more direct path.

As we develop an understanding of story, I move the class toward a student-centered workshop by having students take the lead in minilessons to teach each other what they are discovering or struggling with in texts they are currently constructing. Students begin to learn the skills for providing critical and insightful feedback in my classroom by listening to how writers talk about writing. I can't get to every writer when I'm needed; I want to see students talking to each other about drafts, reading each other's pieces, and using the language I model for them in class to push and prod each other toward greater clarity. That takes confidence many students do not come into class with, and so it is unlikely to develop in a new genre study. It is possible, however, when an extended narrative unit asks students to apply what they've learned in a more complex piece, stretching each student's ability and understanding. As my classroom shifts to student-centered, the peer community is strengthened and students are easier to manage. Students become bound to each other because of the stories they share as well as the expectation that all writers help each other.

I have found this second unit on story extends thinking. There have been times when students were unable to write a complex story centered on theme: The idea of place is just the setting for the story—and the last draft is a simple, chronological detailing of an event, but other students use this construct to craft complicated, moving tributes to their past. It allows students to consider storytelling in new way and to use a familiar backdrop to their scenes that helps the moments connect. I find my students understand the role of theme in literature much better after applying the concept in this unit with their own experiences. But I need to include a caution here as well: Don't let place become just another assignment that shackles writers. You'll notice in several conferences on the DVD that I tell students, "Okay, forget about place . . ." because I can sense that it is getting in the way of the story they want to write. The purpose of this unit is complexity and theme, not place. I learned this by listening to my students and their struggles with the process in this unit.

On our first day of the unit, I tell students we will brainstorm places that are vivid in our memories in our notebooks. Graham Greene said, "For writers it is always said that the first 20 years of life contain the whole experience—the rest is observation." The first twenty years—lots of writing material.

My minilesson is talking aloud as I write a list on the whiteboard, on the overhead, or in my notebook. I say something like this: "So the first thing I think of is my house where I grew up—it seems like an obvious place to begin. I try to think of possible stories or scenes that might come from that topic and write those off to the side of the list in little brackets. Like I went to visit the house when I was already married with my own kids because the house was for sale again. I loved seeing it again, but it was so different. That could be a scene—maybe at the end of a few scenes of something that occurred there. So I think about all of the experiences I had in the house and mowing the lawn comes to mind because our lawn had three levels that had to be mowed and the mower dragged up the stairs in between. We had this little push mower that my mom bought at a garage sale and it had a basket to catch the grass clippings, which I HATED emptying and getting little itchy grass pieces all over my legs. . . ." I talk through each item on the list I am creating as they watch.

1. **My house**—going back when it was for sale, mowing the lawn, the hammock, the robber that broke in while I was in the house, the Valentine's castle my sister, Mom, and I made out of cookies and icing;

2. **Franklin High School**—tennis, skiing, the lobby where we hung out between classes, football games, and cheerleading;

3. **Seaton's Pharmacy**—working there as a teenager, stopping there every day on the walk home from elementary school.

This is about four or five minutes of modeling time. I follow it by asking students to make a list in their notebooks much like mine. I add to my list or extend it while they brainstorm. We share our ideas at the end and I tell students to be kleptomaniacs and steal any good ideas they hear other writers share that remind them of their own stories. I model this as I listen—making a point of taking my pen to record a connection as I'm listening to one of my students share. Sometimes I put the entire list of ideas from the class on chart paper as they talk so that others can see the collected experiences and thinking of the class (especially for those absent).

I usually don't know what I want to write at this point, and neither do students. There is no pressure in this. We study model texts with the rest of our class time that day. I try to ease my students into topic selection by modeling an attitude that I can write about just about anything. My choice depends on how much interest I have in that topic at this time.

On this day, or the next, we sketch in our writing notebooks. I tell students to choose a place from their list and try to draw it with all the details they remember in their notebook. I tell them that when they were children they drew before they could write letters, and drawing still has a way of pulling out details for writers. I sketch in my journal or on the overhead (Figure 7.3) and talk aloud as I sketch to show them how it works with my own thinking. I start with my

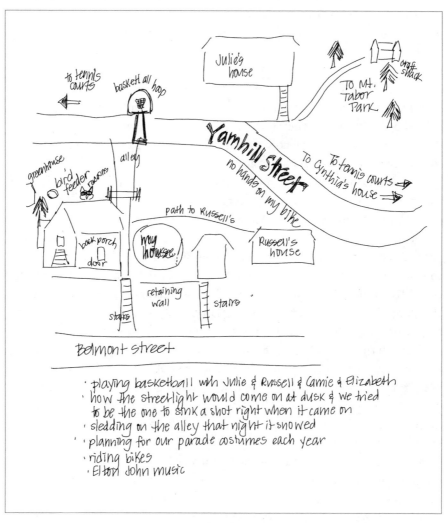

FIGURE 7.3

house, even though I don't feel a strong connection to this topic. I start here because writers just have to start. The process leads to ideas that matter and the urge to write. I sketch the other things nearby as they occur to me, just allowing myself to remember.

I talk aloud as I sketch, "Here's the house, sort of. We had a big porch and stairs on each side from the street below. I'm also drawing in the sidewalk that went from my back door up the alley to Yamhill Street and by these huge trees. And back here is the bird feeder where my mom had visiting raccoons every night, and this is the greenhouse where my friend fell through the glass roof and the pussy willow tree—you know, it is weird, but some of this stuff I haven't thought of in years, but as I'm drawing I remember, like, every single tree in the yard. The deck and the rose bushes that grew around it and the charred hole in the deck when my dad tried to smoke salmon. . . . " I tell students that all of the details that happen during the remembering are the purpose of this activity, not the resulting sketch. I list below the sketch possible stories I'm interested in writing.

After this work we study model texts and notice how writers structure story for the rest of our class period. I ask students to continue considering topics as they live the rest of their lives that evening. I know when I plant a seed like this that most students will continue to think about topics while just driving to work or lying on their bed before sleep.

The next day I ask students to choose something from the brainstorm list or something that occurred to them as they made their sketch and quickly write a moment from that list. Moments or scenes are familiar from our first narrative unit, so this is comfortable territory. I want them to start from a position of strength as a writer—to know what is expected and feel some confidence in that—but also I want them to begin the hard part of writing very early in the unit. I know as a writer that sometimes these early drafts are abandoned, but it is important to jump into drafting, not continue to brainstorm and web or list for too long. This is true for *me* as a writer, that is. I can get stuck in the prewriting stage and use it to avoid the hard work of drafting. I don't try to tell students what their process should be, and I try to be flexible about how different writers approach a writing piece—allowing someone to start writing on day one if they say they know the place immediately, for example, but I also nudge them along continually to allow room for rewriting within a two-week unit.

Again, I model how to do what I've just asked them to tackle. I say, "So I'm rereading my list in my notebook and thinking about what I remember with some detail. I don't need to remember all of the detail before I start because writers say that details come as you write: The brain engages and memories are recovered through the act of writing. Yesterday I drew a sketch of my house because I was thinking about writing that narrative about revisiting it when I was older, but then when I was drawing in that sidewalk up to Yamhill Street, and it reminded me of all the fun I had up there and I want to write about that. I'm just going to write the first thing that comes to me and not worry about how it sounds as a lead or anything because this is just practice writing in my notebook. Remember that the center of quick writing is writing quickly without censoring yourself. Shut off the critic and let your mind go."

I say aloud each word as I write in my notebook or on the overhead projector in front of them. "If you took a snapshot of my childhood—and it was true to my memory—I'd be on Yamhill Street. My house sat on Belmont, but the alley out my back door went up the hill to Yamhill. Everything happened there: the annual neighborhood Fourth of July parade in costumes we planned for the entire year before; the nightly basketball game below the lone streetlight, where we met to ride bikes, swap candy, and gossip about the neighbors; where I grew up. I close my eyes and I'm there.

"I can hear dribbling."

I stop writing and say to my class, "You know, I know that it is easier to write about the past if I write in present tense, so that is why I did that. In those first few lines I was kind of warming up to what I wanted to write—for me and for my reader. Then when I pictured myself walking up that sidewalk to Yamhill Street, I could see myself there and I went to writing in the present tense. When you write today, it can be easier to recall details in a scene as if you imagine you are in it again and it is happening right in front of you."

I continue, "So where was I? I'll reread that sentence and keep going." I pick up my overhead pen and continue to write and talk aloud, "I can hear dribbling. I can almost feel the vibration as the ball hits the street. I tie my shoes, yell a g'bye to Mom and fling open the back door. I hear voices. I leap from the porch to the sidewalk. . . ."

At this point I ask students to put the date in their notebooks and do exactly what I've just shown them. Pick one idea from the brainstormed list and go. By now they've grown comfortable with the quick write process and will write. A few might still sketch, and others might be pondering, but just creating the conditions for thinking and writing always brings results. Silence works. Even my most reluctant writers will rarely sit for the entire time while others write. It is contagious to sit in a writing community. They all write. That silence and writing with them are keys for me. I keep writing the entire time they are: I'm not watching them, I'm writing.

After about ten minutes I stop them and we talk about what we're doing. We share our process as writers, not necessarily this rough writing. I often pair kids up for this, or put them in triad groups. I want everyone to hear and be heard. I wander and listen. Again, for those reluctant to start, they hear a few more examples of how others are tackling the task. It is okay to say, "Not much happened for me today," and learn from the others in the group.

I finished writing the scene I started in class that night at home in my notebook (Figure 7.4):

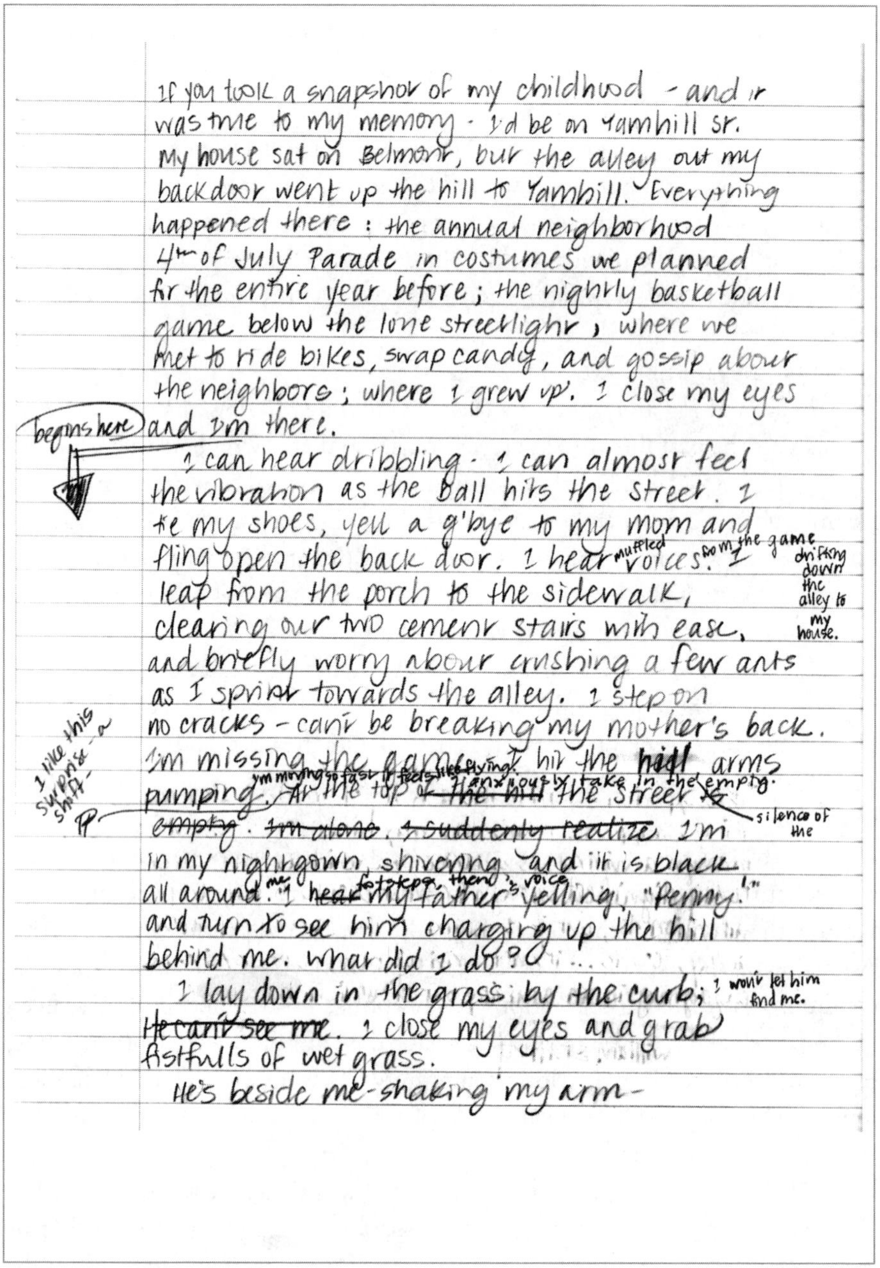

If you took a snapshot of my childhood — and it was true to my memory — I'd be on Yamhill St. My house sat on Belmont, but the alley out my backdoor went up the hill to Yamhill. Everything happened there: the annual neighborhood 4th of July parade in costumes we planned for the entire year before; the nightly basketball game below the lone streetlight, where we met to ride bikes, swap candy, and gossip about the neighbors; where I grew up. I close my eyes and I'm there.
begins here
I can hear dribbling. I can almost feel the vibration as the ball hits the street. I tie my shoes, yell a g'bye to my mom and fling open the back door. I hear muffled voices from the game drifting down the alley to my house. I leap from the porch to the sidewalk, clearing our two cement stairs with ease, and briefly worry about crushing a few ants as I sprint towards the alley. I step on no cracks — can't be breaking my mother's back. I'm missing the game. I'm moving so fast it feels like I'm flying. I hit the hill, arms pumping. At the top of the hill the street is empty. I anxiously take in the empty silence of the empty. I'm alone. I suddenly realize I'm in my nightgown, shivering and it is black all around. I hear my father's footsteps, then voice, yelling, "Penny!" and turn to see him charging up the hill behind me. What did I do?
I lay down in the grass by the curb; I won't let him find me. He can't see me. I close my eyes and grab fistfulls of wet grass.
He's beside me — shaking my arm —

I like this — super stuff — P.

FIGURE 7.4

> I don't see writing as communication of something already discovered, as "truths" already known. Rather, I see writing as a job of experiment. It's like any discovery job; you don't know what's going to happen until you try it.
> ~ W. Stafford

"Penny, you're dreaming! Wake up! You're sleepwalking" ~~arms & feet~~ arms, knees
~~I feel the grass~~ Wet grass clings to my ~~hands~~ hands ~~as I rise to my knees.~~
Daddy holds my hands ~~and lifts me up.~~ running toward home. I don't know what has just happened;
"Come on," he says. I follow. ~~I'm confused;~~ I'm a little afraid, but
~~but~~ Daddy's here; he'll take care of me.

   A photograph fell out of an album I was moving from the basement a few weekends ago. It's faded · but I remember this day. 4ᵗʰ of July of course · we were dressed in a 50's theme for the neighborhood parade. I remember those blue tennis shoes I'm wearing — and I remember those second-hand used clothes next to Cynthia & Michelle's pressed shirts and poodle skirts. I was always standing near them · but a dimmer version - a worn, used version. I remember those long pigtails- my stick-straight blonde hair · the pink lipstick I wore and the blush on my cheeks— my first make-up. I'm leaning on Julia · I stay near her because she always looked worse than I did. Her parents had money, but they never spent it. Her outfit was as dull as mine & her glasses were just horrible. I remember hearing my mom say she was →

FIGURE 7.4 *continued*

and I thought about how I would decide what comes next. I began drawing a storyboard in my notebook. I wanted a visual way to capture the different scenes that were rattling around in my head. I was hoping the drawing might lead to some kind of order or theme for the writing piece. (This is when the lights should flash: danger, Penny Kittle, danger. I know I should just write and let the writing tell me what to write, but my instinct is to jump ahead and plan, thinking that will smooth out the herky-jerky motions of drafting. I want writing to be neat and orderly—planful—crafty. It isn't, but I keep thinking it might be if I just found that magic template.)

Using Storyboards

Day Three I brought in my storyboard. But first a little background: I use the term *storyboard* when I talk about this strategy in my classroom, probably because I learned it wrong the first time. When Roger Essley came to present in Conway, I was unable to go and only caught a reflection of that day from my excited colleagues. Somehow my colleagues and I started calling the sketches storyboards, but the idea is Roger's and he uses the term *tellingboards*. Storyboards have helped many of my writers plan and think as they rehearse an idea. I ask all of my students to experiment with storyboards because they work for me.

The first time I demonstrate using a storyboard in class I bring in large paper and draw in front of students, one idea per page. I then bring up several students to hold the pages for me in front of the class: one kid per page. I talk through my thinking (much like I've written previously) and move the sketches around to show how the story might be told. I move pages off to the side when they don't work with a particular line of thinking. I leave spaces between students for the scenes that occur as I'm talking, but I haven't sketched yet. I am modeling the addition and deletion of ideas as I try to find a focus for a story that emerges. I don't know yet what I want to tell, but at this rehearsal stage, the writing is pliable. I am not tied to lines I've already written. I'm finding a vision for the writing.

On another day I'll bring in a copy of a storyboard (Figure 7.5) and cut it apart in class before them. Then I move the sketches around and talk aloud. I stress how flexible narrative is by saying, "I could start like this: with a scene of my friend and me selling lemonade, and then tell the story of dressing up for Fourth of July." Flexible thinking is needed not only for narrative, it is a process I teach with commentary as well because arguing a position can take many forms.

Allowing students to work through ideas in pictures has been helpful for many of my students: from those who struggle to organize ideas to those who enjoy planning so thoroughly before writing. For many of my students it is a breakthrough. We teach beginning-middle-end in elementary school, then problems and solutions and plot as they grow older. We analyze structure in great novels, admiring flashbacks, mapping out foreshadowing and tension. But it is a leap, a significant one, for students to do this with their own writing. My students are exhilarated by this real writing challenge. There are many ways I can tell this story: which is likely to be most effective?

My purpose is to show how many choices I have to make as a writer—there are many different scenes I could write. There isn't one story of Yamhill Street from my childhood, there are many. It depends on which scenes I choose and how I might put them together. This flexible thinking allows students to see the layers of stories that are in their memories waiting to be told. When we work like this together I rarely hear "I have nothing to write." I hear, "I don't know which story I want to write."

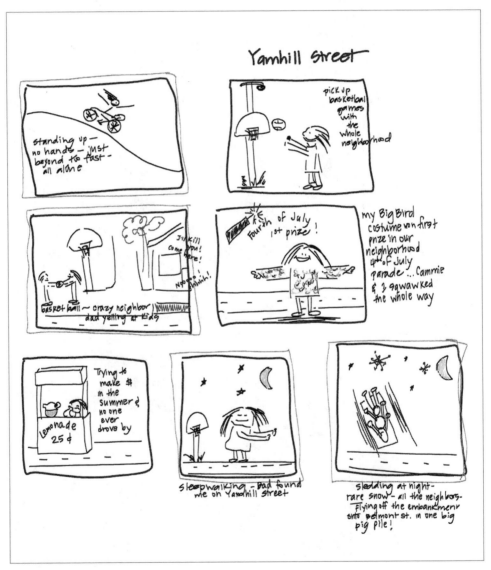

FIGURE 7.5

As I share my storyboard I talk about what I'm thinking as I look at my drawings and remember the scenes. I use a different color to circle four scenes that I think might work together. I know I can't write all of the scenes I remember, or the piece might be many pages long. I'm looking for a narrative essay of about two pages (a good model for my students), so I stick to four scenes. Of course it is easy to change course once I begin and choose different scenes if I want to. With

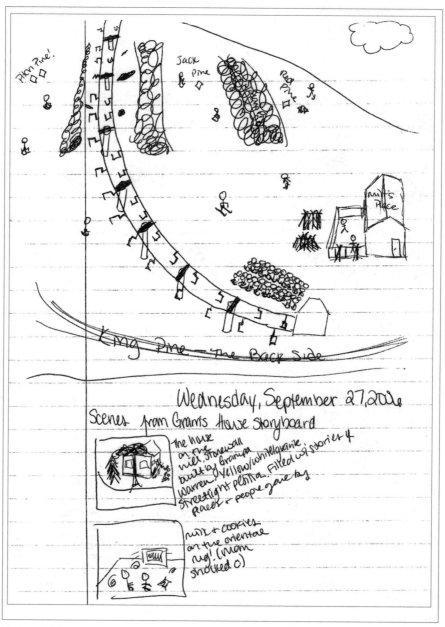

FIGURE 7.6

a storyboard, changes are easy. With pages of drafting, students can be reluctant to cut lines. (The completed piece, "Yamhill Street," is on the DVD.)

Students are encouraged to make storyboards while others can write if they feel like they are ready. Everyone storyboards, at least for a while. Two students create theirs on overheads so we can look at them as a class. In Figure 7.6 is Elizabeth's storyboard from her notebook. Notice on one day she sketched a

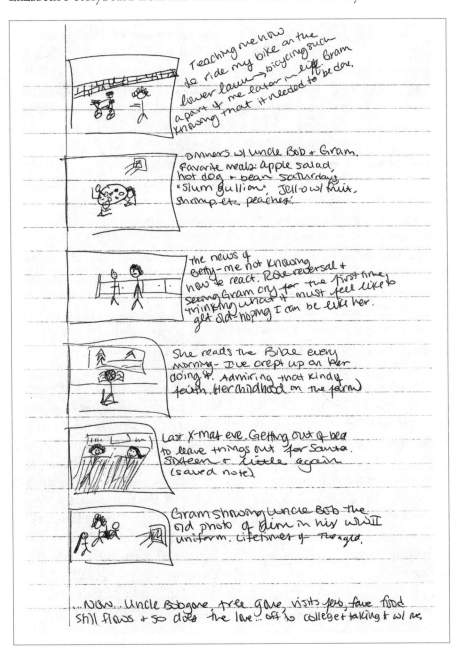

FIGURE 7.6 continued

picture of a ski area nearby and then changed her topic on the next and did a more complete storyboard about her grandmother's house.

Elizabeth is cruising along with a plan and a storyboard and vision for what her writing might look like. She came into my class as a strong writer and needs little to launch herself into writing. (Listen to how the writing notebook helped Elizabeth discover and nurture topics on the DVD, where Elizabeth takes you on a notebook and portfolio tour of her work.)

Others need help getting started. As I make the rounds of the room, Mark and Kate and Ben and Sade are all stuck at a back table. Since none of them has an idea, they reinforce each other and stay stuck. I have to be moving during workshop to see where students are at and what kind of help they need. Conferences are fast. I can't give any of those writers topics; I can only listen and talk to one writer and hope that talk helps the others listening nearby. I want every writer in Elizabeth's shoes, or if not there, quiet and contemplative like Gina who sits beside her. Gina may be as stuck as the kids at the back table, but she'll list in her notebook and think. She might whisper to Jess, but she won't be calling out, "Mrs. Kittle, I don't know what to write! Mrs. Kittle, I don't know what to choose," which makes me want to pass out surgical masks or a little duct tape. I swear as soon as one starts whining, the others will join in.

I say, "I am sure it is challenging. If I were stuck like you, I would be thinking and listing in my notebook until something grabbed me enough to write." Soon I get tougher, "I will get to you in a moment, but I'm going to ask you not to disturb other writers who are working while you're waiting." (This one usually comes with a finger to the lips *shhhhh!* and the narrowing of the eyes.) And I make sure I get there soon. Topic searching is noisier than other writing days, but talk is also essential to writing so I encourage it.

In these moments I try to remember that students carry a lot of baggage into my writing workshop. Some will tell me they don't feel like they can write. They like to be given assignments with ultra-clear parameters like five paragraphs of six to eight sentences each. They don't like thinking through an idea to uncover a natural structure for the piece: That is much harder. These same students would rather I give them a topic (so they can complain about it) than rake through the debris of their life to find their own. But that is exactly why we have to do it. Students need the tough stuff—the work that isn't a formula and doesn't fit into a neat package—the work of craft. That's the work that prepares them for the writing tasks that won't fit a formula: in other words, most of the writing in life.

This first day of conferring is tough. I need to be a lot of places at once. I try to keep track of topics or ideas students are contemplating in my notes as I travel around the room.

STUDENTS PURSUING THEIR OWN TOPICS

I have my clipboard and I'm wandering around the room talking to small groups of kids about their ideas. I choose to sit near a group of five or six at a time so they can hear how others are processing and also so that the words of experience that I offer can multiply . . . as if I'm holding six separate conferences. I start with **Melissa**, and she not only has a topic and a controlling image, it is a stunning idea. Her two older siblings have disappeared from her life. This topic is raw and real and, of course, I have no idea how she should write it, but her search and her decisions will be marvelous teaching tools for the class, or if she doesn't want that audience, just the few nearby who eavesdrop. Her memoir begins with this image of her at three clinging to the leg of her older brother because he is leaving. This weekend she found out that her older sister has a three-year-old son she didn't even know existed. There is a lot to work with and Melissa is a very good writer. I'm encouraged.

I talk to **Corey**. Corey has a 504 for reading and writing challenges. I've spoken at length to his mother about his war with school and multiple failing grades since fourth grade. She told me I was their "last hope." Corey is going to write about Alex (who sits two seats back) and begins telling funny stories about him. I don't push him into "Why does this matter? So what?" because for Corey to be laughing and listing and excited about writing is just too magical to risk halting by pushing him too far. If he can write it first, we can work with it. After I move to the next kid, Corey says, "How do I start this?" I've tackled the same kind of thing before. I say, "You write the individual scenes or moments you remember and then worry about weaving them together later." I know it works. He's encouraged. He can write those individual scenes. Writers typically don't know all the particulars before they write; it comes with the story. So I tell him to write snapshots and go back to insert the theme later. It has worked for me. He can hear my confidence and he begins.

Scott has no idea. He emphasizes, *"No idea."* I tell him to look through his writer's notebook and when he reads his entries to pay attention to anything that has a pulse, anything with a "heartbeat." That will indicate a story he can write or might want to anyway. He seems unconvinced, but I do leave kids like this and move on. I give them a next step (see DVD conference with Paul), but they may not take it. I definitely need to revisit him tomorrow. If I didn't have a clipboard to remind me with a note to revisit him the next day, I'm sure I would forget.

Tom says he thinks he wants to write about his seven surgeries. I say, "Great thought, and it connects to your interest in nursing." I know his interests because of his quick write responses over the last two weeks. Tom talks through how it might work, asking "How should I begin?" Kids seem to always be preoccupied with starting because they don't think they can continue without a place to start. That makes sense, but it really isn't the way writing works. I might write one beginning and find another. We want to provide a simple answer and get them going, but ignoring how complex the process actually is, even at a young age, means they internalize process and techniques that don't work. We are not giving them the tools to tackle complex tasks if we make writing a paint-by-number process. I say, "You could begin with pre-op or waking up after surgery—either of those are probably firmly in your mind and will be available to write rich in detail. It doesn't mean that will ultimately be your beginning for the piece, but it is a place to start. Writers have to get words on paper." Tom asks just moments later, "How do I describe . . ." And he details that foggy, after anesthesia feeling of a film over your eyes.

I move over to the space between the next two rows. I have **Krystal**, whose father has just been diagnosed with cancer, and she says that she wants to write about either family Christmases or her fifth-grade teacher, Ms. Cook, who died of cancer that year. I hear the emphasis on the teacher as she tells me and repeat it to her, "You seem to have more interest in the Ms. Cook story, although I recognize that will be difficult to write." She says, "Yes, that's the one I want to write." But I'm concerned that writing about a death from cancer will inevitably lead to the agony of her father's situation. But the truth is, that's probably why she wants to write it. And the Christmas stories will also lead to thoughts of Dad and what might be. There won't be any escaping this topic.

Shawn asks for help. He's thinking about writing about setting forest fires. I ask him what the reflective part might be. See, Shawn's a stronger writer than Corey. I can push Shawn there before he starts writing. I need Corey just to get started. We talk about it a little and he says he doesn't know if he really wants to write about being a juvenile delinquent or not. So then I look at the brainstorm list he's made in his notebook and I see "Pond Hockey." In our previous unit on narrative, Shawn wanted to write a piece about the state finals tournament the winter before because they lost in overtime, but he didn't. I say, "Hmmm . . . I bet when you played pond hockey you would say things like 'I'm Wayne Gretsky going for the goal. . . .' the kind of thing where you pretend to be a hero," and Shawn laughs. He tells me in his childhood fantasies he was always one of his heroes in a big game. I say, "Now think of this connection, the pond hockey and then the game last year." He goes, "Ohhhhhhhh, that would be good. But that would be hard." This kid gets the power of telling the story like that instantly, but he doesn't want to write it. I can respect that. I hope he does, but I bet he won't.

Now, meanwhile, the time is slipping away quickly. Students are talking through memories and sharing with peers, which is a form of writing rehearsal, but my workshop environment will deteriorate if I let conversations continue for too long. With twelve minutes left in class I direct some students to continue working on portfolio covers and others to list in notebooks while I finish conferences.

Todd tells me he has no idea, but he is such a strong writer that I'm not worried. I say, "How about siblings?" because he has twin younger siblings who are like night and day. His younger brother is a hellion. Todd says, "No." He tells me he'll figure it out. I'm sure he will. **Tanner**, next to him, says he's thinking about writing about the prank phone calls he made that ended up with the state police visiting his house. I say, "What did you learn from that?" and I can tell he's already losing interest in the topic. I used a former student's model of writing in class that day and because it was so well crafted it raised the stakes for my students. Just stories aren't enough anymore: that "write a personal narrative" unit they've completed each year is suddenly much more complex. Tanner says, "No, wait, I want to write about Torin." I put it on my clipboard and meet his eyes, "There's a rich topic," I say. All of these kids know how much a senior in school, Torin, means to me and that I'm struggling to deal with his leukemia as well.

Mackenzie says, "Rain." Then she asks what a memoir is exactly. We are four days into this unit. I've had them record a definition of memoir—"a moment or series of moments, and so on"—in writer's notebooks and I've talked about the differences between memoir and narrative, but she's still not sure. I explain some of the key elements of the student model shared in class that day. She says, "Oh, not rain then. I'll let you know." With Mackenzie's writer's notebook and her first piece, I see a writer of great promise. I do not need to push her any further because I'm confident in her ability to see topics.

Kyle H. tells me he's working on kickball games from elementary school. I say, "What angle?" He says he's thinking of the way they negotiated rules and had fights over them. I say, "Interesting. And now you still have to negotiate things with your friends, but how is it different?" He laughs, "Yes, exactly. We don't punch each other." I think this kid is on to something.

Chris has no idea. He also asks for an explanation of memoir, although he is sitting diagonally from Mackenzie and heard me answer her, he wants it personalized, told to him. I comply. Chris says, "I was thinking about . . ." and he tries out his story on me. Writers benefit from a talk through ideas. I ask him some questions to dig into the story, but neither of us can determine whether it is a good choice for memoir. I say, "My advice: Write it. I find the meaning by writing sometimes, so give it a shot." He seems unsure or unconvinced, but he nods. I know that asking kids to "just write it" makes them uncomfortable. When writing is viewed as assignments and activity, students do not want to start something and abandon it later. I push them to create—to go forward even when they can't see the path—but they are reluctant to follow me at first. Chris returns to reading his book when I leave.

Kyle N. has been out of his seat, out of the classroom door, getting markers, chatting about football practice with whoever will listen. He has been moved to the front of the room for talking, so he's now antsy by himself. I stop by and ask him about topic, pen poised as if I'm sure he has an answer, and he says, "I don't know." I remind (nag) about the first essay, which he hasn't written yet. This is a writer with no confidence and this is exactly how kids fail. They get behind, then more behind, then no-way-to-pass behind, and then it's all over. I have to stop this slide, so . . . what to do? My conference in class doesn't help; my frustration is rising. Kyle is the co-captain on the football team and his coach runs homeroom in my classroom in the morning. I make a point of mentioning Kyle's missing work in front of Gary who needles him about his work habits. More important, Gary tells him to complete his work or forget football practice. I like Kyle and want him to succeed. I may have to keep him after school. That's my next big gun. I refuse to let him sink or swim.

Billy tells me he is writing about a former friend, Cody. I ask him why and he says because. I don't need to push. Billy writes well and on time and is silent most of the time. But notice that this topic choice conference takes about thirty seconds with Billy, but it took several minutes with both Chris and Kyle.

So my last student is **Ryann**, working on the computer. She says, "I'm writing about my boss at work." I don't know what is important to her, and she has a hard time explaining. Finally she says, "Can you just read this?" and I see two paragraphs on the screen. I glance up and see that a student I bypassed on the first run through around the class has returned from the bathroom and we only have four minutes of class left. Before I get lost in her writing, I say, "Brian, do you know what you are going to write about?" He says, "No." I say, "I have noticed a lot of your entries are about baseball. It might be a place to think about." He nods. His story came out at lunch yesterday, and he's a kid with a huge hurdle in his personal life, but is surviving. I don't think he can write this piece without a lot of structure, but it can't happen today. I have to finish Ryann's conference.

The two paragraphs written are about being raised by neighbors, basically. She says her parents are the kind who are never there. Never home. Never involved. Pretty disconnected from her life in general. She mentions her boss, and as I struggle to connect the parts, Ryann tears up, "She's got cancer and she's got about three weeks to live. This is so not what I need right now with Torin and everything." I say, "I'm sorry, Ryann, that sounds like a rich but difficult story to tell." She keeps writing. At the end of class she's still typing. Her boyfriend brings her backpack over and waits while she keeps at it. I leave them and head to my office.

The things they carried.

End of day total: **Twenty-four kids. Four absent. Seven with no idea yet. Thirteen ready to draft.** This teaching of writing work cannot be sequential or logical or magically organized. This work is circles. Introduce, confer, draft, confer, revise, confer, draft more, introduce for the one absent, confer, and it means keeping twenty-four separate kids in my head at all times for just one class. I need to know what Shawn knows in order to push him to write. I confer with **Elliott** about his siblings to try to help him find a topic, and after several minutes, he's not going to use it. I have to help him tomorrow when the search begins again. One student goes confer, confer, confer, list, confer, draft, give up. Another goes: quick write, draft, type, "I'm done!" And next time they might reverse roles because the writing focus changes, and one student has nothing to say and the other an idea burning to be brought to life. I can't define these writers.

In these examples you can see a range of student topics, far beyond a list I could create on my own and give to them. I want all students to have topics when I stop by to check on them, but most do not. Most need a little conferring mini-conference with me to sort through ideas.

I think about how I might use student topic ideas in my minilesson the next day. "Several of you are writing about sports highlights, and I wanted to share with you a golf match story by a student from last semester. As we think about how he organized this piece, I'd also like for you to consider what the writer's 'so what?' might be. Why is he telling this story in this way?" If I can match the model text to the beginning ideas a few are sharing, I'm more likely to be placing the vision exactly in line with what students need. Students like Elizabeth won't need this match this unit. She may struggle in the next, however, since some genres come more easily to writers than others.

I close this day with something like, "I want these ideas rattling around in your head tonight when you're trying to watch TV or do something that isn't homework. I hope you'll remember something you sketched in your notebook today or caught a glimpse of in your writing. Writers write without pen and paper: They write in their minds. Let a little of that work happen tonight so you can make use of it tomorrow."

How Minilessons Happen

If there's one thing I want you to learn in the following examples it is this: You have all the tools you need to plan minilessons in the students before you. The secret is to be willing to flail around together through the murky mystery of how to get to the heart of story. This process creates the mental flexibility essential to making your students independent, thoughtful writers. It starts with you. You put your early, predraft thinking out in front of the class and talk about how you might get the writing done, then respond to the ideas your students have and their process in clarifying them. Students mimic what we show them. Look for lessons in your writing conferences with individual students and, especially, in the moves of your struggling students.

Figure 7.7

On the first day of our work in this unit, I saw Marc working on the storyboard in Figure 7.7 during class. We talked about what he had before him. He mentioned that although he enjoyed being outside, as he'd gotten older so much more of his life was inside, from school to work to playing video games. He didn't know where his place was, but he felt like he wanted to write something about how these two places showed different times in his life.

I suggested we let the class look at his storyboard and help him consider the possible ways he could write the story. He was anxious about being in front of the class, but equally anxious about his progress with this writing. I think he was willing to try anything. I try to seize moments like this in my teaching: when the struggle of one writer might help others. Marc's storyboard became my minilesson the next day. Because of a fluke—an unexpected snow day that postponed school until the next week—we caught it on video. On the DVD you can watch Marc tell the story of his storyboard and then watch as students help think through ways he might write the piece. Two things impressed me about the work my students did this day: the flexibility in thinking they demonstrated, and their respect for Marc and his ideas. These kids understood what Bruce Pirie said about writing: "The five-paragraph essay doesn't 'teach structure' any more than a paint-by-numbers kit teaches design. We teach structure by sitting down with students who have something they care about saying, *helping them sort out how they might try to say it*, and looking at examples of how other writers have structured their work" (italics mine).

The reason I asked Marc to do this with me in front of the class was to empower all of my students in this kind of thinking. By participating or watching it happen, struggling writers expand their understanding of what can be done with story. Storyboarding is not just for struggling writers, although it provides a smart and efficient scaffold for those kids, all writers benefit. Jake, a confident writer, mentioned in his place narrative end notes that he figured out how to write his piece the day we looked at Marc's storyboard in class.

Mentor texts are important in my units, but a moment like this with writers is more important. It's the active processing of ideas that might make a story work *before the piece is written* that energizes the class. All is possible: There's no failing here. There is only free thinking and creativity and possibility. Where else do they get to exercise this kind of thinking in school? Students want to write what they think they can't—and do it well. Being able to lead students there is one of the gifts in this work.

Marc's next step is familiar: Write one scene from your storyboard. Again, all the choice is in the writer's hands: Which scene do you want to write? Start there. (On the DVD in Sara's conference she is making this choice as well.) I look for energy, I tell my students. I write the scene that I most want to write or the one that is the most vivid in my memory. I write it as best as I can. Figure 7.8 shows what Marc tries in his notebook.

3/5/07

Working at Hannaford I am on the move. Bagging, restocking bags, cleaning registers, and pushing carts ~~no time to hang out with freinds and just simply having fun outdoors.~~ ~~An accident has just occured~~ ~~The customer what was bagging~~

While I bag for the costumers groceries an ache occurs in my shoulder after bagging over a bazillion groceries. It's a pain that sticks with you till night.

Watching the conveyer belts move in a constant motion it's almost hypnotising until ~~products~~ food products go down it. An old grumpy lady, or old miserable guy ask for specific thing. Things that are so detailed they are like instructional demands. You could almost tell them, "stop fussing you old grump." Chew on some more of your pills. They might help you die quicker. But I am a nice person I would never say such a thing.

Ever ... a bad day you have to look motivated and ready to work

The Front End shift Leader asks me if I wanted to push some carts. I say like always, "o.k., yea, or alright". That's the favorite part of the job. Mainly because I am outside. When there are no sign of carts out there I wander around the parking lot and breath the exhaust from cars and avoided the big puddles that are deep enough to soak your whole shoe. The snow hills created by big plows.

FIGURE 7.8

He has decided to take a student's advice and begin in the present day with his work bagging groceries at a local supermarket. We had a conference during the writing of his draft shown earlier. He had written the first three or four sentences when I stopped by to see how he was doing. I asked him to stay in the moment of bagging before he moved on to what it meant. He scratched out the two sentences following the first details and added much more about just bagging. Marc was in class during our first unit when we looked at the elements of scene, and he's heard my emphasis on details and stretching out a moment that matters, but he hadn't applied it. Here his first piece was mostly tell, and as he sat to write this piece he zoomed right past one idea and jumped to the next. This isn't unusual. I have to remember that writers often learn the same lessons over and over again as they apply them to different contexts where they need them. When

I slowed him down and asked him to stay in the moment, he provided every line of detail you see. But without the conference, he might not have noticed. I'll say it again: Conferences are the in-time teaching we need to move writers. They are the backbone of the writing workshop—the simple importance of nudging a writer along in small steps.

At the end of class that day, John handed me a list (Figure 7.9). You see, John had tried to start writing, but couldn't, so he typed a list called "Everything I want to put in my piece but don't know how." He wants to write about mountain biking, and the sport holds so much of what he values about life that he can feel how big the topic is. I said, "Can we look at this in class tomorrow?" He agreed, and my minilesson is ready for the next day.

John Atkins
Everything I want to put in my story—but how?

My bike
Holds most of my most thrilling memories
Trust
Confidence
Accomplishment
Bond
Becoming one—like another body part
Passion
Comfort zone
Work of art
What its like
Friend
Feelings
Its own mind
Nobody else can
Adventure
How it brings you closer to other people
Some people bike because they need to—I love to—find time and
    reason to go biking
Treat it as you wish to be treated—even though everyone has had
    a bad day
Building bikes
Learn through experience
Build it to break it
Fix it even though it's not broken
Learning to leave stuff alone when it's not broken

FIGURE 7.9

Learning from mistakes
Learning determination—or does it come naturally
How did I start biking and why did I fall in love with the sport
Getting dirty
Work to earn money for parts and racing
8th grade racing team
Vermont racing
Building trails
Tricks
Wounds—how they feel good in a way—shows that you doing some-
  thing wrong or you need to do it again—in my mind
Disappointment
Thrill
Seems so normal—why do people call it extreme?
How can anybody not want to do this?
Why biking?

FIGURE 7.9 *continued*

My students worked with John's list in much the same way they had worked with Marc. There were theories on what he might include and how he might show what matters. In doing this, they would say, "You could take this and this and this and then write a scene where . . ." in a natural grouping of ideas and experiences. There were several paths created for his ideas, and then we all got to work on our writing and John got out a pen. He created a code of squiggly lines and scratchouts to group things in the list into categories. Then he developed scenes that might include things from the list that we had grouped together. I would never have envisioned teaching this strategy for finding the writing from a big topic. I probably can't mimic the energy we found in class that day from playing with John's ideas and the flexibility of thinking it required, but I imagine I'll suggest this listing idea with another writer who is stuck some day in class.

FINAL THOUGHTS

Yesterday we met my husband's family at Popham Beach in Maine for an end-of-summer wave-riding, picnic-sharing day of laughter and story. Our boys will be returning to college soon and the girls, both sixteen, are entering junior year of high school. It was a brilliant day at the beach: the water still warm from summer sun and the hours longer somehow as we walked barefoot from sand to water to the rocky places that appear for exploring only at low tide. The eight of us have met often since our boys were infants, sharing our thinking and our parenting challenges along with cheddar fish crackers and baguettes. But what binds us is story. The kids swapped tales of tourists from their experiences working this summer at a clothing store, at a water park, as a housepainter, and as a babysitter. Storytelling brings family together. It brings students together. It is shared experience that helps us see and understand each other. It is time well spent in the teaching of writing.

CHAPTER EIGHT
The Art of Persuasion

Writers don't need to be given formulas; they need to be shown possibilities.

—BARRY LANE

You would love to watch democracy in our small collection of towns here in the White Mountains. We shrug off scarves and winter coats in early April and gather just after dinner in the high school gymnasium for a town meeting, followed the next night by the school meeting, where any registered voter may rise to take a position and defend it while grandmothers click knitting needles and old friends sit together to whisper and plot responses. There are rules of order and yellow card ballots we wave to vote. Each warrant article can spark a debate, from the raises for local policeman we know by name to the nearly free afterschool programs for elementary kids. The discussion of individual issues can stretch to more than two hours. People call, "Move the question!" if the discussion begins to repeat, and others yawn and fidget, checking a watch that crawls past 11:00. It's a marathon for a school night. I sit on a folding chair with a stack of student papers and my notebook and listen. This can be hard when a citizen (or school board member!) spouts statistics that warp facts or insults a group of people I love, but we don't interrupt. We wait as white-haired Mr. Lucy, a town patriarch, slowly approaches the microphone with his notes in one hand. He'll question the school board about rising taxes and he'll listen hard to the response.

I remember well when a student, Todd Frechette, took the microphone and turned to face a packed gymnasium of voters there to debate building a new high school. He gave us a brief inside tour of our crumbling facility, with carefully considered details like the brown water trickling from corroded water fountains and plaster falling off classroom walls, and then asked for the adults to build a school the kids could be proud of—that his kids would someday be proud of. You can imagine the sound of that standing ovation. I was grateful to be there that night.

Words are potent. I remind my students of their obligation as citizens in a democracy, to be informed, but also of the power their ideas can have when presented in an oral argument at town meeting. They know the importance of writing to persuade a college admissions director to consider their application or a scholarship committee to award them money, but argument should be about more than self-interest. It is an opportunity to address the inequities in our town, our workplace, our world. Teenagers like to argue more than anyone I know, but the art of well-reasoned argument—nuanced, multifaceted, credible—is about more than passion. It rests on research and clarity of thought. It can be taught. We enter our four-week study prepared to analyze its structure and apply what we learn to the issues that startle, amuse, or frighten us.

I begin with stories and issues that can wake me up at night. I use Mitch Albom's 1997 editorial "A Deadly Decision" about a car wreck that took the lives of three teenagers, one just days before her high school graduation. I read this out loud and students hold a colored pencil as I do, listening for phrases or language patterns they appreciate. As Katie Wood Ray said in *Wondrous Words*, "Read aloud is the single most important tool we have in the teaching of writing. If students of any age don't know what good writing sounds like—how it is different from speech—they will have trouble revising for sound. We must read aloud differently than we speak to our students and ask them to listen for how it is different. We must read their texts like art and immerse them in what good writing sounds like." In this article, the drunk driver who killed the young adults is one focus of this editorial, but as in all good argument, Mitch broadens the debate, asking each of us to consider how we allow it in our society. How do we look the other way?

This argument uses a well-crafted, vivid story to draw readers in, and I begin our unit on persuasion with editorials that use story, so that students can see the connection between what they learned and practiced in our last unit and the possibilities of this one. Story draws people near—you can feel the leaning in, the close connection between reader and writer when an essay begins with story. Of course the tragedy of drunk driving is a familiar story, repeated in local papers all over our country far too often, but the cliché becomes new in the hands of a smart writer. I also know that too many high school students drink and drive; this article makes them think.

I then read "Proof We've Failed to Teach What Children Should Know" by Leonard Pitts, Jr., who won the Pulitzer Prize for commentary in 2004. He tells the story of a high school soccer initiation ritual that sent several students to the hospital, and then asks readers to consider how the students and parents reacted to the school's punishment. This piece gets my students talking. There are hidden rituals among our own sports teams as well as the larger issues of bullying and parenting that hound every high school. There are no easy answers. I choose these editorials intentionally; I want stories that command the attention of my soon-to-be-graduating seniors. My mentor texts must have tight writing that shows what I want my students to imitate: clarity, specificity, and thoroughness. We focus our discussion of each piece first on the central idea or purpose of the writer and the credibility of evidence presented, then on the specifics of craft that move a reader to embrace that evidence. In the first days of our study, we listen, we respond with our thinking in quick writes, and then we analyze the text. There is no workshop time yet because students are not ready to write. We study the form first and begin considering ideas we care enough about to spend hours articulating our views.

Mitch Albom's "A Bullet's Impact" moved my entire class from middle-of-the-week, first-block complacency to vigorous debate yesterday. (Although known primarily for his moving memoir, *Tuesdays with Morrie*, Mitch Albom often writes commentary on local and world events as well as sports in his regular column for *The Detroit Free Press*, available at www.freep.com.) In this story a sixteen-year-old is shot execution-style in the freezer of the pizza store where he works and the police arrest two dropouts for the crime. The story forces us to look at stereotypes and prejudices while absorbing how the loss of one kid in a small, rural high school can disrupt the entire community. We then read Robert F. Kennedy's speech "On the Mindless Menace of Violence," given the morning after Martin Luther King, Jr.'s death, and talked about the parallels between 1968 America and our current culture of violence. We look at the claims made and supported in each piece.

This complexity of argument is not what most students have been writing for school. What kind of evidence is most convincing in this essay? How is it presented? The best writers assemble ideas like a tower of blocks, one thought resting on the one before, all supporting each other to create an imposing final product. My students' prior experience has been too often argument in its most simplistic form: the five-paragraph essay. Take one idea and present all of the evidence to support it, pausing to address the issues raised by the other side, then wind up with a finish that restates your thesis. It is a formula of topic sentences, prescriptive paragraphs, and a test-ready structure students master easily. You've seen the workbooks for this writing, complete with planning organizer and rubric. It is a rare and determined writer who makes something stunning from this simplistic formula. Most of my students have practiced it in courses throughout high school, particularly in social studies. I couldn't defend writing more of the same. I focus on broadening this understanding, and again, raising expectations for my students by giving them vision for what's possible in this genre.

In the first few days of our study we read for main idea: *What's the claim?* And persuasive technique: *How does the writer make you take his side in this debate?* Students respond briefly in their notebooks with impressions, their own stories, their own debates. Each day we read several editorials from a current edition of a national paper and respond with quick writes. Editorials are current, explosive, fact-based, and organized in myriad ways. This is where we start. I use one of the arguments I have written in the past during our study (like "What Forty Cents Can Buy You in November" on the DVD) so that I can answer crafting questions as we look at the piece. I also want students to know that argument is not something just written for school.

Students focus better on craft once they are allowed to respond to the content of what they're reading. Quick writes allow us to discuss the issue and our own thinking in response before breaking down the piece into an analysis of its structure and tone.

We analyze and annotate these editorials. We put brackets around the story, for example. Many arguments begin with a story that illustrates an issue. Take a look at Sarah's (Figure 8.1).

> We tucked our arms under our chests, unfolded our hands up towards our chins and rolled. Down the hill we spun, a crazed grin of childhood ecstasy plastered across the face of my little friend. Saydee's bald head peaked out from her leopard-print hat as she tugged its corners over her pale ears. Breathing heavily, sprawled out on the ground she took a minute to catch her breath, then promptly grabbed my hand and pulled me back to do it again. Saydee's sick. But Saydee's just a kid. She's resilient and tough and open, a model cancer patient, but her luck stops here. Seven-years-old and thousands of dollars in debt, it just doesn't make all that much sense to me. I mean, what exactly are we gaining from this? Saydee's mom has been dealt a hard hand. She's a single parent with bad insurance and two young girls, one of which requires weekly trips to Maine Medical Center. She has more responsibilities and heartache than hundreds of mothers combined, but you're right. We should definitely make her pay for that.
>
> Universal healthcare is like a distant beacon to the children of the United States. We're a modern country with technology and policy that often serves us well. However, somewhere along the line we decided to back away from the global trend of insurance for all. We decided it wasn't important enough. Well, I've spent time with these families, these innocent victims, and I can't think of anything more important.

FIGURE 8.1

Illness and injury, we've all been there. The difference is for many of us this is routine, a minor blip in the radar of our dual-income families. We fall down the stairs, we go to the doctor, and we don't give it much thought. We focus on getting better and recovering, not on the co-pay that our insurance picks up. Imagine your kid's lying in bed with a fever, has been sick for days and you are nothing short of stuck. You can't afford to get help; you can't afford to do anything. So you sit and you wait it out. You hope for the best, because the last thing you need is that bill sitting quietly unpaid on the table.

So it'll be hard. I understand that. As a country we seem to be constantly under an impossible wave of debt, but it is certainly not because we've put the health of our citizens above all else. Let's prioritize. Logically, a nation based on the feats of people would want to keep those same people alive, but no, history proves otherwise. Why the United States chooses to keep universal healthcare so untouchable, I cannot tell you. But it is the most important thing. It's a land where chemotherapy isn't covered by many bottom-of-the-line insurance companies, and insurance, let alone good insurance, isn't provided or required. It is a wonder any of the lower middle class gets any attention as to their wellbeing at all.

Should we go back to the ideals of our country, we could realize that not offering free insurance for all is essentially denying the American public of their basic birthrights of life and the pursuit of happiness. Neither of which are possible with a portion of society unable to afford the rising costs of health. It is time to follow the lead of our northern neighbor, of the United Kingdom, France, and Germany and create socialized healthcare, covered under an established tax. This is where our priorities need to be: in Saydee, in the chance to get better, to be well.

FIGURE 8.1 *continued*

This editorial includes the same elements we studied in our last two units of story (detail and voice) but in a compressed version. We underline the claim and find the supporting evidence for each subclaim. We look for how the writer addresses the other side of the issue, and then how the writer responds to this other point of view. Last, we identify where the writer involves the reader. Is there a call to action? I find students need a lot of practice with this. The work reinforces the elements of argument they may already know while also demonstrating the flexibility in structure that draws readers. We want to see an issue in a new way—that's why we read the Op-Ed page or skim the letters to the editor in the paper. Can you imagine how fast you would lose interest if each letter and editorial was written in five-paragraph form? It's insulting to consider. It's insulting to our students to expect strict adherence to a form that has so little currency in our world. I wouldn't bore you by bringing this up if I didn't see this form steadfastly a part of my colleagues' assignments. I can't imagine a more punitive punishment than a weekend with 100 five-paragraph themes on *Romeo and Juliet*. O happy dagger! Indeed.

I assign another editorial to read and analyze at home at least twice during this first week, but I'm careful to choose current issues and smart, smooth writing so this homework is interesting as well as relevant.

I read at home and on vacation with this unit in mind much of the time now. I take notice of how persuasive writing works. It is the best preparation for my teaching and it is in reach of anyone. Read, notice, think, and make theories about how the writing works. Imagine possibilities; write one yourself. Those are the habits of an empowered writing teacher. It isn't magic; it's just slow, creative work.

Figure 8.2 is a sample of my reading of "Blank Checks and Party Hats: Unworthy Charity?" written by a former student. I model this annotating of a piece of writing to show students how carefully I want them to read our model texts.

Unit Planning

Figures 8.3 and 8.4 (pp. 138 and 139) are sample unit plans from one study of argument. I list model texts we use each day (as well as our daily poetry), and I include the goals for the week. These plans are flexible and I change daily focus if I discover areas of weakness that must be addressed with a particular class. After the initial days of analysis, students choose topics and writing workshop consumes one-third or more of our eighty-five-minute block. I confer with individual students about their drafts and often stop mid-workshop to teach something that occurs as I work with students on their drafts. This is, of course, the craft of our work as teachers. I trust you to know what your students need and how best to give it to them. I find that having a recipe of essential ingredients for my argument study simply helps me stay organized and focused as students' individual creations begin to bubble and sizzle each class period.

In the second week of the study our analysis of published work is briefer, and often student-centered. It is, of course, a thrill when a student brings in a piece of writing for the class to consider. I leave time for a student draft to be at the center of a class conference. Student drafts provide vision of how to struggle and how to succeed and often have the biggest impact on the collective understanding of the class. A draft in progress may be missing something essential. For students to wrestle with that nagging feeling of something missing and then discover together what it might be is as powerful as it is unpredictable. It creates a deep understanding of the genre that will serve students well throughout their lives.

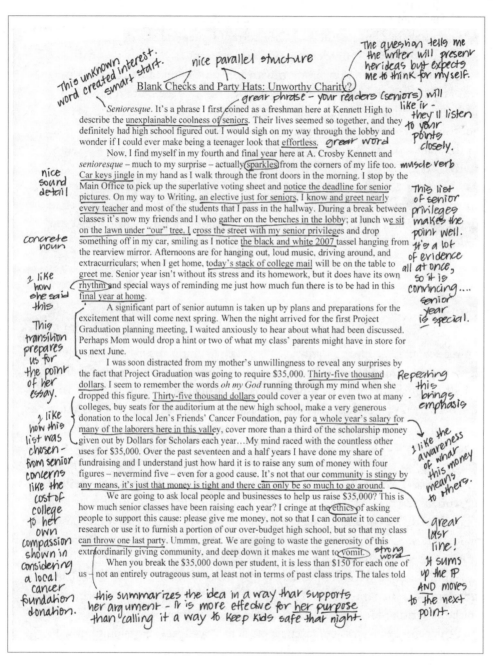

The question tells me the writer will present her ideas but expects me to think for myself.

This unknown word created interest. smart start.

nice parallel structure

Blank Checks and Party Hats: Unworthy Charity?

great phrase - your readers (seniors) will like it - they'll listen to your points closely.

Senioresque. It's a phrase I first coined as a freshman here at Kennett High to describe the unexplainable coolness of seniors. Their lives seemed so together, and they definitely had high school figured out. I would sigh on my way through the lobby and wonder if I could ever make being a teenager look that effortless. great word

nice sound detail

Now, I find myself in my fourth and final year here at A. Crosby Kennett and *senioresque* – much to my surprise – actually sparkles from the corners of my life too. muscle verb Car keys jingle in my hand as I walk through the front doors in the morning. I stop by the Main Office to pick up the superlative voting sheet and notice the deadline for senior pictures. On my way to Writing, an elective just for seniors, I know and greet nearly every teacher and most of the students that I pass in the hallway. During a break between classes it's now my friends and I who gather on the benches in the lobby; at lunch we sit on the lawn under "our" tree. I cross the street with my senior privileges and drop something off in my car, smiling as I notice the black and white 2007 tassel hanging from the rearview mirror. Afternoons are for hanging out, loud music, driving around, and extracurriculars; when I get home, today's stack of college mail will be on the table to greet me. Senior year isn't without its stress and its homework, but it does have its own rhythm and special ways of reminding me just how much fun there is to be had in this final year at home.

This list of senior privileges makes the point well. It's a lot of evidence all at once, so it is convincing.... senior year is special.

concrete noun

I like how she said this

This transition prepares us for the point of her essay.

A significant part of senior autumn is taken up by plans and preparations for the excitement that will come next spring. When the night arrived for the first Project Graduation planning meeting, I waited anxiously to hear about what had been discussed. Perhaps Mom would drop a hint or two of what my class' parents might have in store for us next June.

I was soon distracted from my mother's unwillingness to reveal any surprises by the fact that Project Graduation was going to require $35,000. Thirty-five thousand dollars. I seem to remember the words *oh my God* running through my mind when she dropped this figure. Thirty-five thousand dollars could cover a year or even two at many colleges, buy seats for the auditorium at the new high school, make a very generous donation to the local Jen's Friends' Cancer Foundation, pay for a whole year's salary for many of the laborers here in this valley, cover more than a third of the scholarship money given out by Dollars for Scholars each year…My mind raced with the countless other uses for $35,000. Over the past seventeen and a half years I have done my share of fundraising and I understand just how hard it is to raise any sum of money with four figures – nevermind five – even for a good cause. It's not that our community is stingy by any means, it's just that money is tight and there can only be so much to go around.

Repeating this brings emphasis

I like the awareness of what this money means to others.

I like how this list was chosen - from senior concerns like the cost of college to her own compassion shown in considering a local cancer foundation donation.

We are going to ask local people and businesses to help us raise $35,000? This is how much senior classes have been raising each year? I cringe at the ethics of asking people to support this cause: please give me money, not so that I can donate it to cancer research or use it to furnish a portion of our over-budget high school, but so that my class can throw one last party. Ummm, great. We are going to waste the generosity of this extraordinarily giving community, and deep down it makes me want to vomit. strong word

great last line! It sums up the ¶ AND moves to the next point.

When you break the $35,000 down per student, it is less than $150 for each one of us – not an entirely outrageous sum, at least not in terms of past class trips. The tales told

this summarizes the idea in a way that supports her argument - it is more effective for her purpose than calling it a way to keep kids safe that night.

FIGURE 8.2

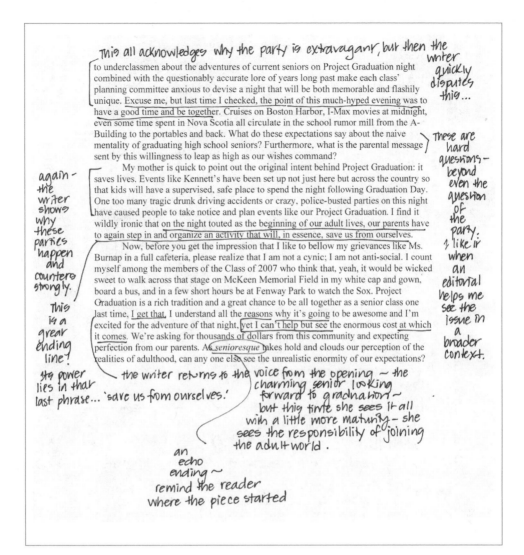

The handwritten annotations on the figure read:

"This all acknowledges why the party is extravagant, but then the writer quickly disputes this..."

"These are hard questions – beyond even the question of the party. I like it when an editorial helps me see the issue in a broader context."

"again – the writer shows why these parties happen and counters strongly."

"This is a great ending line! Its power lies in that last phrase... 'save us from ourselves.'"

"the writer returns to the voice from the opening – the charming senior looking forward to graduation – but this time she sees it all with a little more maturity – she sees the responsibility of joining the adult world."

"an echo ending ~ remind the reader where the piece started"

The typed text within the figure reads:

to underclassmen about the adventures of current seniors on Project Graduation night combined with the questionably accurate lore of years long past make each class' planning committee anxious to devise a night that will be both memorable and flashily unique. Excuse me, but last time I checked, the point of this much-hyped evening was to have a good time and be together. Cruises on Boston Harbor, I-Max movies at midnight, even some time spent in Nova Scotia all circulate in the school rumor mill from the A-Building to the portables and back. What do these expectations say about the naive mentality of graduating high school seniors? Furthermore, what is the parental message sent by this willingness to leap as high as our wishes command?

My mother is quick to point out the original intent behind Project Graduation: it saves lives. Events like Kennett's have been set up not just here but across the country so that kids will have a supervised, safe place to spend the night following Graduation Day. One too many tragic drunk driving accidents or crazy, police-busted parties on this night have caused people to take notice and plan events like our Project Graduation. I find it wildly ironic that on the night touted as the beginning of our adult lives, our parents have to again step in and organize an activity that will, in essence, save us from ourselves.

Now, before you get the impression that I like to bellow my grievances like Ms. Burnap in a full cafeteria, please realize that I am not a cynic; I am not anti-social. I count myself among the members of the Class of 2007 who think that, yeah, it would be wicked sweet to walk across that stage on McKeen Memorial Field in my white cap and gown, board a bus, and in a few short hours be at Fenway Park to watch the Sox. Project Graduation is a rich tradition and a great chance to be all together as a senior class one last time, I get that, I understand all the reasons why it's going to be awesome and I'm excited for the adventure of that night, yet I can't help but see the enormous cost at which it comes. We're asking for thousands of dollars from this community and expecting perfection from our parents. As *senioresque* takes hold and clouds our perception of the realities of adulthood, can any one else see the unrealistic enormity of our expectations?

FIGURE 8.2 *continued*

THE TEACHER'S MODEL OF PROCESS

During our daily quick writing and analyzing of argument models, both published texts and student samples, I am composing an argument for my class. As I walk through the steps in my thinking, I include students in responding to my thinking and my process. I model topic search first, using my writing notebook, then show how to think through and organize my idea before I draft. For years I have used Jim Burke's Argument Organizer to begin. You might notice the

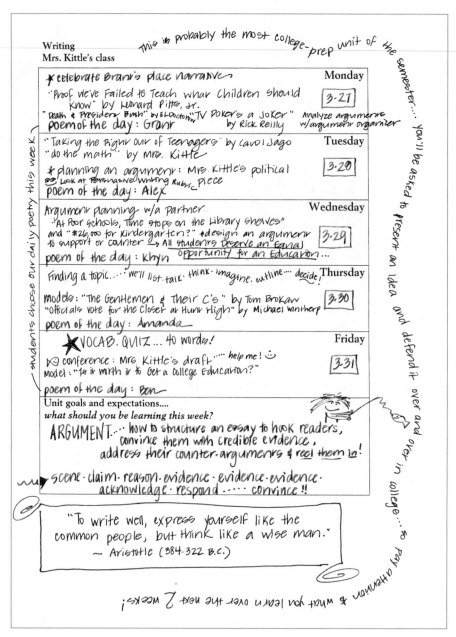

Figure 8.3

structure could frame that dreaded five-paragraph essay, but I tell my students these parts are like building blocks to me. Even if I gave each student in class the same handful of blocks, no doubt a glut of creations would result. I hold a blank organizer before my class and cut the components apart. I can then arrange them however I want—however my topic and ideas might drive me to write.

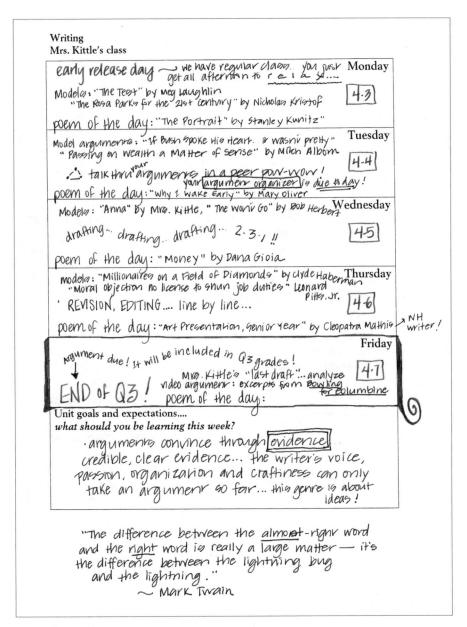

Writing
Mrs. Kittle's class

early release day → we have regular class. you just get all afternoon to r e l a x....	**Monday**
Models: "The Test" by Meg Laughlin "The Rosa Parks for the 21st century" by Nicholas Kristof	4·3
poem of the day: "The Portrait" by Stanley Kunitz"	
Model arguments: "If Bush spoke his Heart.. it wasn't pretty" "Passing on wealth a matter of sense" by Mitch Albom △ talk thru your arguments in a peer pow-wow! your argument organizer is due today! poem of the day: "why I wake Early" by Mary Oliver	**Tuesday** 4·4
Models: "Anna" by Mrs. Kittle, "The won't Go" by Bob Herbert drafting... drafting.. drafting... 2·3·/ !! poem of the day: "Money" by Dana Gioia	**Wednesday** 4·5
Models: "Millionaires on a Field of Diamonds" by Clyde Haberman "Moral objection no license to shun job duties" Leonard Pitts, Jr. ' REVISION, EDITING.... line by line... poem of the day: "Art Presentation, Senior Year" by Cleopatra Mathis → NH writer!	**Thursday** 4·6
Argument due! It will be included in Q3 grades! → END of Q3! Mrs. Kittle's "last draft"... analyze video argument: excerpts from Bowling for Columbine poem of the day:	**Friday** 4·7

Unit goals and expectations....
what should you be learning this week?

· arguments convince through evidence ·
credible, clear evidence... the writer's voice,
passion, organization and craftiness can only
take an argument so far... this genre is about
ideas!

"The difference between the almost-right word
and the right word is really a large matter — it's
the difference between the lightning bug
and the lightning."
~ Mark Twain

Fᴇɢᴜʀᴇ 8.4

I show them a draft (Figure 8.5), for example, of an essay I wrote in response to a news story that detailed a ninth grader's expulsion for writing in her private journal a fictional story of killing a teacher. I began my essay with an opening scene, and then the teacher's point of view, which is an acknowledgment to the other side of the issue I'm going to argue.

I imagine this 14-year-old gifted writer in her first quarter of high school being called out of class by the Vice-Principal. All of the students whisper, "Ooooo, Rachel!" causing her to blush a furious red from her collar to her hairline.

She follows him to a conference room in the main office where serious adults surround a table watching her enter and fumble for her seat. She sees her journal, the one the art teacher confiscated second period the day before; now she panics. Have they all read her private thoughts? Her notes to her boyfriend? She's going to puke if someone doesn't start talking soon.

Travis Carr is several hallways from the main office helping a student with a perspective drawing in his second period class, but he can't quit thinking about that journal. He remembers its path around his room yesterday, passed from one student to the next, the snickers and huddled students pouring over its pages. He took it. Rachel protested, but he ignored her. Forget it. He was sick of warnings. If her privacy was so important she should have left it at home.

He tossed the journal on his desk and didn't think about it until late that afternoon. He started flipping through it, ignoring the poems and sketches, skimming the writing. Until he read that one passage, blood spurting out the side of the head of the teacher she had just shot. His heart pounded in fear. Rachel? Who was this girl? Is this what the other kids were laughing about?

Travis didn't have a choice. He left it with the principal the next day. There was no way he would be blamed if this girl brought a gun to school. The school's new "zero-tolerance" policy was explained in detail at the start of the school year, and Travis agreed with it. Schools have a responsibility for keeping kids and teachers safe. He wasn't going to bet the lives of his colleagues on his limited knowledge of Rachel Boim.

But here's where my fictional version ends, and the real world steps in, because when Rachel Boim left that Indiana conference room that afternoon she was expelled from high school for the remainder of the school year, and that's not only wrong, it's ridiculous.

At the hearing both parents testified about Rachel's character. She's a vegetarian because she abhors the killing of animals. She has never had a disciplinary issue before, is slow to lose her temper, but she's a voracious reader. As Gary Paulson says, she reads like a wolf eats. And that means everything: poetry, literature, horror, comedy. Rachel experiments with these forms in her private journal as writers do. Does that mean she's dangerous?

FIGURE 8.5

Schools are on trial in the media for everything these days. Test scores that stubbornly refuse to rise, lazy students who fail courses and then drop out, teachers who don't inspire adolescents the way their video games and DVDs do. And then there are the school shootings. Armed students entering classrooms, teachers held hostage, tiny caskets buried in flowers as weeping parents watch. If we can't squeeze enough dollars out of the budget for modern textbooks or classrooms, at least we can write a plan to prevent a massacre. And then follow it, no matter who is ensnared in the catch.

Rachel will be allowed to attend another high school in the county for the remainder of the school year and transfer back as a sophomore. This is a solution for adults, not teenagers. As if she could ever go back to her school, ignoring huddled whispers as she passes students in the halls, slithering into art class with Mr. Carr, avoiding his eyes, then waiting to be questioned when a rowdy student scribbles a threat on the bathroom wall to avoid a math test in the afternoon. She's marked. She's guilty. She cannot possibly return to that school "ready to learn," giggling at lunch, playful and creative in English classes, gathering vocabulary and skills to prepare for college. Her school life is over in Fulton County; her ability to tolerate this dramatic change of events is exactly zero.

We can't save Rachel Boim. But we can think through a policy because of her story. All schools struggle to maintain order and be fair to teenagers who make mistakes. Schools respond to anxious parents with a flurry of suspensions then agonize over their drop-out rates. It all comes down to knowing the kids well enough to make a reasonable judgment about character, and that will take smaller classes, more guidance counselors and millions of dollars.

Will we pay, or just sigh and pretend students like Rachel will take care of themselves?

FIGURE 8.5 *continued*

In another class I crafted the plan in Figure 8.6 in front of students early in our unit as a model of process. I was determined to write a letter to the editor of our local paper regarding an upcoming vote. In Conway, local taxpayers must approve raises in the teachers' contract, and our budget committee had recommended that year against support of the warrant article that would provide funds for those raises. I had to organize an argument to address the issue in hopes of seeing this article passed. As I worked through my thinking on the overhead, I discussed the way argument is organized, including how to present evidence. I teach students the thinking behind a formula called 2-3-1, another lesson I learned from Don Murray. Which line of evidence is most persuasive in my plan? It should be the last one presented in the essay since readers remember the last information with greatest clarity. The second most convincing evidence will go first, and the least convincing evidence should go in the middle since it will least likely be remembered. We had quite a lively debate in class over which evidence was most convincing as well as other evidence students felt I had left out.

The following day I brought in a rough draft and we did a whole-class conference on it. I took notes as my students offered suggestions.

Here are two student comments from our work that day. Garrett waited until class was over to pass me a note with a question about my last sentence. He said, "This is kind of picky, but *game* implies 'fun and games' and that doesn't seem right. So Grant and I thought about *battle* but that sounds like war. We both think you should choose another word, but we don't know what." I love that the two of them were still discussing the piece even after the lesson was over, and especially that they were so attentive to the impact of word choice. (I changed it to *salary competition* for the final draft.)

Andy said, "I feel better now that I've seen this. This draft is just what mine looks like. I also want to say that I like the second choice for your first line in the letter. It makes me think 'what is that important decision?' and I keep reading."

Argument Organizer: Reading, Writing, Speaking   Name: Mrs. Kittle's plan

Claim
What do you want people to know, do, think, or believe?
that they must reject the budget comm. recommendation and vote yes on warrant article #7 (teacher raises)
Who am I to act as an authority on this issue?
K-12 Mentoring Programs for new teachers - director for 6 years- also hiring NT- interviewing

Reason(s)
A sentence or two explaining *why* you are making this claim.
It is essential to pay good teachers well in order to retain them as well as to attract new teachers to Conway. Failure on this article will hurt our ability to attract good teachers.

Evidence — Facts · Figures · Statistics · Quotations from the text · Expert analysis

Evidence	Evidence	Evidence
Teacher salaries (2005) state of NH: 43,941 Conway: 40,395 (9% below the average) Hanover 59,000 minimum starting salary: state of NH: 28,279 Conway: 26,900 (112th! out of 154) bottom 30% in state for new teachers critical shortage areas: math science, language, special ed., reading specialists, etc.	Our compensation system: performance-based pay (6 years) · 66 items based on planning & preparation, classroom environment, instruction, professional responsibilities · Allows basic teacher to be removed if performance doesn't improve · rewards excellence ~ · this system was requested by the ___ form & implemented successfully.	Teacher = Student Achievement "Numerous studies reveal the tremendous impact schools and teachers can have on student achievement. In classrooms headed by teachers characterized as "most effective," students posted achievement gains of 53 percentage points over the course of one academic year, whereas in classrooms led by "least effective" teachers, student achievement gains averaged 14 percentage points."

It is already hard to attract the best & brightest to Conway - please don't make it harder.

Good teaching is worth the investment.

Acknowledge and Respond
Discuss, address, and respond to alternatives, criticisms, and objections.

Acknowledge	Respond
The burden of CSD taxpayers, especially with the new school - that the budget comm. was trying to 'send a message' about health care costs w/ this vote ... that it was a tough winter for many businesses in the valley	* not one penny of this article is for health ins. * CSD teachers already pay 20% of costs when most NH teachers pay 10% * this vote will send a message alright, this vote will tell teachers we're going backwards in a salary game that Conway is already losing.

this vote would sabotage our efforts.

© Jim Burke 2003. May reproduce for classroom use only. www.englishcompanion.com

FIGURE 8.6

I continued crafting this letter and sent it to our paper just days before the vote. (The final draft is on the DVD.) I'm thrilled to say that warrant article #7 passed, although by a margin of only thirteen votes. More than thirteen of my students voted that day, and I hope that in working through the process of drafting persuasive writing they learned a path through their own thinking as well as the power of their participation in our democracy.

COMMENTARY

After reading and writing argument for two weeks, we step into the murkier waters of commentary, which draws on the structure of argument, but can often contain several claims and rely more on the writer's facility with language and thinking than facts and figures. It is a "comment on life" essay, one writer's views or wonderings, but written to make readers consider their own. Commentary is often persuasive and in this unit we study how it is convincing. There is no one definition of either of these forms, but I think of argument as the simpler version of crafting commentary so it comes first. In the first two weeks of studying argument I push students to write with power, but only some of them are confident enough to do so. When we follow up with commentary, more students step forward with commanding voices and convincing details simply because they've learned more, read more, and have an opportunity to practice a developing skill again.

I imagine you see the similarity in planning this work in persuasive writing to the structure of our foray into story: write one, then raise the quality of the next in a more complicated version of the first. Write argument, then try commentary, more complex and craftier. As always, we are also working on the skills and habits of a writer simultaneously with the content of this particular product. This work in persuasive writing builds a foundation for writing research in our multigenre unit. Students will use research in persuasive writing, but often without citation, as we see in newspaper editorials. When we move to multigenre, cited research is an expectation.

LETTERS

The origin of commentary is the letter. I have asked students in the past to compose a letter to someone as the first step in understanding this genre. Students can choose any issue, any person, but they must use their understanding of evidence and point of view to be convincing to the audience they imagine reading their work. Here are a few topics from this past semester: a letter to the superintendent asking that participation in a dance company be considered for P.E. credit; a letter to a local business complaining about recent service; and a letter to a parent asking to be treated as an adult. Mary's letter (Figure 8.7) is a remarkable model of this form. She certainly understands how evidence can support a position.

> Dear Mom,
>
> I'm writing to you on the subject of my age. I am in fact seventeen years and eleven months old! Of all people I would expect you to remember my birthday, the day on which you supposedly brought me into the world. Maybe there was some mix up in the hospital and that is the root of our misunderstanding; we never seem to be on the same line of thought. Seventeen years and eleven months, that means I'll be eighteen in just one month! I can leave the house, move to Iceland, change my name, sign my own legal documents, and never see you again. How do you feel about that? If you think you'd like to avoid any or all of the above then I would strongly encourage you to begin treating me like an adult and not a juvenile delinquent.
>
> I am sick of being interrogated on a daily basis. I am sick of being told I am not allowed to partake in normal activities for teens. I am sick of your constant spewing of disgust at everything I do from eating a carrot before dinner to volunteering at the nursing home. I am sick of the answer always being NO! I am sick of your constant criticism: when I write a letter you notice there are two spelling mistakes, when I get a report card all you care about is the 89, and when I do a race all you ask is did you win? I am sick of suspicious looks, searches through all my belongings, eavesdropping on my phone calls. I am sick of getting in the car or walking in the door and finding myself, within five minutes, engrossed in an argument that drains all the happiness out of me, saps all the motivation from my body, and leaves my face streaked with bitter tears. So many tears, so many nights of frustration, so much wanting to give up, writing about it makes me cry.
>
> Why? There has been no need to wreak this havoc upon my life. I am Mary, remember, a girl most people consider to be a good person, one who works hard and can be trusted. The families I baby sit for hand me the keys to their luxury vehicles and tell me to go have fun with the kids. Yet as you take off for a weekend in Boston with my sisters, you tell me I'm only to use the car for the purpose of transporting myself to and from church! This is the height of lunacy. I'm giving up three days with my

FIGURE 8.7

sisters, who I rarely get to spend time with, so that I can go to ski camp. Why? Because I care about skiing; I am actually willing to spend all of my Thanksgiving break training. You don't recognize my drive as something rare and hard to come by in seventeen-year-olds, as my coaches do. You don't have an ounce of respect for my training efforts; you, in fact, discourage them! I've had to beg to go roller-skiing and running. Now that I'm coming back for training camp you expect me to be housebound at the neighbor's whenever we're not out skiing.

I realize your twisted mentality, which deems teenagers undeserving of any degree of freedom or license to have fun, is rooted in your upbringing. You are the sheltered child of an overly strict, completely unreasonable father. You didn't have any fun when you were young, so why should your daughter. Let me tell you, having this sad, sick outlook is only damaging my development into a normal young adult. I've rarely gone out; I don't have a boyfriend; I've slaved away trying to live up to expectations set by you—someone who doesn't appear to hold themselves to any standards whatsoever. Now, a senior, your little wonder-child is finally realizing that she is done. An urge to get away and go absolutely crazy, to pull out all the stops, grows inside me every day.

This will be a shocker, but I'm seriously considering taking a year off to (This is going to kill you) volunteer in a foreign country teaching English. I sound sure of myself, saying I want to study history and teach and coach for a few years before possibly going to law school. But frankly, I don't know what the real world is like and it might be a good idea for me to do some discovering after I'm removed from the extreme climate control of your household and before I'm thrust into college where the forecast is never predictable.

I need to escape like my sisters have done. Being the youngest, the lone warrior fighting to evade insanity as induced by you, I consider myself at the highest risk of landing on a leather couch for counseling in twenty years. Maybe this letter will make you see the light: if you really care about me, you need to let go. You need to respect me and consider your own faults at least as much as you focus on mine. Please change. Imagine waking up to find me gone.

Love, Mary

FIGURE 8.7 *continued*

The letter unit is all about voice. In commentary, voice is central as well. It is an easy move for students from letters to essays, especially given strong models of both product and a path through this territory in my model of my own process to produce one. I tend to write a lot about teaching because those issues gnaw at me, and as I explained to students, my voice has credibility because I've worked for more than two decades in this profession. It seems to me, as long as the topic feels fresh to the writer, it shouldn't matter how many times or ways one tills similar ground. I remind myself of this when one student writes mostly about football throughout a semester or one writing piece after another on a loss that follows a student like a dark kite bouncing in a stormy sky behind. Writing is enriched by personal experience, so I lead with my passion and look for theirs. This unit I wrote again about education in our valley. I was struck by the contrast between students who succeed and those who don't, students who attend Ivy League schools and those who drop out. I told students I had two ideas in my head: the power of public education to provide opportunity for those who could not afford to attend private schools, and the sometimes empty promise of an equal education for all. I put the two words *power* and *promise* on the board and brainstormed phrases and ways to think about each.

I then composed the first paragraph of a draft on the chalkboard as they listened and offered suggestions. When students went on to their own writing, I often referenced my thinking in our conferences. I didn't complete the writing until weeks later, however. I was too focused on their drafts to work on my own. I don't believe we have to write finished products each unit, but we should, as Don Murray said, have recent experience in the genre.

FINAL THOUGHTS

I tell my students that persuasive writing is the most directly "college-prep" of the units in our course. Students will be asked to defend a position often in college and will be expected to be flexible thinkers, smart in their construction of ideas and clear about supporting evidence. But even for students who don't go on to further schooling, persuasive writing can help convince a neighbor to a halt a lawsuit or fellow citizens to support a candidate's election to senate. It just might bolster a marriage proposal or assure a promotion. It is writing worth doing well for our democracy and for our lives.

Phillip

Every compulsion is put upon writers to become safe, polite, obedient and sterile.
—SINCLAIR LEWIS

Phillip sits in the worst seat in the room—my colleagues and I think it is cursed. The back corner seat wedged between bookshelves and the windows, it is the least interactive place to be. A student who chooses it signals that he doesn't want to be a part of what we're up to as writers. I watch Phillip as he takes this place and then hides behind his computer screen. Day after day I wander the room conferring with writers, and he is usually buried in the pages of the book he says I must read. It's historical fiction—a shipwreck—and I just can't muster a lot of enthusiasm for it.

I can't seem to move this kid toward writing. Phillip quick writes with little enthusiasm. He gives up short of the time, unlike most of his classmates. He makes a production of it, tossing his pencil at the desk and closing his notebook with a flourish. He isn't defiant, he's just doing what's required of him and that's it.

During our first unit Phillip writes a truly compelling story hidden amid short, uninspired sentences and jumbled paragraphs. I think of a quote from poet Jane Kenyon, "People don't know how hard it is to write, what a struggle it is to know what you want to say and then to say what you mean." Here's Phillip's story: He was injured as a child and developed seizures. He became determined to be seizure-free in the two years prior to his sixteenth birthday so he'd be able to take driver's education and get his license. He watches what he eats, he monitors his environment; he approaches it all with maturity and discipline. No such luck. He has a seizure in school just a day or two before his appointment to take his driver's test. He has to give up the thought of ever being able to drive and live with the humiliation that these unexpected seizures bring on in the middle of a class, in front of a girl he likes, in the locker room after a game. He spits out a draft that is all tell, no show. He's a limited writer so this doesn't surprise me, but even after we confer and he seems to understand what I'm saying about sensory details and image, he makes only the most superficial changes to his draft. What to do?

I meet with my colleagues every other Thursday morning for our writing professional learning community. We often look at student work and talk about what we see and would say to the writer. On this day I have Phillip's draft. Since it is Thursday, he still has two class days to revise before he turns in a last draft. My colleagues read and mark up his work, high-fiving the lines and ideas that resonate and asking questions, suggesting places to develop, and so on. We have a lively discussion of this piece and how Phillip might work with it. I think it is amazing that this student will get not only a rough draft back with feedback after he just turned it in the day before but a rough draft with the feedback of three determined writing teachers—that's something.

When PLC ends, class begins. I'm energized by the talk with my colleagues so I approach Phillip as he arrives. One of my class requirements is to discuss a rough draft with the class at some point during the semester and elicit feedback. I ask Phillip if he'll be the first to go through the process by letting the class look at his piece and talk about revision. He agrees.

My students are lively, informed, and far smarter than I expect. They end up narrowing down Phillip's information to three key scenes and they suggest cutting several other moments that distract from that focus. I take notes on the whiteboard as several students talk through his piece. They've learned much of the language I had hoped, with references to detail, dialogue, scene, momentum, zooming in, and so forth. Phillip seems pleased and encouraged and works all period. Well, he looks like he's working, that is. His computer is on and his piece is on the screen and he stares at it for most of the workshop time.

Friday when I get home with the stack of essays I rifle through to find his and move it to the top of the pile. I read eagerly. It doesn't take long to realize he has made not a single change to the text. It is so discouraging I don't quite know how to comment on his work. It is as if the entire experience washed over him. In his end notes he credits the class conference and the feedback from three teachers in helping him write, but why? He uses none of the advice.

It's a good reminder that we coach and lead and don't always succeed in a way that is immediately evident. The writing must remain in the hands of the writer and the suggestions made are not orders. Phillip's piece was what he wanted, and he either didn't know how to make our ideas work or he didn't want them to. Either way he has had good teaching, and that is not a waste. I used to get discouraged when I focused too much on the writing, not the writer. If the piece didn't improve I felt like my efforts were wasted. I've just seen too many kids use something I've taught them months later to worry that nothing sinks in. It does. We're just impatient. Phillip was connected those two days; he was thinking. He made decisions. I can respect that and look for signs of my teaching in another piece. It has happened so many times before. Sometimes it takes a new writing piece and a new need to bring back the teaching we gave him. That's when a student's learning will surprise me like a carefully wrapped present delivered after my birthday has passed.

Months later we begin multigenre, and as I confer with students about possible topics, Phillip surprises me. He says, "I already know what I'm writing about: the Iraq war. My brother came home five months ago and he's different. I can't explain it. But he's just not the same. He stays up all night watching TV. I came in the room one night and it was just fuzz on the screen—static—and I thought he was sleeping but he was just looking at it, with his eyes open, staring."

"That must be hard," I say to fill up the space he's left in a long pause. I want him to keep talking. I know I need to listen. He's already connected to a topic, which usually takes him days to uncover. I want to ask how he'll write about the war and his brother, but I'm afraid to turn this experience he's had into an assignment. I *will* myself to be quiet.

"We don't do anything for the guys coming back, you know?" he's troubled and sad. More silence.

I say, "I think that's a strong topic, Phillip. You could teach all of us to understand all we hear about the war in a different way. I don't know much about the Iraq war, but please let me know how I can help you." I leave him thinking and move to confer with other writers nearby.

The next day Phillip begins his project with a map of Iraq. He fills it in with the names of soldiers killed this year to create a concrete poem. He writes an editorial on the conditions of Army hospitals, but nothing about his brother. I feel his project is almost there, as if he's on the brink of a great leap that will connect his experience with his writing, but we're running out of time. It's June.

On the day of his multigenre presentation he bursts into class late with a mini-movie he's finished that morning. In a series of photos, quotes, and clips of speeches he's gathered and assembled on his computer, you see and feel the anguish of this war on the families of those who serve. It's brilliant work—and so complicated in its construction with one layer of song and another of image and then another layer of concise quotes that bring the three strands together. It is complicated story: ideas written in image and sound. There are repeating lines—like poetry—and symbols seen in a new way, like an image of soldiers in wheelchairs with missing limbs followed by a stoic American flag waving behind them. I wonder how all of the elements of story and persuasion came together for him—when and how. He told me he spend about twenty hours crafting his eight-minute movie, but how did he know to make all of the decisions that piece required? His mini-movie was a tapestry of anger and confusion woven with experience and image into a thoughtful commentary on the most important issue of our time. It was a tribute to the loss of some part of his family and his life, and it gave my classroom of young voters—young citizens—something to think about as they left class for graduation practice and all of the responsibilities soon to be theirs.

I'm not convinced Phillip could compose an essay that would be as skillful as his mini-movie. I know his movie counts as commentary in our world today, but I wonder about school. Do we honor the talents of the Phillips in our rooms as readily as those who compose writing of depth and complexity? Perhaps we need a new vision of crafting ideas to embrace the technology so available to our students. Certainly we need to make that technology available to all students so that all can realize their talents in this medium. Writing is as simple as pen to paper and as complex as orchestrating scene within video.

I have work to do. I need to broaden my understanding of writing to include digital storytelling and video commentary. You know how I'll start. I'm learning to lay down tracks of music, image, and text on my computer. I'm asking for help from smart people I know at my school and watching my students work in our graphic arts program in the Career and Technical Center. I'm zipping around Youtube.com looking for model videos that I can learn from. I'm watching my process as I work, considering how I might guide my students.

I feel incompetent and slow.

I can't believe I'll ever create something worthwhile.

I keep trying.

Sometimes I give up.

I tell myself to try for just fifteen minutes and see what happens.

I recognize this process: It is too hard, but exhilarating in the same moment. I discover all kinds of things I didn't know I could do and ideas for things I need to say. There's so much to learn, but if I want to lead students I'd better muster up some courage for the task. I have teaching to do.

CHAPTER NINE

Seeking Balance
Writing About Literature and Writing About Life

Reading makes immigrants of us all.
It takes us away from home, but more importantly,
it finds homes for us everywhere.

—HAZEL ROCHMAN

I love literature: an over the moon, can't eat or sleep, Stanley Cup kind of love. I love the revelations buried in a text that allow me to see in a new way. I've read all the Brontë novels several times and Austen's probably a dozen each; they will never age for me. What an exhilarating way to spend an afternoon: reading and rereading language that sings. Bring on *Anna Karenina* one more time, please. I'll always long for those lovely evenings in graduate school buried in British literature; I came home breathless. "Line my coffin with books," I would say to my husband, "I want George Eliot near when I cross over."

Ah, he just didn't get it.

I hustled to the portables behind our school when it was time to teach American Literature. They pay me for this? An hour to talk about Stella? Oh, sweet life! There's literature, and there's everything else. And in the beginning of my years teaching high school, there really wasn't much else. I followed the advice of my department chair: There wasn't enough time to teach all the literature that should be taught, so writing about it was a way to kill two birds with one stone. It seemed sensible; all teachers know this familiar race against time.

But even in my first semester I could feel a shift—something had died alright—the writing. My transition from middle school was challenging in many ways, but this was the most disheartening. Many of the papers I read were distant, shallow, and lacking the passion I had come to expect from teenagers; why had they stopped revising? I went back to the writing of Donald Murray, Donald Graves, and Tom Newkirk to search for answers. Choice was at the center of what a writer needs. What real choices did my students have? I believed I was preparing them for college, but I didn't ask two questions that seem so obvious now: How many of my students would likely major in English? And if they didn't, what kind of writing would they be doing either in school or in life that I was preparing them for? The trick was to match the literacy expectations in many fields with my students' experiences in English, even when the focus was a course in literature.

I began to email college professors in all fields: What do students need in writing? The same themes emerged: to pursue a line of thought, to provide credible evidence to support an idea, to be flexible with thinking as well as sentences, and to write with power, grace, and style. I've found that sometimes those qualities emerge in papers on literature, and sometimes they emerge in narrative, fiction, or poetry. To gather more of my students around good writing, I backed away from many of the assignments connected to a novel and explored instead issues and personal experiences that led to commentary, memoir, literary nonfiction, and argument. I made an intentional move away from product and immersed my students in process. It was challenging to plan, but the payoff was huge.

I have many stories I could share since I confronted those questions in my teaching: Michael's failure in ninth- and tenth-grade English where he wrote in incomplete sentences with multiple errors of logic about *To Kill a Mockingbird* and *Hamlet*, contrasted with the provocative essays he wrote about an adopted brother, assisted suicide, and his own CD label he was managing outside of school. Or Josh, who suffered English courses, one after another, so he could move on to computer programming in college. His narrative on the impact of his parents' divorce spanned nine pages and remains one of the most complex pieces of high school writing I've read in the last decade. And then there was Johnny, who wrote about growing up on the football field, and was so intent to get the story right that he reviewed game tapes at night and revised his piece more than a dozen times.

Some colleagues, however, clucked their tongues and said, "Well, of course if you let them just write about what they want, they will. That's easy. Literary criticism: That's rigorous." And it hurt. Teachers can be like catty high school girls. At night as I wrestled with sleep I'd wonder, what if they were right? Perhaps if I just taught literary analysis better, all of my students would become super-critical thinkers, slaying symbolism with one flick of a polyester super-cape. But a question still nagged at me: Would that be enough?

We know we need students to write about literature because writing about it improves their reading. We need deep readers. They will likely learn and understand more about their reading when they write. The problem is, they will not necessarily understand more about writing with this work. Rewriting is, after all, what writing is all about. When students summarize chapters or write journals in the voice of a character, no one rewrites anything. This is not writing process work, it is all about product. And some of the time we need to make that trade in order to advance the reading. But we have to recognize this is a trade—not a genuine engagement with both reading and writing. Writing skills (except on the most superficial level) will not improve with these activities because there is no deep engagement with the process of making meaning.

It's like taking me to the hardware store. My husband knows better now, but we had a few unfortunate trips to the home improvement store before he figured it out. I just don't have any enthusiasm for tools or bolts or large sheets of plywood. He would patiently point out the differences in electric screwdrivers while I picked dog hair off my coat. "You aren't listening!" he'd rant. True, I'm afraid. Unless all of this attention leads to something I value, I'm just along for the ride. Too many high school students are along for the ride in English; you and I both know it. It doesn't satisfy them to say they need literary analysis for college. All we have is now. Today. This moment with these writers. We need a full-on embrace of writing process in order to teach writers. To get to amazing products, we have to change our focus to the process. We have to let go of products to get them. I know that's enough to make you crazy, but stick with me here.

We know that students will revise with more energy if the topic is personally meaningful to them. They will revise little, if any, if the topic is not. Sometimes the passionate engagement with a text they're creating comes from literature, and I stand up and do the twist at my desk because a student is speaking my language. But I've read too many of those other papers that were revised little, or I suspect, not at all. There's nothing like a multipage horror of literature analysis to send me straight for a couple of strawberry-frosted donuts. Likewise, when you give a whole class the freedom to choose a moment from their lives and illuminate it with all the creative expertise they can, many revise and rethink the piece a dozen times, and then others revise little, if any, and toss it on my desk. I wish there were a secret formula to ensure that all students will revise everything, but kids are different, passions are different, and the writing process changes according to the needs of both the writer and the piece of writing.

So we need both: writing about literature and not writing about it. We need students collecting evidence to support an idea from a text and making discoveries about meaning and their own life experiences so they can bring to those stories, and then we need students making choices about topics they want to write about, so that they are forced into the chaos of thinking that must somehow transform itself into a draft that represents what they believe. How do we divide our time? Fifty percent of each? 70/30? I don't know The Answer. I know it is a question we must ask in our departments and in our own teaching, because it can't be 100 percent of either.

In my high school we created a course devoted to writing. It is a semester-long elective for seniors. Students at Kennett are immersed in literary analysis during the study of American Literature as juniors, but won't write any in this course called writing, which is one reason I teach it. I am not an expert teacher of literary criticism and I don't desire to be. I know if I need help I will go to Carol Jago or Robert Probst who have both written many fine things on the topic and I will be guided well.

We have adjusted more of the writing work in courses taught to freshmen and sophomores. We made a list of all the writing students were doing in a quarter, then in a semester, then in a year. It is called vertical alignment and it is smart work for any high school English department. We studied the balance of genres. We discovered that students wrote more literary criticism than anything else in their first three years of high school; that's a problem.

Here is an example of how we have adjusted curriculum since we made that discovery: students read and write about *The Great Gatsby* (and talk about how it was written as they study it for about three weeks) and then study writing on its own for a few weeks. And I don't mean just "write a personal narrative," but studying writing and creating something original and meaningful. If it is some half-hearted-must-do unit interrupting what the teacher believes is really important, believe me, the kids will get that. And their work will reflect that. If we try to craft meaning from our lives right beside them, they'll see that story is more than a formula and writing is more than an activity. And it will entice more students into rigorous work: rigor in process, rigor in thinking and imagining what's possible. Rigor that interrupts their crazy-busy lives outside of the classroom and demands attention. That's our goal—rigor in process. We want students haunted by writing. We want topics that grab them and won't let them go. As much as we embrace the literature we are privileged to share with students, we now seek to embrace the craft of writing as its own subject, worthy of its own time in our curriculum.

WRITING WITH STUDENTS ABOUT LITERATURE

Picture Jason Wood, otherwise known affectionately as the Wood-meister or The Wood Man by students. He's grown his hair long this year, the wavy locks curling just beyond his ears. He is always in a wrinkle-free shirt and tie and this man follows the rules. Don't even try to bring that cell phone to class. He's been teaching in this cave at the bottom of the stairs in the English wing for a couple of years now. It is probably in the running for the smallest room in the school with exposed pipes and general nastiness collecting in all corners. It was a janitor's closet for the first sixty years, then converted to a classroom as the population pushed the limits of our school. But life percolates in this dark space; Jason lives literature. Mr. Wood has been teaching at Kennett High School for the last five years. Even as a rookie he was thoughtful and reflective about teaching as well as madly passionate about literature. He is the American Literature Professional Learning Community leader in our department now and even teachers with decades of experience recognize his commitment.

Jason and I have often battled over the value of literary analysis. It is a friendly duel: I take shots, he returns them. I send an article his way; he stops by to talk about it. I send him to a conference on reaching struggling readers; he takes on our lowest-level juniors and tries to reach them. He's everything I love about new teachers: He still believes he can reach everyone; he's willing to work most weekends to make it happen; he admits mistakes and revises his teaching in response.

So when Jason told me he was starting the year with juniors reading *The Scarlet Letter*, you can imagine there was smoke coming out of my office. "Could you have chosen a more distancing book for these kids? It's downright cruel." He smiled at my predictable ranting. I finally asked, "Why?" He talked about chronology in American Literature and the importance of Hester's coming of age in the novel. Just listening to him made me want to read Hawthorne's work again, and his team of teachers had decided on the text together: that matters. In our organization as a school over the last few years into professional learning communities, we have embraced teacher collaboration as essential.

A few weeks into the unit Jason stopped by to talk about literary analysis. He had heard my "write with the students" mantra enough and he had tried it. I think this is remarkable. Most literature teachers I know don't write analysis, they assign and assess it. They'll tell me they don't want students imitating their thinking or ideas, so they can't do model writing. But when we read literature together, aren't we seeking that rich, personal connection between reader and text? Where, as Louise Rosenblatt said, the reader's experiences help make sense of the novel? I imagine that individual connection to literature allows myriad ways to analyze. There aren't really people out there teaching one way to understand a book, are there? (Okay, okay, you know this isn't a serious question. We interviewed someone last summer who told me there was only one way to understand Mark Twain. I just believe that is a narrow and untenable position from which to teach.)

So here's what Jason did. He believes that narrative-style introductions can improve the quality of literary analysis and help students personalize their reading, so he brought two possible introductions to class of his own analysis of *The Scarlet Letter*. He put both on overheads and had students help evaluate the merits of them.

INTRODUCTION A

According to *Adventures in American Literature* Nathaniel Hawthorne was descended from John Hawthorne, who was "active in prosecuting suspected witches and committed about one hundred of them to jail." Hawthorne was ashamed of the atrocities committed by his forbears, which was probably why he temporarily changed the spelling of his name, and he believed that he too was guilty of their crimes because evil was "a force that (left) its mark on generation after generation." Perhaps he wrote novels and short stories about sin and guilt because he felt that, by sharing them with the public, he was somehow repenting for the sins of his forefathers, and that keeping them secret was the worst thing he could do. Similar sentiments can be found in his writing—for example, in his novel, *The Scarlet Letter*, he uses symbolism to reveal that keeping secrets can be self-destructive.

INTRODUCTION B

A few weeks ago I drove down to Connecticut with my wife for her grandmother's celebration of life ceremony. Lilly was going to perform a number from the Broadway musical, *Wicked*, with my mother-in-law, and while they were preparing for their time on the stage I observed an interesting exchange between my father- and sister-in-law: He was sharing his opinion on same-sex marriage when she stopped him with a cautionary, "Be careful, Dad. What you hate might end up in your own family." Whether her comment or my wife's sudden appearance on the stage ended this line of discussion still remains a mystery.

Later that day, when my father-in-law and I were making the long drive back to the Mount Washington Valley, he suddenly brought up the discussion that he and his daughter never had the opportunity to finish. He told me that he should have asked her whether she was finally coming out of the closet, and how frustrating it was for him as a father to have a daughter, whom he loved dearly, that kept secrets from him. My sister-in-law thinks that it is for the best that her father doesn't know that she is a lesbian, but I could see how keeping this secret put stress on her and the already strained relationship that she had with her father.

Nathanial Hawthorne offers me a similar moral in his novel, *The Scarlet Letter*: no matter how good the intention, a secret kept will ultimately hurt its keeper and those who they believe they are protecting.

Students were predictably enthusiastic about the second and less interested in the first. His modeling of a personal connection to theme inspired students to reach in their analysis and produced some truly fine papers. Lauren wrote of the pain of losing a teacher she adored in a kayaking accident and then how keeping her feelings a secret had cost her something as well. She understood Hester's struggle with secrets through the lens of her recent experience.

Jason shared his thinking and a bit of his own struggle in his model introduction for students. I believe for his students it was an invitation to explore the transaction analysis Rosenblatt spoke of within the lens of personal experience. It was a risk for Jason, but one that offered students a way to connect to reading in deep, lasting ways. I don't believe we have time for anything else.

FINAL THOUGHTS

Our English department has made hard choices about time and balance in our curriculum. We studied the parity between reading and writing as content in our school because there are two costs when 100 percent of the writing is connected to literature.

1. **Students become topic dependent.** Students who write their way through high school from one book to another forget that their entire lives are topics. They sit and wait to be told what to write, so their brains are disengaged from writing most of the time when they aren't in class. They do not read their world like writers—ever. We lose all of that rehearsal time, that opportunity to consider the ways to craft a piece while riding on the bus to an away game or folding shirts at Aéropostale. After all the energy put into showing elementary writers the plethora of choices writers must make, we narrow those choices too much in high school. It isn't smart. We need writers, not just students who can respond to books. We need writers prepared for the literacy expectations of a variety of fields and the literacy demands of a variety of life experiences, not just students who will excel if they major in English.

2. **The writing task drives revision; if the task is an assignment, the student will depend on the teacher for revision suggestions, editing, and so on, focused on what the teacher wants instead of what the writing needs.** The student asks, "How long does this have to be?" and we create nonsensical responses like "size twelve font, two pages double-spaced" instead of "As long as it needs to be to argue your position effectively." We give time for revision—setting up "workshops" in class and they don't work. A teacher tells me, "These students won't revise." It isn't about them. The task doesn't drive them to revise.

Dependence does not prepare them for college. We need writers who can imagine multiple ways to present their understandings and ideas. My need to make sense in this chapter—to present evidence that will convince you right now as you read this, wakes me up at night, causes me to ignore the dishes and the buzzing of the dryer when it finishes. My shirts wrinkle as I write, but this writing is too important to me. I reread and adjust words, sentences, paragraphs, because I care. That energy times dozens of teenagers can rock a high school classroom. How quickly that happens when students find writing that matters to them—that they are invested in as human beings. It might be literature; it might not be. The key is balance, so that during the school year every student in the class is invested in the process of making meaning.

In a perfect world, there would be enough time to teach each well—an immersion in literature, then an immersion in writing as its own subject. Somewhere in four years of high school we have to make it happen. If we don't, we'll continue to have students playing the game of school, hardly engaging with our writing topics from books, and not improving as writers.

My students are no different than yours. I didn't hit the student lottery here in the White Mountains. My students are disobedient, rebellious, candy-smuggling-even-when-I-told-you-no-food-in-class adolescents similar to yours. Mine won't revise writing they don't care about. Not even once. They won't engage during workshop and stay focused on their own work so I can confer with others if what they're writing has no value to them. In fact, I would bet you wouldn't either. We have to let go of some of the writing we want them to do about literature and just let them write. Give students models and vision and good teaching and thinking about writing, and then force them to make decisions about how to craft their ideas. Once you hand over the ultimate responsibility for product to students, you can teach structure and organization and voice and they'll listen. You will stand back and wow at the products that come.

CHAPTER TEN
Finding Form for Ideas
Blending Genres

An effective piece of writing is produced by a craft. It is simply a matter of working back and forth between focus, form, and voice until the meaning is discovered and made clear.

—DONALD MURRAY

When I discuss what I believe about teaching writing in high school I find myself reciting the same particulars: story lays the foundation for our workshop, argument raises the quality and flexibility of the writers at work, then creative work in many genres allows students to bring all their skills to a final, cohesive project. But this feels more orderly and certain than honest. It's my one-sentence summary, not the vision I hold inside me. You see, I grafted my thinking from reading and listening to Donald Murray, and Don believed that idea was primary, then form. My one-sentence summary is centered on form. I struggle with this. The vision is pure, but the application in high school is complicated. I make decisions about teaching and then wonder if it is the best thing just about every week in my class. And every year I struggle with letting go of control once we've negotiated and practiced the twin arts of story and persuasion. I like my orderly plans with weekly goals and clearly defined products. But I know as the semester nears the end, that it is time to reach for something greater. My goal is for writers to find a form for their ideas. If they can do that, they can do anything. My students have accumulated some tools and some confidence in our work during the first two-thirds of the semester, so can I step back now and give them more freedom?

It's tempting instead to jump into another unit. Let's all write fiction. This is a powerful genre for teenagers and I've had many twenty-page stories result from a study of it. I would argue it's worth studying, but not once has that unit inspired every student in the room. Why not poetry? Or I know, we'll all write letters to the principal suggesting changes in our school.

I feel like I'm walking the plank.

This is not what I believe; this is not where I want to be with writers.

So what to do?

I look at my own writing. For years I've tried to work through the death of a friend at nineteen. She appears in my thinking of childhood over and over like a record album with a deep scratch. The needle returns to that spot and stays. And I've written about her—about us—many times, but the need to explore my memories with her remains. There's a reach for clarity. Randy Bomer wrote in *Time for Meaning* that memoir was "the making of sense from the chaos of experience." I wrote that phrase in my notebook over and over through the years. I believe it, but Cynthia's tragic death still doesn't make sense to me. There is no wearing out of this topic; I'm always circling it.

> *If you lead the way by committing yourself to honesty, clarity, and discovery, you will share your students' experience and earn their respect. In fact, writing with your students is such a powerful force that that one activity alone can change and revitalize a classroom. It can even change and revitalize a teacher.*
>
> —DONALD MURRAY

There are others in my life. There are unsettled relationships and experiences that my thoughts drift toward when I'm driving on a long stretch of highway with no one in sight: my father and I, an estranged friend, students I couldn't reach. No doubt you have your own list. Atwell called them writing territories, and I like the word because it is big and impossible to know completely—like the Northwest Territory or the Rocky Mountains. Within those territories are an endless collection of trees, views, streams, moments. And within my memories of my childhood friend, there are many ways to write. Those ways don't always have a name.

I taught a class on writing memoir for our adult education program last year. Each week we brought a piece of writing. One night I sat on my dining room floor with an old scrapbook on my lap that I created after Cynthia's funeral looking for an idea, a spark. The tan, wrinkled newspaper article detailing the accident fell onto the floor beside me. I read it and thought about each line—each word. And I thought about all it didn't say. I wrote this in response:

Student dies in wreck

EUGENE—A 19-year-old University of Oregon student from Portland was fatally injured Friday night when a car on Oregon 126E slid on ice and careened over a 75-foot bank about 30 miles east of Blue River, state police reported.

This is not the girl I knew: dark-haired beauty with strawberries gummed up in her braces, singing along to the radio as we tanned in the sun. We hadn't spoken in weeks when the car she was riding in careened over a 75-foot bank on Santiam Pass—a road I recalled with a sudden chill.

    I looked across the couch at my silent father who'd answered the phone. It was early morning. Childhood friends don't die on Saturdays.

    "I was just on Santiam Pass without chains in a snowstorm." I spoke each word with a muffled horror.

    "Don't tell me that! What were you doing there?" His eyes flash and he clenches his armchair, swiveling his neck to watch me like an owl.

    "We were going to Mt. Bachelor, you know, two weeks ago. And my windshield wipers stopped and Yukari had to hang out the passenger side door and move the wiper back and forth—in the snow—so we could keep going. We had borrowed chains, but when we finally had to stop I had no idea how to put them on. Two guys stopped and did it, but they were disgusted with us."

    He has stopped listening.

    "I'm calling Julie," I say to no one. Mom has returned to her dishes; Dad glares at the television.

Authorities said Cynthia Jane Epley, 6371 S.E. Yamhill St., a passenger in the rear seat of the car, was tossed from the vehicle when it went over the bank. She was dead at the scene.

    6371 S.E. Yamhill St.: 232-9312.

    "Cynthia Jane Epley calling. Are you coming over?"

    "Yes, I'll be there in nine minutes. No hands." I see myself on my bike, rounding the curve on Yamhill Street with my bouncing Schwinn Varsity 10-speed frame between my knees. The deep green of Mt. Tabor Park blurs to the left beside me; my blonde hair whips across my face. I love speed and the fear of crashing and the rush of my arms stretched out wide at my sides. The hill drops to my right towards Russell's house, I can feel it, but I don't look. Keep your eyes straight ahead and watch for cars.

And I see her tossed from the vehicle when it went over the bank. Did she tumble in the air or burst through the window in a flurry of broken glass? Did she scream? Did she enjoy the fall—suspended in air—even for a moment?

The driver, Christopher Foley, 19, and another passenger, Jamie Brishchle, 19, both of Eugene, were treated at Sacred Heart Hospital in Eugene and released. State police said another passenger, John Lowell, 20, of Eugene was not hospitalized.

Her house is strangely cool; there are platters of food in the dining room, but no chairs. We are lined up near the front door talking in whispers. I see myself climbing the stairs to her room, but I can't seem to. I've never been in this house without her.

Ken says in my ear, "Her head hit a rock and she died with one ski boot on."

I hold my stomach with both hands.

"She wasn't wearing a seatbelt."

I never liked him. "Ken, you have to be wrong about that." I won't look at him; my eyes follow the worn path at the center of the golden carpet stair upon stair.

"The police said so," he stares hard until I meet his eyes.

NO, Cynthia was nuts about seatbelts, I don't say. I can't have this conversation with this ex-boyfriend. I know what you did, I glare back.

"That's why she died. She was thrown from the car."

No, tossed.

"He was with her," he motions towards a boy leaning on crutches, his leg in a long, white cast. "Ask him."

I watch the sky darken out the dining room window. There is ham and turkey on a silver platter; charcoal dresses rustle beside me and pale hands clutch damp tissues. I reach for my coat and almost start up the stairs, but instead I feel the brass knob in my palm, turn it, and step into the rain.

The car was eastbound on the highway about 6:50 p.m. Friday when it hit the ice, bouncing off a guardrail and going over the bank, state police said. It came to rest some 125 feet from the roadway.

At Cannon Beach she braided my hair in the morning, her long nails click-clicking as she wound the strands one and then another. She pronounced me lovely and sprinted for the water, her jeans dragging across the sand, her sweatshirt pulled tight against the wind.

"We'll make sandcastles," she called to me.

There are four in the picture—spread across a bank far from the hungry, advancing tide.

After, we rested flat beside them, squinting our eyes against the sun, willing our summer to last.

Cynthia Jane Epley
March 30, 1961 ~ February 6, 1981

Nature never repeats herself,
and the possibilities of one human soul
will never be found in another.
Elizabeth Cady Stanton

It is a blended genre, an alternating style as Tom Romano (2000) defined in his book that launched a multigenre sensation. I know because of Tom's great passion as a writer and his deep thinking as a teacher that the definition of this writing experience—this thing we call multigenre—was never meant to be as categorical and orderly as we teachers have created plans in response. At its core, multigenre means letting go—letting writers decide. If the territory drives you to write, then I trust you to determine how to write about it.

So I may write "Student Dies in a Wreck" about Cynthia and then sit down with it beside me and ask, what else do I have to say? And I wonder and doodle and find a way to that next writing piece. That's creation. That's the struggle that leads to the most satisfying, lasting experience with writing. That's the process that leads me to confidence as a writer. What I don't need—what will get in the way, in fact—is to look at a unit plan with a list of genres and try to write something the teacher thinks I should experience.

So at the end of the semester I lead my students to the foggy world of blending genres, finding form, as a culminating experience of being a writer. This is the time when I feel closest to Don Murray, when I hear his voice in my classroom. I like to begin with a launch into the possibilities of this kind of writing by orchestrating a class experience and then having students play with different forms of writing in response.

BLENDING GENRES

This unit works the way others have during the semester.

1. We have daily quick writing to experiment with genres we haven't talked about yet: One day we read brilliantly written obituaries, on the next we experiment with multi-voice poems, then fiction, newswriting, cartoons, or recipes to name a few. I present published pieces of writing and student models of these genres and we experiment together.

Here's one sample. Sarah created a multigenre project on the woods that surround her house. She did research on deforestation and global warming, wrote narratives of hiking and camping with her father and the two-voice poem in Figure 10.1. We read her work and then experimented with a quick write two-voice poem in response.

Walking Sarah
By Sarah Morrison

S: Tucker! You wanna go for a walk buddy?

T: O Boy! O Boy! Taking Sarah for a walk! This is good! This is good! Gotta get up from under the table. Damn my back end is getting hard to lift. Okay here we go. Stiff legs are on the move.

FIGURE 10.1

S: Tucker come on!

T: I'm comin'. I'm comin'. O boy it's nice outside. Where's the woods? Where's the woods? O there's the woods!

S: Come on buddy lets go!

T: Why the heck's she runnin'? What's she gotta run for? I hate running. It's making me pee. Gotta pee. Darn I'm dribblin'. Find a bush. Find a bush. Damn I'm getting too old to lift my leg. I'll just squat.

S: Good boy buddy! You want a treat?

T: O boy! A treat for peeing! Lets see if I can squat some more!

S: Come on Tucker. That's enough! You already went. Let's go!

T: O boy! I love the woods. *sniff sniff* I love the woods smells. All the rabbits, and squirrels and poop....POOP! I smell it! O boy! Where is it? Where is it? THERE IT IS! I'm gonna roll in it! O I love rolling in poop. Where's Sarah? She's missing out. There she is. Sarah look at me I'm rolling in poop!

S: TUCKER!!!!!!! Get out of that!!!!!! Get over here!

T: O boy! Now it's time to run. Gotta go! Gotta go!

S: TUCKER!!!!

T: O man! Keep running! Gotta make it home before she does. Whew...this is quite the work out! There's the house. Okay I made it. Gotta find a place to hide. Under the truck looks safe. Whew that was fun. I love taking Sarah for walks....and boy do I smell good!

FIGURE 10.1 *continued*

For my quick write I tried to capture two voices in "Listen, Hannah" (Figure 10.2). I was thinking about how Pat and I parent our daughter differently sometimes and I tried to write words that would intersect so we would speak those lines together in performance. Two-voice poems are, of course, written for two speakers to read separately at times and then in unison.

Listen, Hannah
Penny Kittle

MOTHER	FATHER
Life is short and **You must live life**	**You must live life** With purpose
With joy	
	Your personal integrity Depends on your work ethic
Work To bring beauty to the world	work
Work hard To be kind	**work hard**
Other people	**other people** Expect you to work
Have their expectations For you	
Don't listen	**don't listen** If they tell you to slack off Party Call in sick
Life is short. Live well.	**Life is short**
	Make me proud.

FIGURE 10.2

When I put "Hannah" on my topics list that week I could feel the energy: so much to say . . . so much to think about. Sometimes quick writing leads my students to this same place.

2. I bring in binders of student work and students review multigenre projects from the past. They choose five to read carefully—every piece, every end note—and then respond in their notebooks with their thinking. (There is a student project included at the end of this chapter that you could begin your own study on.)

3. I model my thinking with a topic I want to write about, and I experiment with form in front of them, working toward a final product I can't yet imagine.

4. Daily workshop time with conferring, reader-response groups, and time to write.

WHAT DOESN'T WORK

1. *Narrow topic choice.* I know this sounds obvious, but since both of my children have experienced this in the last two years, I know even well-intentioned teachers can stumble here. My son was assigned a multigenre project on *The Great Gatsby* for American Literature in his junior year.

   I said, "Oh, cool, multigenre."

   He groaned, "Mom, I hated the book and now I have to write about it in five genres!"

   And I'm not saying literature isn't a smart launch for a multigenre project. It is a vibrant approach to this work. In fact, on Tom Romano's website at Miami University you can review student projects on *Dracula* and *Speak*. My students have been inspired by this creative work. But I believe the writer must choose the novel, not the teacher.

2. *Trying to teach content through multigenre writing.* Don't try to teach some other content through a complicated writing project like multigenre. My daughter studied China in her World Cultures class and had to choose five genres to show what she'd learned. This is more school stuff—not an authentic writing process—but the bigger mistake is asking a writer to be an authority on a topic she barely understands. So much of good writing rests on the writer in command of a subject: We want the confident voice, the clarity of idea, and the orderly and effective balance of image and information. When writers are just given stuff to do, they operate asleep at the wheel. Somehow they end up at the destination, but the journey is unremarkable and seldom lasting. There are few discoveries in completing assignments. Hannah's final project didn't even make it home: She tossed it.

broth · er (bruth 'ər), *n., pl.* **brothers. 1.** a male sibling who is convinced he is better at everything **2.** a source of entertainment, i.e., *I enjoy annoying my brother.* **3.** someone who is always there for you

sis · ter (sis 'tər), *n., pl.* **sisters. 1.** female sibling whose main purpose in life is to bug her brother **2.** an embarrassment, i.e., *My friends are here, so go someplace else.* **3.** someone who is always there for you

FIGURE 10.3

In contrast, when given choice she wrote about her relationship with her older brother. She spent hours on it, including the definitions in Figure 10.3 that opened and closed her project.

3. *Narrowly defining the product.* In my writing professional learning community this year, we struggled with defining the parameters of this work. How many genres should students explore? We settled on big vision first, a definition of the holistic impact we were searching for. The definition in Figure 10.4 was written by Tom Romano.

	Holistic impact of the paper
186–200	Knocks me off my feet, **bowls me over**, so informative and emotionally moving is the paper. Throughout there is evidence of **original thinking**, depth, *specificity of detail*, **delights of language** or insight. The MGP is rife with **excellent writing** that includes attention to a pleasing visage of the page, *action verbs*, varied sentence length, effective word choice, skilled placement of payoff information, strong leads and endings, visual and other sensory **imagery**. Research is interesting, surprising, and deftly and creatively incorporated into the paper.
170–185	A **good** paper. I'm upbeat because of some of the solid moves the writer pays attention to that are mentioned above. I learn things about the topic. While the paper didn't blow me away, I am happy with its competent execution. Research is good.

FIGURE 10.4

150–169	This paper is complete but the writing hasn't much used those qualities that make writing sing. There is a feeling of **middle of the road** about it.
132–149	This is not a **good** paper. The writing shows almost none of the skills mentioned above. Some pieces seem perfunctory, as if written hastily and never revised. Content shows little depth or insight. More telling than showing.
0–130	An insult to turn in, an insult to the teacher, to the disciplined, creative act of writing, and to your own mind.

FIGURE 10.4 *continued*

If you've read Romano's *Blending Genre, Alternating Style,* you know the potential of this project, but it's tricky. For some students there is an engagement with writing I haven't seen all semester. Some writing produced will rival anything most students will write in four years. But you can feel what's coming, can't you? There are kids who go through the motions here and throw something together the night before. I remember Catherine's ridiculous tribute to high school. I won't even define the details it was so bad. It was a waste of time to create; an insult to read. If I knew how to avoid it completely with every student, I'd tell you. What I know is that more students reach for something almost unattainable—so big and complex—in this last unit that I am delighted each semester with the results.

A LAUNCH INTO MULTIGENRE

This year I decided to set up a scene that would surprise my students. I wanted to define the concept of multigenre by creating one as a class from a shared experience. This idea came to me while I was at the National Council of Teachers of English conference in Nashville listening to a young teacher who was so filled with sparkle I wanted to follow her around all afternoon.

I made up index cards with the name of a genre on each one. I then arranged a scene with our school resource officer. T. J. Herlihy agreed to visit my class soon after silent reading one morning. Of course the minute my students saw him they thought he was there to see one of them. "Uh-oh," several said.

He came into class—"Can I speak to you for a minute?" He looked directly at me with serious eyes that scared me a little.

I planned my first response, "Is my son okay?" Cam's away at college as a freshman and my students know I worry.

"Oh yeah, no, I just need to talk to *you* . . ." but he came all the way across the room to where I was standing at the back of the class as he said this. He's 6'2" at least and intimidating. "Can you come out in the hall?"

I glanced at my students, "I'm in the middle of class. Can this wait?"

Again, all seriousness. "No. Did you get a speeding ticket on the North-South road last week?"

I looked at my class, "Uh, yeah, thanks for sharing it with my whole class." They howled. I had everyone's attention, that's for sure.

He continued, speaking quietly but insistently, "Well, you wouldn't come outside so I *had* to share it with your class." Not a trace of humor. "That ticket had a court summons on it for excessive speed."

My students smiled and nudged each other. I'd picked a violation I knew the kids would believe. I am the law-abiding type, but I drive a Mini Cooper and they always think I drive too fast. You know rumors.

I snickered, "Oh, I didn't even look at it; I just put it in the glove box. Sorry," I added.

T. J. was not amused. (He was brilliantly serious!) "I need to take you in. There's a bench warrant for your arrest."

I laughed nervously, "Are you kidding me? I'm a good person. I've never been arrested. Right here in front of my class?" You can just see my seniors— wide-eyed, nudging each other, open mouths, watching me. I continued, "You don't have to do this, I'll come and see you when my class is over."

He played it perfectly. He said the chief said to bring me in as soon as he saw me. I followed him to the door. He ignored my students (several on their feet) and waited while I buzzed the office to send someone for coverage. I'd prearranged it with a colleague and while we waited, I said to my class, "I can't believe this is happening."

Kate said, "Oh, don't worry, Mrs. Kittle, we won't tell anyone!"

Shaina added, "I'd be crying if I were you."

When my friend Amy arrived, T. J. took me by the arm out the door, then in front of our glass window, put the cuffs on me. The kids went wild. Amy played this perfectly, "What happened? Oh my word! She didn't pay her speeding ticket? See what happens?"

T. J. and I went down the hall and around a corner so he could take the cuffs off. We passed three students from other classes, one who text-messaged students in my class to find out why I was in handcuffs. Gossip in high school: that's what travels at the speed of light.

Within a minute or two we were back and I told the class it was all a joke. Oh, this was fun. I gave them a moment to calm down and talk about what they were thinking. I passed out the index cards with genre names on them and said we were going to create a class multigenre project. They were allowed to trade cards if they got a genre that they felt they couldn't possibly work with. It was only a minute or two before everyone was settled. We wrote for about fifteen minutes and ignored the vibrating cell phones as kids in other classes tried to confirm what was seen in the hall.

When the writing was done, we had a recipe for disaster, an invitation to appear in court, a thank-you note for taking me away, a ransom note from the Conway Police Department for my return, a biography, a haiku, a news report, a diary entry, an instant message, an email, a cartoon, and a script. The most memorable were from two boys who are not often my most diligent, on-task writers in the room. They find school a bit silly, and although both are creative and funny, they don't find those qualities called upon much during the school day. Isaak volunteered first. He had "song," and he stood, stepped back, and began singing, "A policeman came to class," in this dreamy, 1970s croon that had us in tears from laughing so hard. Matt followed with his rap. Isaak gave him the beat and Matt pulled it off perfectly: rural white boy plays gangsta. There was lots of impromptu applause, a high five or two, and most important, a shared experience that morning.

Class multigenre woke us all up. I had been sleeping a bit in this class; I was feeling the November blues, the post-Thanksgiving slide. All of a sudden in the days before this lesson I was brimming with energy again—looking forward to the skit, nervous as I dried my hair that morning. I felt the difference. I knew what had been missing. And the writing we created that morning was just a bonus, really. Multigenre now had a roaring start. My class was back—ready for more. My intent was to open up possibility. Now I could follow up with a daily study of one genre at a time with their own personal explorations of topic and theme.

FINAL THOUGHTS

In conferences as we begin this project I find myself saying some version of the following to students, "Take on a big idea that's circling in the back of your mind that you know is important, but that requires an emotional investment to create and work through. Don't choose a topic like 'soccer' unless you have reasons why this topic and all you might do with it in writing matters in your life today. Don't make a list of the greatest golfers of all time with little summaries about each and call that research. Dig in. Learn. Ask authentic questions and search for answers."

When we dive into research I say, "I would suggest that if your questions for your research component of this project aren't making you *want* to research, they're the wrong questions. It is human nature to be curious, so what are you curious about? That's what you go after."

The qualities of writing that we value are all evident in a multigenre project. A topic should gain clarity through the use of different genres to broaden the reader's understanding of the issue. A research report about depression won't enlighten readers the way that report combined with the dialogue between three sisters as one tries to explain it to the others, coupled with poetry, narrative, and fictional letters that try to capture the experience through the voice of those involved (doctor, parent, friend) might. The writing helps us see and feel, not just know the facts. That's the essence of multigenre work—a broadening of understanding through the use of different forms of writing.

This project requires more because the qualities of writing change according to genre. A letter has a conversational voice that draws the reader near, whereas research is more likely to allow distance between writer and reader and between writer and topic. A narrative will make use of sensory detail, and a business letter will not, although the letter will likely have supportive detail to anchor an argument of the position.

In this unit students will see the distinction in word choice and conventions by genre. Muscle verbs help a narrative move and bring originality and spirit to a poem, but the technical language of biology that might lend credibility to a narrative on the blue whale is quite different. A strong multigenre project will make use of those distinctions. The use of conventions is traditional in prose and creative in poetry. Yet the conventions of research writing mean readers pay attention to citations and sources and a clear organization through paragraphing and sentence structure for complex ideas.

Organization assists a reader in following ideas and arguments. In narrative how you open the piece determines how the rest is read. Poets use stanzas and other formatting to organize ideas. Friendly letters are organized more loosely than business ones. The point is that good writers understand how the qualities of writing will most effectively present their ideas in each genre.

In this project students have to think about the organization of the entire body of work. The first piece of writing in the project (the lead) is critical to establishing the theme, and song lyrics, photographs, and other visuals can help pull the pieces together.

I will end this chapter with showing, not telling. I hope you will take time to read Logan's multigenre project and end notes on being bullied in elementary school. My best advice for understanding how to teach multigenre is predictable: Study what this writer has done and then craft writing on a big topic in your life.

<u>Youth</u>
The Truth About Elementary School
by Logan Dwight

Kindergarten:

Look
Look at Gwen
She has the blocks

I want the blocks

Blocks
Blocks in a castle
Big castle with all the blocks

Mine

Smash
Smash Gwen's blocks
No more castle

My blocks, all mine now

Mine
Mine Mine Mine Mine
My blocks now.

1st *grade:*

Writing Prompt: How do you feel about school?

I luv skool. I hav fun. My teacher is real nice. Recesss is good. Sumtims I jus wanna hav skool all the time. I hav a redsox lunch box. It's red. I hav power rajer pensils to. I gav the gren rajer wun to paul. Hes my frend. We draw alots and he is funy. My techer sez im good at math. She make me do times tabuls sinse im so smart. I luv skool alots.

4th *grade:*

who do you think you aRe you're nobody
buy better shoes cut your hair changE your clothes
you're not one of us you Do not belong here leave
uselEss do nothing going nowhere with your life
don't even try you're a Failure give up
you don't even deserve to lIve
No we don't want to be your friend
loser loser losEr

whY won't you just go away
yOu smell funny look funny act funny
we don't need to Understand you you're just a freak
you're too quiet too loud too stupid no one caRes
shut up shut up shut up shut up Shut up
we are bEtter than you and you know it that will never change
you're hardly human you're an animaL go live in a zoo
we wish you would just disappear Forever

. . .

Home Town... Those words have a foreign air to them, overused but non-existent. "Home is where the heart is," they say. Well, if that were true, I guess I would be homeless. The truth is Barrington is more like a pit, a black crater of intolerance lined with dollar bills and insecurity, cleaned so slick you can't climb out.

We are going nowhere.

I can't remember the last time this felt good. In my fifteen-dollar Adidas shoes, beyond broken-in and far out of style, I make the long trek to Hampden Meadows Elementary. The sidewalk is too clean, like it's some crime to show life's residue. That just wouldn't be proper. I pass bleach white fences boxing in lawns so green a football field would be envious. This is the American dream: a small town on the East Coast.

The American dream is surprisingly desolate.

No one talks.

No one plays.

No one lives.

Welcome to Barrington, Rhode Island. Please stay off the grass. Even the sprinklers are automatic, the pop-up variety that often makes you wonder "Does anyone even live here?" *At least we can take comfort in the fact that, even if we all die, our lawns will thrive for an eternity.*

Even at 9 years-old, I find myself disgusted with such impersonality.

And then, there it is, looming over me, my own red-brick personal slice of hell. Walking the same black-tar walkway, passing the same deceptively bright sign that reads "Hampden Meadows Elementary, Learning is Fun!" I have become used to the pit in my stomach. This is how I learned routine. I could ace any vocab test with ease: *Define Routine. Routine is repetition and pain, doing the same thing over and over, no matter how it hurts. Routine is that dull ache right behind your eyes when, every day, you're pressed further into the one place you don't want to go.*

It's loud inside, the way a pack of wild animals is loud. In the corner, the same twelve kids snicker through sly smiles as I walk by, hyenas of the suburban jungle. The clean white of their new shoes is so finely polished I can see my reflection, should I care to look. I don't look.

This is what school has taught me:

Be ashamed of yourself. You will never be good enough.

"Hey Loogey!" is the closest thing I get to a greeting. Sometimes I forget my own name; it's rarely ever used. Do you remember, when you were younger, trapping flies under glass for torture? I imagine this is what they must feel like.

This is torture; this is hate.

This is three hundred rabid dogs all pissing on the same tree.

This is praying to get picked *last* in gym, because you rarely get picked at all.

This is not knowing what "best friend" means.

This is wanting to cry, but not knowing how.

This is true pain.

This... is the fourth grade.

Today is my birthday. This morning my parents surprised me with a brand new bike. Eager to show off my new 12-speed orange center of joy, I ride it to school. *Maybe someone will like it. Maybe they'll want to be friends with me now.* For once, I'm happy.

Placing my new bike in the old, rusty rack; I'm proud of the contrast. I charge into school like a champion, and sit down in the cafeteria, my usual corner. Then it happens. *Welcome back to reality.* Someone calls "Loogey" and soon it seems like the whole room is up against me.

How could I be so foolish?

Did I really think today would be different.

Suddenly, I can't control myself. Every fiber of my being wants to scream. I do.

"Shut up! Today's my birthday! I just want it to be happy!"

Then I sit down…

And cry.

I cry for myself. I cry for all the hate and pain in my life. I cry for every lost happy moment.

A hand touches my shoulder. "Are you ok? What's wrong?"

This part of my life, this is where I learn compassion.

She was beautiful. Maybe it was because she was a grade ahead and older, but she was the only person who cared. Long blonde hair, round blue eyes shaped like almonds, and she cared. I never knew her name, never saw her again, but she taught me something that day.

Never, ever, give up on people.

The day passed smoothly after that, not happily, but smoothly. I let comfort creep up on me.

Big mistake.

As I walked back out to the bike rack that day, some kids were trying to cut the chain of my new bike. They stopped when I arrived.

"Hey Loogey, nice bike," one of them sneered at me. Something was in his hand. He wasn't going to make me wonder what it was.

Wham! There is egg on my shirt. Suddenly, they're all armed, school-yard soldiers. Eggs are on my clothes, my face… my bike.

Again, all I can do is cry.

This time, no one comes to save me.

This time, I'm alone.

Today is my birthday.

Welcome to Suburbia. All things beautiful are ugly inside.

5th *grade:*

Writing Prompt: How do you feel about school?

I hate school. No one likes me. My teacher even hates me. She made me stand up in class yesterday and appologiz because jimmy threw a paper football at me. She said I made it. I didn't make it. I promise. She just hates me. Everyone hates me. My closest freind is john and he just likes to teas me and make me eat gross things at lunch. He made me cry last week. I eat alone sometimes so I don't get made fun of. At recess everyone tells me to go play with someone else. There is no one else. I hate school. I want real freinds. I want to go home.

(I did not turn this in. The teacher made me stand in the corner for the rest of class.)

. . .

You hurt me. Now you will hurt.
I will never forget that day. Standing over him, fists clenched, filled with hate. The blood on my hands, the flush tone of my face: all the same red. *They say rage is red.*

The names will not be changed to protect "the innocent." No one is in-nocent here. *Raymond Dederyan* was his name, and he taught me all too young what it was to hate.
He wasn't just another kid who poked fun at my jeans, or played games with my name. No, Raymond was the ringleader, the source of it all. His sick pleasure was my misery, and he made that abundantly clear. The things he did, no child should do. *It's inhuman.*
In the winter, he would throw snowballs filled with rocks through my bedroom window. In the summer, I would find bags of feces, broken paint balls, or other messy trash chucked at my tree fort; the one my dad spent a whole summer building, one of his many attempts to brighten what had be-come a bleak childhood.
My parents tried time and time again to confront his parents: a broken drunkard father and an apathetic chain-smoking bitch of a mother. As expect-ed, the results were less than stellar.
Now, let's back up here for a second. Raymond Dederyan is *not* some-one to feel bad for. Some PHD wielding, tight pants super-shrink might say

he is a victim of a broken home, and that his personality isn't his fault. Well, Raymond had three siblings, and they all turned out fine. His oldest brother went on to pursue a successful military career, his sister went off to a high-class college, and his brother, Scott, was one of the smartest and kindest kids in his class. The reality is this: Raymond was a bad seed, a demon child right from the start.

Raymond sat in the back of all my classes, surrounded by his white-gangster super-jock lackeys. I don't even dare estimate how many rumors and bad jokes they spread about me, but it was enough that kids I had *never even met* shunned me in the halls. I was an outcast, marked before I ever had a chance to act.

Then one day, I did.

5th grade, I was riding my bike home from school, the same way I always did. I would struggle to leave early, so that Raymond couldn't catch me on *his* bike. On this day, I didn't leave soon enough.

He was waiting. Half a mile up the road, he stood off to the side, balancing his spray paint black bike on one leg, a crooked, devious grin stretched across his face. Even in silence, he mocked me. *You could see it in his eyes.*

As I got close, he pulled out in front of me. "Hey, Loogey!" he shouted, "where you going *Loogey?* Going home to play with your friends? Oh, right, you don't have any friends. You're just gay, a big gay fag. Go home and be gay with your little brother."

That was it. I was done. *He was done.*

I dropped my bike on the side of the road, and in seconds, I was on him.

He had strength, athletic build, speed, but he didn't have what I had. *I had hate.* No force on earth could have pulled me off of him.

Wham.

I hit him. Hard.

Wham.

Feel my pain.

Wham.

Feel my anger.

Wham.

Feel my sorrow.

Wham.

Feel

my

hate.

Everything in me, all the days I spent alone, all the tears I cried, all the names tossed my way, all the bad pranks, all the bad laughter, all my ruined childhood moments, were poured into him. I felt no pain as my knuckles broke the skin on his cheeks. All my pain was now his. *I will make you hurt. I will make you bleed.*

And he bled.

From his nose, lips, cuts on his cheeks, thick red livelihood poured onto some nameless rich family's lawn, dark maroon contrasting the chemical green rug beneath us. It streamed onto the sidewalk and pooled near my feet.

This is for every happy moment you never let me have. This is how it felt.

He was crying. His eyes, once filled with mischief and scheming, now begged me for mercy. Our roles were reversed, and now he was the victim.

I stopped.

My god, what had I become?

I looked down at the bloody, crying boy in front of me. *This was wrong.* I had done something horrible. I had become like him, I had become a monster. I made a promise to myself that day. *I will not become that kind of person, I will be better than that. I will not make people hurt the way I hurt.*

I got back on my bike and rode home.

I wonder if he still remembers that day, because I will never forget.

8th *grade:*

My mother told me we were moving.

I cried.
    tears of joy
Finally
                leaving behind this broken childhood.
Finally
    I can start over.
Finally
            I can escape.

Today:

So I'm surfing the Internet, looking for information on "bullying," and it's slowly dawning on me. No one *really* gets it, this bullying thing. What I see are conglomerates of parents, teachers, and other adults making unrealistic claims about a subject they no so little about. Campaigns to stop bullying try to appeal to kids, but the reality is, these people have no idea what kids *really* think, what they do, what they want. It's becoming redundant. A teacher of mine once said that words overused often lose their meaning. "Bully" is such a painfully butchered term that all it invokes is sighs and rolling eyes from today's youth.

Everybody, wake up.

Websites for these anti-bullying groups are plastered with cartoon graphics and happy-go-lucky slogans like "Make a stand, lend a hand," or "Let your light show." You know what kids think when they see these sites? They think it's all a big joke.

The other approach is to avoid cartoons and try and make the campaign "cool" with stereotypical "trendy" graphics and pictures of "cool teens." Most kids today just see it as mocking them, and it is.

This whole anti-bully campaign insults the intelligence of our youth. It's a small wonder they don't take it seriously.

One website stoops low enough to ask "are you a bully?" and has a little bullet item guide to see if you are, in fact, a "bully." Again, we are not that stupid.

It seems a sad and sorry state that adults think they have to disguise such a major problem with cartoons or hip graphics in order for today's kids to accept it. The effect is precisely the opposite. Kids are turning away from these organizations, seeing it as embarrassing and under-informed.

Well, people, the truth is *you are embarrassingly uninformed.*

You want to fix bullying? First of all, we need to bring seriousness back to the issue, to the concept of "bullying." How about a campaign that just flat-out says it how it is, no fancy graphics and gimmicks? How about you talk to kids like they are adults? When they see they are treated with maturity, they will face the issue with maturity.

But me, I'm just one youth among many, and since so many adults think they "totally understand children," I have serious doubt that anything will ever change. Bullies will keep ruining kids' lives, and no one will fix it because our youth is being given the impression that it's all a joke, a farce.

Personally, I'm done with soccer-moms, guidance counselors, and psychologists saying they know how it works, that they know what I went through. And who cares, it's all a big joke, right?

. . .

I came back to Barrington last summer. I made a stop at Gwen's house, one of the few people I considered a friend growing up. We talked about what any late-high school students talk about: college, trips, classes, friends. It was nothing too exciting, just normal talk. Even so, we were enjoying it all.

"You know, I remember in kindergarten I used to really hate you," Gwen said to me.

"Oh really? Well, I'm glad we're past that now," was the best reply I could think of. Honestly, what do you say to that?

"Yeah, I remember there were these blocks at recess. Everyone always took them before I could. I was always really quiet in class, so I just waited my turn to use them. There was this one day when I finally got to play with the blocks. I had been waiting for months to play with them."

"Oh? And what's that got to do with me?"

"You took them from me. I had built a big castle and you just smashed it and took all the blocks away. It made me really sad."

It made me really sad too, to think I had done that to her so young, that I had caused someone to hurt at 5 years old.

"Wow, I'm really sorry. That was a jerk move."

"Yeah, but it's OK now," she smiled at me.

It might sound silly, but it's not OK now. It breaks my heart to think I would have done something like that to a friend, even something so small as steal some toy blocks. It was a big deal to her back then, and it stuck with her all the way up to now.

When you're little, everything counts, even blocks.

End Notes:

Kindergarten
➤ "Blocks" poem
   • I wrote this poem in very simple language, as to emulate the language of a small child. The poem represents the thoughts in my head when I took the blocks from Gwen during recess in kindergarten. I wrote this piece to show me being a bully, and it connects to the final piece in this paper. "Blocks" is a short poem because I felt poetry was the best way to get the simple thoughts of a kindergarten student on paper.

1st grade
➤ Writing Prompt
   • When I was younger, I used to love school. I use two "writing prompts" in my piece to show the change in my feelings about school as I got older. This first prompt shows me loving school and having friends. I specifically talk about my friends and my teacher so that they can be contrasted in the second prompt.

- 🍂 4th grade
  - ➤ "What you say, what I hear" poem.
    - • This poem is done in free-verse so that I could simulate the mish-mash of comments thrown at me from every direction. I bold certain letters to spell out a sentence in the piece. This sentence, "Redefine yourself," is meant to show that through all the teasing and misery, I only took away one message, and it was positive.
  - ➤ Place Narrative
    - • I decided to include my place narrative in this multi-genre because it is also about my elementary school years, and it really captures the heart of the problem. All of the other pieces in this paper build off of the ideas present in my place narrative, so it is only logical I would include it.

- 🍂 5th grade
  - ➤ 2nd writing prompt
    - • This is the second writing prompt. It shows how I felt about school in later years. I use the example of a best friend and a teacher to show how much of a difference there was between my early elementary years and my later ones. I had many horrible teachers and peers in that time, and this "writing prompt" represents something I would have actually wrote at that time.
  - ➤ "Raymond" narrative
    - • Anthony was the number one worst part of my childhood. When I confronted him that day, it was a major turning point in my life. In this piece, I sought to capture the feelings I had for how he treated me, and how they changed me in the long run. It is probably the most emotional part of this paper, as it is my strongest memory from my childhood.

- 🍂 8th grade
  - ➤ "Moving" poem
    - • Again, I used a poem to represent thoughts. This time it is more of a reminiscent view. The poem is supposed to feel like flash thoughts when I think about that day. I spaced the lines out all differently to show random thoughts that all still were part of a whole. I wanted to capture how I felt, not necessarily the moment, which is why I kept it minimal.

- 🍂 Today
  - ➤ Research Commentary
    - • This piece is very interesting to me. It started as a research report on "bullying," but it quickly became more of a commentary rant.

In looking for resources, I stumbled on to all these web sites concerning bullying. I was so upset with how poorly these organizations were going about stopping the problem that I chose to write about that instead. I believe that all these "anti-bullying" programs are doing nothing to really help solve the problem. As such, my research paper has become a commentary on how we should *really* approach bullying.

➤ "Gwen" narrative

- This piece ties everything together. It is connected to the poem in the beginning, which details the day I took Gwen's blocks. This narrative shows how even small things can affect a person years later. The point I try to make here is that children care about the little things, and that "bullying" is far worse for small children because of that. Gwen's conversation was a real-life example of such an impact.

Aaron

Fear is the highest fence.

—DUDLEY NICHOLS

So we'd been struggling, Aaron and I. It was not just his absence every Thursday morning for a doctor's appointment; it was an all-around lack of value for the writing workshop. I have procedures in place for missed class time, and he didn't follow them. Not just the first week or two, but every week. Missed work was piling up; missed momentum was more serious. Aaron didn't share the text studies I carefully chose for the class and often seemed out of sync with the gathering understandings of his peers. Now add to this his exceptional ability in oral storytelling and you would hear a constant chatter from his corner of the room, see me approach his desk and his blank computer screen and question, prod, encourage, listen, and get nothing. Not a line. Weeks passed; I was losing ground.

He made it through first quarter by pulling his writing together at the last minute for each deadline, but that wasn't working for either of us. For all of his skill with humor and story, it just didn't transfer to the page. Since he rarely wrote in class I had little to work with. I resist kids who arrive and complete work like they're at a docking station, a quick stop on their way somewhere else. I want students who discover and grow and expand as writers and human beings. Aaron wasn't. But there was such potential; I felt a gnawing inside, the need to crack his code.

So second quarter started and the missed assignments cycloned together, dropping him into failure. He was frustrated by an early grade report; I told him he needed to make time to meet with me. He finally agreed to bring his lunch to my office. I said, "Don't forget: If I'm giving up time to work, I better see one of those chewy molasses cookies from the pizza place across the street." He laughed. It never works, but I keep asking.

He was thirty minutes late. I barely contained my annoyance, "Yeah, Aaron, tell me you're coming in and then arrive a half-hour late. Nice. I feel your respect."

He leaned against my door, offering a cautious grin; this conversation could go either way. He didn't have gym class so he had gone out to breakfast with his friends and couldn't get a ride back. I wish he'd thought of something better than that. I fumed. I could make him pay for keeping me waiting, or just realize it was an opportunity and let it go. And don't think this is an easy choice for me: At that moment it was a force of will.

I invited him in. He stretched his heavy legs out beneath the table by the window and ran his fingers through tight brown curls. He was all antsy movement, toes bouncing to an internal beat, head swiveling as he looks out the window then meets my eyes, looks away. We zipped through homework, missed text studies, his responsibility when absent, and finally to the heart of the conference. "We started working this week on finding topics for the multigenre project, Aaron. I'd like to talk a little about what you might write about. Usually students choose something important—something they want to write a lot about because we'll be considering it from many angles."

Aaron scanned the floor, pawed through the basket of candy on the table beside him, looked twice up at the door and out into the main office. I said, "Would you like for me to shut that?" He looked at me, then away.

"Yeah."

How do I describe the weight of that one word? It came from his gut and dropped on the carpet between us. I stood up and slowly kicked the door stop, letting the door slide into place. For just a moment I wanted to freeze time—before I knew.

I feel privileged to be a teacher: I'm in a place to listen and encourage a student who is desperate or alone, but I also feel burdened by all of the troubled stories that repeat in my head deep in the night. Aaron jiggles his leg constantly, tells me that is part of his constant anxiety. He doesn't sleep. There's a small pause then, "I was sexually abused by my adopted older brother." He tumbles out with moments from two years of hell: threats, knives, atrocities. He is safe: The boy is out of his house, but Aaron is a wreck. He is terrified of night: He waits in his room and listens for footsteps on the stairs. He lies awake until 4 A.M., arms clasped around his dog, until he drops into sleep. Two hours later he startles awake in a half dreamlike state for school.

And oh yeah, meanwhile, his father is an alcoholic and his parents have just split up.

His eyes are deeply sad.

I never feel prepared to say the right thing.

"Aaron, I'm so sorry," I manage.

He has always wanted to write about the abuse, but he wonders about the boundaries in class. And this isn't simple. Should students go after topics like this in our rooms? A year ago when Julie told me she wanted to write about cutting herself, she first said she'd bring it up as a topic in class and see how the room reacted. If she felt she could trust her peers to take her seriously, she'd write it. If she sensed they'd use it against her or not listen with their whole hearts, she'd write about her obsession with Johnny Depp. They listened, she wrote it, and we all grew.

I tell Aaron he should try to capture small bits of all he's been through. Sometimes confining something scary takes away its power. This experience is in his soul; there is writing to do in response. I tell him it can be between the two of us. He can tell students he's writing about childhood and when others share drafts in progress, he can choose not to. When we present projects and portfolios, he can present to me alone.

He says he'll think about it, and I almost hope he'll choose something else. I don't want to read the details, but it is likely a topic that will bring his invest-ment as a writer. That matters.

When he leaves my office I find a colleague who listens. I watch the buses pull away from the school and consider all the stories seated there that we don't know. I am stunned and angry and helpless; my stomach churns. It's a fault of mine: I can't just hear your story, I experience it. The emotional investment is a cost of this work. It will come to me when I don't expect it and from kids I don't expect it from, but it will come.

Aaron emails me the next morning.

> as i sit back thoughts run through brain
> the shit iv been through maken me insane
> its been a struggle ever since i was a kid
> fightin all the time like mom and daddy did
> But im solger been through alot token gats and token pot
> brothers been shot fathers been caught every fucken day im put on the spot
> its no biggie as the demons chase through my head
> one day i though maby i wish i was dead
> but you keep the fight alive till your barely breathen
> emotions runnin high up to the ceilin
> Just a good kid never drank shit like my daddy did
> this fucken me the real one
> big fat kid brother hurt me then desert me don't fuck with me im scared of me
> and im the real muitha fucken peoples MC you feel me
> You know if you went through this shit try and hide it to the world
> but you still feel it.

Sleep is few and far between and if you do you have some fucked up dreams
it seems your the only one alone on this earth
but stay strong keep your head up and carryon

And what is this English teacher to do? This is not Acceptable, I'm sure the school board would say. This is not allowed under our student handbook: this language, this raw anger and emotion. This is not what we want our students to write. If you allow it, you encourage it. If a student writes this instead of something academic, how is it useful to his education? And if he can only write this—this garbled no-grammar confusing rhythm and rhyme—what have you taught him? What is the use of this?

I can't escape the voice of those I report to.

Why not "school" him instead of counsel him?

Because this is what I believe: My work is about the process of writing, not the product. The process is about rough language and rough ideas and a search for meaning. The products are just a small part of my mission. The products will not teach more if they are Acceptable. The products will still just be products, only part of what I teach.

How can I say this and live in our world of relentless accountability? Because students get to a place of greater clarity and freedom with writing when allowed to follow topics that nag at them. They seek their own clarity, so they rewrite and rethink and massage one piece for days. Engaging a student in that process is the best work I do. No-investment products are the easy stuff. Write-this-way students will struggle with the flexible thinking required in college and life and never believe they write well. Perhaps they will be like my mother. She played the game marvelously in high school, rising to valedictorian and a full-ride scholarship to a university. But she will not write the stories of her childhood for her grandchildren because she is afraid of those products and what they might say about her. I think we're all a little afraid of writing.

Aaron is swimming in fear. I ask him if he can imagine living his life without constant trepidation. He shakes his head and his eyes grow dull: No, Mrs. Kittle, I can't imagine that. I tell him fear might be the topic he is reaching for.

What if in writing this brutality, he manages to overcome a small part of it? Would that be worth my acceptance of his rage? I cannot answer that for you, but I believe that when we choose to teach we have to ask the question. What are we called to do? What can we teach in writing that will be worth something to the students before us?

No matter what I do, Aaron will leave my class still carrying this burden. It will impact his writing in college, his ability to hold a job, his fit with the world he lives in. But it also might be something he can wrestle to the ground and begin to overcome. If he works through the motions of some other topic—like a superficial review of his years in football—it will likely teach him little and matter less in the years beyond.

But here's another truth: If his writing finds its way to our local paper, I will be ridiculed and likely lose my job. Perhaps I can't risk that.

Perhaps I can.

PART FIVE
MECHANICS

CHAPTER ELEVEN
Grammar, Punctuation, and What Keeps Me Up at Night

Grammar is a piano I play by ear. All I know of grammar is its power.

—JOAN DIDION

The image that comes to me is a toolbox: punctuation is nails, screws, nuts and bolts, the means by which you secure things in place, maintain the space (time) between them, put the rhythm into sentences so they become comprehensible. Punctuation as fastener.

—JOHN JEROME

I think it's a disturbing little secret of high school English teachers like me: This grammar stuff is like fresh garlic in the hands of a chef—let me at it. I love the symmetry of sentences with semicolons and the perfect poise of parallel structure. I get paid to talk about it like a great evangelist of grammar, and I *love* that. Here I am in a book talk one morning in class after I'd spent the night reading *Eats, Shoots and Leaves* by Lynne Truss. "Class! Get this! There's a whole *chapter* on just the semicolon!" And my students smirk and titter as they catch eyes across the room. Yes, this is what happens when you take all of this mechanical stuff far too seriously; exhibit A: Mrs. FreakaKittle.

So you can imagine just how my spine straightens and my mouth turns in a prim little line when grading student papers full of errors. *No. No. No.* My hand itches for that red pen. It is important to get this stuff right, people! *That apostrophe means possession; what is possessed here?* You can hear me grumbling on my couch night after night.

And during those moments when I'm not exactly sure about a usage question asked in class: what a happy little problem that is. I have to consult the Holy Grail: the reference section of *Writers, Inc.* I reveal this with a flourish to my distracted teenagers, my hands elegantly sliding across the pages and pages of rules that govern writing. How can they not be impressed by the immensity of detail? But even if you (and my students) say I care far too much for these intricacies, I also know how quickly a teacher or school is judged based on the spelling or punctuation of students who share their work in public. There is no tolerance in the world for errors. You know what a misspelling can mean on a college admissions essay. It matters.

I must teach grammar and punctuation well, and success with it takes three things in my classroom: patience, repetition, and teaching, both in conference and in minilessons. And it works! With persistence and repetition, almost all of my students retain the essentials by the end of a semester and become strikingly better writers because of their understanding. Grammar converts: what a payoff.

PATIENCE AND REPETITION

It all begins with attitude. I used to see myself as a toy doll with a pull string, robotically repeating the same rules over and over: "Its" is the possessive without an apostrophe; two complete thoughts are not connected with a comma; we put the punctuation inside the quotation marks in America. And still they made the errors. As each class revealed the same mistakes semester after semester, I was tempted to bark, "Why don't you know this by now? What have others been teaching you?" But you can imagine how effective that would be. Now I begin each semester with a little self-talk. Patience, Penny. Quit being a know-it-all. No one likes that prim little, bun-wearing, English Teacher alter ego. And worse yet, she's not a very good teacher: No one listens to nagging. I take a breath and start at the beginning.

I think of grammar, I tell my students, as a list of expectations and clarity that most readers know; we measure the credibility of the writer by adherence to this code. As Joan Didion says, it is a piano she plays by ear. There is a sound to sentences that make up our writing and grammar mistakes are the misplayed notes we hear and want corrected. Of course, as readers we expect some variations, particularly in poetry, but most writing should adhere to this code we know by heart. I can feel an incomplete sentence because I'm listening to your text. The problem is many of you don't listen to your own writing, and worst yet, you don't know the code. I say you can't misplace an apostrophe in a possessive noun and expect most readers not to notice, and you laugh at me. It is a tough sell because you don't notice. None of your friends notice. But I can sell you with this reminder: Adults notice, colleges notice, your grandparents notice. Your boss will notice. And in your life this semester one person who matters a lot to you will notice: the one who determines your final grade. I don't expect you to know all of the rules now, but with daily, short practice, you will. I promise. And if you don't, I have this jolly little event I call "grammar lunch" where you bring food to my room and we practice. I'm not kidding. You will leave my classroom at the end of the semester as Grammar Kings and Queens, able to slay a comma splice with one swift slice of your punctuation sword. (You can imagine their raised eyebrows. They're asking for a pass to get to guidance and transfer out of my class, right?)

I get students to really pay attention to mechanics by holding to this standard that I explain during our first week of class: It is impossible to get an A on a paper that has more than a few mistakes. Remember, I teach seniors. I don't think I can hand out exceptional grades for shoddy work, even if it is beautiful prose that captivates me. Polish matters. I stick to this, although I do allow students to revise and improve their work to raise the final grade on a paper. This standard allows me to really push kids who are driven by grades, but are not used to editing their work. I win by getting students to reread and rework their ideas, but also to understand why they are making convention errors in the first place.

Disengaged students have little use for grades or other methods typically used to motivate students. If high school students are not concerned about pleasing their teachers or don't value success in school, the threat of low grades or failing state tests has no impact and is of no value in engaging them.

—BROWNSTEIN, DiMARTINO, AND MILES 2007

But we all know there are plenty of students not at all driven by grades.

They need to know that a real audience notices and cares about the polish of a piece of writing. I work hard at this. We create class books that stay in my classroom long after students have moved on: They see the books created by former students (and, of course, it is the student photos that get their attention first). They want to look good and leave something behind that is sharp. As my colleague Ed says, you might spend a lot of time picking out the pants and shirt when you're going out for the evening, then the right shoes and perhaps an earring that looks good, but if your tie is crooked, people notice. The little details distract from the whole package. We work hard to get the details right, so the reader can live in the story without the distractions. I create binders of student work by genre that students read to think about structure and ideas during writing workshop. They know their work might be seen again and again in the years to come and they like that, but they also are challenged to produce graceful work because of it.

My goal is not catching students making mistakes and penalizing them; it is motivating them to listen and learn. Patience is important here because they are going to make the same errors many times before they begin to change. I wish they'd be transformed after my first brilliant lesson, but often I continue to work with mechanics all semester. My goal is lasting understanding. To get there I challenge their thinking with practice and variation.

I ask them to question every single mark of convention that they put on the page. I want them rereading a sentence with an apostrophe to determine if the word with the apostrophe is a contraction or a possessive noun. I want them rereading for usage whenever they encounter a homonym and I show them how to do this in a minilesson. I do not spend time on spelling with a whole class since most have mastered it (or use spell-checker), and it is rare when I need to address it on a final draft. I also review capitalization only rarely, since again, only a few students don't know most of the particulars by now. But if they don't know it, we study it; each semester I determine areas of study in mechanics based on the errors most students are making in class.

John Jerome's quote at the opening of this chapter speaks to the subtlety of punctuation: It creates the scaffolding for building the beauty of a piece of writing, but it should sit in the background as screws do in a handcrafted maple bed frame. Punctuation as fastener, indeed. I teach students how to listen to their writing through reading their work out loud. I want them to hear how a piece reads and how it might read: the risks that are possible and the rhythm that is expected. Readers want the smooth hum of a British racing car taking a corner on a mountain pass, not the lurching and bumping about of a misfiring engine. I ask questions, "Is this how you want your work to read?" and I read it back exactly as it is punctuated. Readers often won't stand for anything less than cruising, I say, so tune up this piece.

TEACHING MECHANICS

Punctuation and grammar are taught both in the context of their writing and outside of it: as a whole-class minilesson. I have an area of study on the schedule every week of class and we practice with the concept in very short bursts. I remember when I first started teaching and studied lesson design. We spent a good deal of time on Madeline Hunter's retention theory. The gist is that to learn something you must practice it every day for a week or two, then a few times a week, then less and less. I remember trying to apply this to my elementary classroom with these elaborate drawings and arrows across my plan book. I tried to follow this for every new thing I was teaching across seven subjects and just about drove myself crazy, but when I accomplished it, my students really learned the skill. That's how I approach grammar and punctuation and all things mechanical.

It begins with determining a need. I look at what students are writing and go after the big ideas first. We almost always begin with sentence structure. Years of cryptic notes in the margins of student papers—"run-on," "frag," and "c-splice"—have not resulted in lasting learning if you've noticed. Many students just recognize something is wrong, not how to fix it. So we begin with sentence combining. I often lift a sentence or two from a student's writing and use it to teach crafty ways to punctuate. Attitude matters here: It is never "look what someone did wrong," but rather, "look at the possibilities we have with these ideas and the myriad of ways this could be structured." We experiment with punctuation in our writing notebooks. Recently sentence combining was listed as one of ten strategies that make a difference in student writing (Graham and Perin 2006). Without explicit teaching of the possibilities, there is only correction and frustration, for both the student and teacher. With focused teaching on sentence work, students improve.

I put the following four sentences on the board. (I use myself or a student in class as the content since they are typically more alert when it is all about them.)

Mrs. Kittle teaches English.

She has taught for two decades and in lots of grade levels.

She loves teaching.

This year she teaches writing to seniors at Kennett High School.

I show them how I might combine the ideas into one sentence by making some ideas subordinate to others. One example: *Mrs. Kittle, who has taught for two decades in lots of grade levels, loves teaching writing to seniors at Kennett High School.* We then talk about other possibilities for combining.

- *Mrs. Kittle loves teaching—even after two decades and lots of grade levels— and this year she's teaching writing to seniors at Kennett.*

- *This year Mrs. Kittle is teaching writing at Kennett; she loves teaching seniors and brings two decades of experience to the classroom.*

I give them language for this through my discussion of a possibility. *I can use a semicolon in the second example because there are two main ideas in complete thoughts that are closely related. Semicolons can't connect just anything; they must* connect ideas that are related to each other. I remind them of the independent and dependent clauses, and so on. It is important to establish this language, so I can use it efficiently in individual writing conferences.

Another way we look at sentence combining is through the lens of voice. I want my students manipulating structure, but I don't want them losing their voices in the process. I tell them the previous example isn't how I would relay this information; it doesn't sound like me. So we practice telling the same information in our own voice.

- *Mrs. Kittle is one of those crazy old teachers who still loves teaching—every day, every class, every student. She's been teaching writing for two decades now in all kinds of grade levels, but has found a home with Kennett seniors.*

We can spend five minutes on this in class—one combination a day like lightweight training—and build punctuation muscles in the process. I take a student and list a few things about him: *Jeff is an only child. He is a wicked cool baseball player. He lives in Redstone. His pitching put our team in the state championship this year.* The students create their own combinations and we share. Try it. Come up with three ways to combine those four ideas. It is problem solving and thinking and it reveals a lot of what our students don't understand about punctuation. Students are happy to take over this teaching once they understand it—either creating combinations for us to work with or in leading class discussions of possibility.

We need these daily conversations about grammar and punctuation because students won't get this anywhere else. And I'm sorry to say, they won't get it from the "context of their writing" alone. I often hear teachers say, "I teach conventions in context," which I agree is more effective than the old grammar texts we once used, but it just isn't enough for me. I can't spend as much time on mechanics as I need to in order to move a writer during our writing conferences. I have to work on ideas and organization and voice and word choice and encouraging a writer to move forward with a little fledgling of an idea. I can't spend every conference teaching parallel sentence structure or comma splices or I'll risk having the student think that is all I care about. (And yet if I am focused on ideas and voice and I never get to mechanics, they'll be sure to think it doesn't matter.) So, left with those realities, I do both. I teach and practice with the whole class, then reinforce what we're studying in conferences when I can. Like this: Imagine you're eavesdropping on my conference with Chris during workshop.

Chris has written, *I played hockey for five years with my younger brother; who is better than me.*

Now first I talk about the writing piece and the help he needs from me, as usual. Then before I leave I say, "Tell me about how you used the semicolon in this sentence, Chris. What do you know about a semicolon?"

He repeats what he's learned in class: It combines two complete ideas that are closely related. I say, "Show me the two complete ideas." He can find only one. Then we talk about his other options, like using a conjunction and a comma, so that the sentence will be correct.

I can't have that short conventions conference with him if I haven't built the foundation in daily class practice. I used to get frustrated when I tried to approach conventions in conference because it was never short and easy to do so. We know we can't confer for twenty minutes with one student, and we certainly don't want to lecture about conventions and move on. No one learns that way. I've found the combination of whole-class foundation building and in-context reinforcement works. Combine it with expecting all finished writing to be "darn near perfect" and most students really start to change their writing habits.

I have been amazed at the lack of conventions muscles my students have. They'll tell me no one has taught them these things before, but I don't believe it. I have great respect for teachers at all grade levels. I know we're all out there teaching, but almost all of my students haven't *learned* enough about grammar and punctuation before their senior year. Perhaps that is because it isn't taught enough or practiced enough, but raging about teachers who don't work hard enough never helps me. I just make sure they learn it from me.

POSSESSIVE NOUNS

Learning takes practice. How much? Here's an example of work with one class on possessive nouns. I kept track of the steps I took to reach mastery with most students in one class in one semester.

1. The need for initial practice was determined based on repeated errors in essays. All students struggling with single possessives, plural possessives, and contractions. Corrections were made on drafts of essays (in context) and individual conferences were held with many as we worked on our first piece of writing, but final drafts showed little improvement.

2. I introduced a study of apostrophe use with four sentences: one with no apostrophe—a PN (plural noun), one with a SPN (singular possessive noun), one with a PPN (plural possessive noun), and finally one with a C (contraction of noun + is) because my students often spell contractions as plural nouns.

Students practiced with a second set of sentences in writer's notebook (not graded) as I walked around to see how they were doing. Many errors.

3. I teach this each day of this first week of our study with sample fill-in-the-blank sentences like these:

boys (PN) boys' (PPN) boy's (SPN) boy's (C)

- *If the _**boys**___ in class don't stop talking, I'm going to sing for them.__**PN**__*
- *The _**boys'**___ papers were filled with humor and made Mrs. Kittle laugh. _**PPN**___*
- *One _**boy's**___ story of winning the soccer tournament had a very crafty ending._**SPN**___*
- *You know the _**boy's**___ going to be late when he's still toasting his bagel as morning announcements start._**C**___*

Notice that our initial practice involves only four choices, which makes this task easy. I soon make six sentences with the same four choices, requiring more thinking. We review the answers together briefly and move on with our work for the day. This is a five-minute exercise at most, and students begin to develop confidence quickly. Soon I can assign a pair of students to create the sentences for the class each day and others to lead the discussion of answers. Students begin to notice apostrophes in model texts we use in our genre study.

4. I begin class with a quick quiz after two weeks. In this particular class the results were: 25 percent solid understanding, 65 percent developing understanding, 10 percent no understanding. I'm discouraged, but not surprised.

5. I continue discussing corrections in conference on essays (in context). I find that even with good intentions I get involved in the piece of writing and often just don't have time to also work on the conventions. This reminds me of why I must do some of the work with the whole class or it won't get done at all.

6. I continue to review this skill once a week for two more weeks. I create review groups of mixed abilities with at least one student with a solid understanding assigned to each group. Students are given several sets of sentences and work through the same process and thinking, but turn in one paper with all four names on it and share a classwork grade for this activity. Cooperative work

allows me to circle and listen, while allowing students to have another teacher. The truth is, they're just more attentive to each other than they are to me. I can't imagine why.

7. After five weeks of work focused on possessive nouns and sentence combining, I create a quiz with many variables and much greater difficulty. Results are better: 52 percent solid understanding, 22 percent developing understanding, 19 percent with only half correct, but I still consider that little to no understanding, and one student missed almost all of the questions. (He and I schedule a grammar lunch for the next day. Grammar lunch sounds like torture, I know, but I keep candy in my office and students are usually willing to stop by for help as we eat. I also have scheduled times before and after school when students can count on me for individual help.)

8. At this point our class study ends. I will review this once every two weeks or so (retention theory) while I also continue to work with the few individuals who really need it in conference. All of my students think differently about possessives at this point and often notice errors in their own work without me. They also get high fives for finding an error on a sign in town or in the paper.

This isn't a plan that I can give you for your class, since your class may have better or worse skills than mine did this semester, but I can tell you it takes this kind of effort in order for many students to finally learn the rules. I watch my students, read their drafts, and decide on a grammar or mechanics study based on what they're able to do as writers. One semester it was dialogue and homonyms first, then possessives, with lots of sentence structure all semester long. They still weren't completely independent by the time they left me, but thankfully, that was an unusual group. With a strong class the year before we zipped through every review with ease and speed and they had it.

LEARNING TO LISTEN TO WRITING

I ask students to reread their writing out loud for sentence structure. I ask them to reread their drafts with a highlighter for marks of convention. We practice one day in class. Every mark of convention is highlighted in a paragraph from a piece of their current drafting. I tell them about the cool history of many of the punctuation marks (Atwell 2002) they use today. How the circle at the end of an idea meant going all around a subject and evolved into just a period.

How quotation marks were first lips on each end of what was said. How comma meant "little knife" and cut off one thought from another. Then I talk about how it is a conversation between reader and writer. We are following directions for how to read. What directions are you giving a reader? Of course, I do this with one of my drafts in front of them. I want you to pause here (there's a comma) but not come to a full stop. I read it out loud for them. Now here's a paragraph because this is a new idea—I want you to feel a transition to something else. I show them a few paragraph changes that don't work from anonymous student drafts. It might be beautiful writing, but it feels wrong if it should be broken apart based on a change in time, location, or movement; all of the information cannot be crowded into one long paragraph.

Just like with all work on conventions, I repeat this lesson over several days. On day two, I use a student's draft (with their permission, of course) and ask the student to talk through convention decisions. This is marvelous thinking in front of a class. The student will often discover errors as he reads and make the changes in front of the class. This is important because it teaches the student presenting as well as his peers.

PARALLEL SENTENCE STRUCTURE

Helping students to write with grace and style comes from a continued focus on how other writers accomplish this. I have used the Poynter Institute's website (www.poynter.org) and in particular, Roy Peter Clark's Fifty Lessons for Writers, to help zero in on particular strategies that lead to smooth writing. One of those is looking carefully at the use of parallel structure. I use Martin Luther King, Jr.'s "I Have a Dream" speech as our mentor text for this lesson. As we read the speech I ask students to underline phrases that repeat. After we've heard the speech we go back and look at examples of repeating patterns.

I also bring in picture books like *Scarecrow* by Cynthia Rylant and *The Paperboy* by Dav Pilkey that are fine examples of word choice and parallel structure. It is easier for students to focus on phrasing if they have the text typed out to study as I read aloud. Parallel structure has a repeating rhythm that adds style to an otherwise ordinary text. Once we have identified it in a whole-class lesson, I ask students to include one example in their current writing piece. When it comes time to turn the piece in, I ask students to highlight the section where they used parallel structure. This reinforces their learning and is much easier to assess.

I used to be afraid to teach wacky, creative exceptions to traditional mechanics because my students didn't seem to know the rules. You know what people say: Writers must know the rules before they can break them. I don't buy it. I've found that teaching the exceptions also help students learn (or realize they know) the rules. Instead of having a lesson with seniors on what *is* a sentence, I teach that lesson within what is *not* a traditional sentence but effective writing. I teach lots of "look how odd this punctuation is" lessons, and they allow me to remind students of what is traditional form and why breaking form works only some of the time.

Here's an example: the one-word sentence. We see this in real-world writing all the time. If the entire idea can be contained in one word, it works. Cool. (Or if you're from New England, you have to use two words: wicked cool.) The reader can imagine *That is cool* to understand the writer's meaning. The reader draws on an understanding of context. I show my students this in a piece of my own writing from *Public Teaching: One Kid at a Time* (2003).

> "*Miss Ostrem! Make him stop!*" *I heard from across the room, turning to see a frog with at least three crickets hanging out of his mouth, the terrified legs doing a slow death dance as they advanced farther into his grinning lips.*
> *Oh.*
> *My.*
> *God.*
> *Hysteria once again took over my classroom. In those final moments, I managed to traumatize the room. The cricket population disappeared with incredible speed. . . . (9)*

It is important to notice how the preceding section reads if punctuated differently. I give students three possibilities: Oh my god, omigod, and Oh my God! and we talk about what changes in the mood of that section, and the voice of the narrator, depending on the choice the writer makes. Punctuation is all about choices. In sentence structure those choices must be intentional, or the reader doubts the writer's credibility. In other words, fragments just read wrong unless they come after a whole sentence and the reader assumes the beginning that is missing. (*I want mashed potatoes for Thanksgiving dinner. And turkey. And stuffing. And don't forget pumpkin pie.* That works.) We've all read many, many fragments that don't: The reader feels something is missing and wants it fixed. *Women should stay in the kitchen where they belong because.*

I needed that section of my story to read like I felt it at that time:

Oh.
My.
God.

I want the reader looking around at the chaos in my room and saying each word on its own. I want the horror of the situation compounded by this slow beat of realization.

The day after I taught this, I read Matt's story of realizing his girlfriend didn't like him much.

I've talked with my friends Logan and Caleb about my most terrible secret: I hadn't gotten over Molly. They both suggest I talk to her, so I do. Worst. Idea. Ever. Every terrible emotion comes crashing down on me the moment I hear her voice on the other line…

With Matt's permission I shared this draft in class. We agreed it was perfect sentence structure for the moment. It brought the writer's voice to the center of the scene: You feel his pain. Soon after Kate imitated this in a story about living with an alcoholic and again, it worked. My students love the freedom of breaking the rules and using punctuation to determine how their work will be read. It is the best way I've found to get them to really listen to the construction of their writing.

CORRECTING GRAMMAR ON DRAFTS: MY TEXTS AND THEIRS

There has been a tension between what to write on drafts in our field. Many believe the final piece is a work of art and shouldn't be written on. Some believe it is the last chance to give feedback and so they do. Then there are those who barely find time to read and grade, let alone correct a lot of errors, so they don't put feedback on final drafts because they can't manage the time to do so. I was either of the first two, and went back and forth depending on who I was reading at the time. I wasn't sure that either approach was enough to change writers, so I kept vacillating, hoping that one way or another somebody would learn it all and I'd no longer have to make the corrections.

I learned one thing in those years with absolute certainty: Correcting errors on final drafts does next to nothing to improve a writer's skills. Kids I know skim by our comments on a sprint to discover their grade and then toss the piece in a notebook or the trash. I just don't have that kind of time to waste. I have to give myself over to reading rough drafts and helping with punctuation and grammar *while the piece is in formation,* when the writer wants to learn and I can be helpful, not a judge. Once the piece has reached an ending, the piece is over. The lessons are often useless. I record errors made on a final draft on the qualities of writing sheet, not the piece now, because I know this. But don't think by saying this that I'm letting you off the hook from correcting errors at all. Don't tell me you can't find the time to read rough drafts and then don't give feedback on the final because it won't help anyway. That's malpractice, as Carol Jago says.

We must do more than correct errors. We must teach punctuation and grammar in their writing. We must. This means I read ten drafts most nights. I don't spend more than two or three minutes per draft, just getting a sense for the piece and pointing out a few glaring problems, but turning over drafts each night helps writers progress through a unit with feedback that helps. And yes, to do this I take drafts everywhere I go. I read them at basketball games and during commercials and definitely during faculty meetings. It's a daily task that pays off in a huge way with my writers. It is worth it.

I've found that a lot of grammar and punctuation teaching can happen while sharing the decisions I am making as a writer in my own texts. If you've read this far in my book you realize that a teacher's writing is fundamental to a workshop in my mind. I use my drafts in lots of ways, but almost always as a vehicle to talk through the options I have as a writer regarding punctuation. I explicitly model how I decide which way reads better (and they love to help me with this). Then in conference I ask students to do the same thing: Show me a few sentences and the options you have and how you choose. They are manipulating their own writing, for a useful purpose—since one option will be chosen for the final draft—and learning grammar in context, the way it will most likely be lasting and useful to them. This works and it is important.

Kristen

Surely there must be times when the sculptor laughs for joy
at the hardness of the stone.

—GARRETT KEIZER

She saunters into class on our first day like a gangster with low-slung jeans and a long T-shirt hiding her solid build. Her dark hair frames her face in soft waves against creamy skin, but her eyes narrow at me and dare me to notice anything soft about her.

"What's up?" she says, tossing two words into the distance between us. She doesn't want or expect an answer. I've seen her around school and felt a little afraid of her—knew she'd challenge me, wondered if I was up to it. Now the semester starts and we'll find out. I remind myself I'm taller and older. I'm the teacher; she's not.

We aren't even through our first week when she says, "That little shit always . . ." and I stop her mid-sentence with a, "You can't say that in here," bringing those dark eyes in a sweep across my face, measuring me. An inevitable but pesky showdown has arrived.

"Say what?"

"You know: profanity. No warnings: You need to be in my office for lunch. Today."

"That's not a swear—everyone says *shit*."

"Not in my room. Lunch today." I turn my back to her and my attention to the class. She growls something to Courtney, but the confrontation is over. This isn't a win exactly, more like she takes the pitch and fouls it out, but I'm still standing, so I'll take it.

She enters my office at 12:20 and wedges herself between floor-to-ceiling bookshelves and boxes of senior class T-shirts, keeping her fists deep in her pockets as she slides onto a chair. She looks out the window to students on the front lawn. "Hey, Chris!" she bangs on the glass.

"That's privacy glass; he can't see you."

She turns, amused, to look at me. "So—what—do you just sit here and watch everyone?"

"Sometimes. Most of the time I'm facing the other direction," I point toward my desk, "working."

"I bet," she zaps me with a head nod and a smirk: *I don't believe you, but we'll both pretend I do.* I snicker.

I "reinforce my expectations," which takes about thirty seconds. Kristen tolerates me. I want something more out of this moment with her because there's always a story, every kid has one. Don Graves would say, "The question is: will they tell you? Will they tell me?" Kristen's not telling. She does her time: eyes watching me, then back out the window. The silence lurks there as I return to reading papers. *Try harder*, it nudges. I don't.

I get another chance the next week, and the one after. She earns lunch with me regularly: four times in one week. I refuse to give in. I won't even refer her to the assistant principal; this will be solved between the two of us, but I'm resentful of all the time I'm spending with her. I want her to just do what I ask—just try.

She's having trouble getting started. Her notebook is filled with tiny print, but one line tells me how to help. *Everyone I knew in Haverhill is either in jail or dead.* I sit beside her, "There's a story here; tell me more."

For the next few days in class she writes, deletes, writes, deletes. "Just write one moment," I say.

"I can't write, Mrs. Kittle, I suck at writing. I can't spell anything," she says.

"Drafts are messy, I know. You've seen mine! But at the start I just tell myself to get the story out and fix it up later."

Kristen shuts off the computer and wraps herself around her notebook. Pages fill.

Kristen writes of being expelled from eighth grade. "I never got to tell my side," she says. And she needs help. She knows so little about conventions (contractions, possessive nouns—forget paragraphs or ending punctuation even) that I feel words I shouldn't say rising up inside of me—*How come you don't know this? Why didn't anyone teach you?* But instead I focus on slow conferences. "Can you feel the ending of this thought—that's where you put a period. It's a pause for the reader to take a breath. Now read it to me."

There's too much ground to cover and days when I'm impatient: There are twenty-eight other writers in my room. Kristen's mouth helps me out: Our lunch detentions become writing conferences. We finally have all the time she needs. And Kristen finally has a story she cares about writing, so she wants to learn. Those four words mean everything, of course: She listens hard; she asks questions; she tries to use what I'm teaching her. She sustains this effort for weeks—one writing piece after another—one lunch detention after another.

And what a joy it is to know this girl; she is intense and grateful and true. She wants to become a teacher, she tells me, and help out kids that everyone else gives up on. She tosses a smile across the hall between classes and reminds me that my work matters. She came to me not even knowing the months of the year—*I know, I know*—but she kept showing up, giving me a chance to teach her.

Here I am learning those same teaching moves again: Believe any kid can learn, no matter how far behind and how resistant; try in as many ways as possible to connect and teach; love each student unconditionally with the patience and faith it takes to see it through.

Kristen Hughes and I are at her graduation in June 2006.
She is now studying to be a teacher.

PART SIX
ASSESSMENT

CHAPTER TWELVE
Leading Students to Reflection and Independence

There is an hour when the work, at last, must be passed in and the writer revealed. Writing is never completed; the process of revision, reconsideration and editing goes on until the final deadline is met.

—DONALD MURRAY

Writers need feedback, not evaluation. I believe this. I embrace it. I seek readers as I struggle with my thinking, but I don't want a letter grade on my writing. It won't help me with that piece; it will likely damage my confidence and disrupt my process. For example, the draft of "Combing Through" that I took to my writing group (see the DVD) had construction issues and was likely a "B." If I left group that afternoon with a letter grade, the label would get in the way of my work, especially since I am writing about a personal experience. As Joan Bauer wrote in *Hope Was Here*, how can you put a grade on grief? But I also won't pull out a tissue with one hand and slap an "A" on a piece with the other just because the student had the courage to write it. Who could defend that? I'm not going to suggest we stop grading altogether, unless you work in a place that would allow it. I've always taught in public schools, so I've never been permitted to write narrative summaries of student learning, although I believe it would be more helpful and more informative. I've always had to determine an average—a number—that can be defended when there's a challenge and computed with all the other numbers over four years to determine class rank. I'm left with this conundrum: Letter grades on individual writing pieces—*bad*. Individual grades that can be averaged for a progress report, parent phone call, or request form guidance, special education, or administration—*necessary*.

What is a writing teacher to do? I try to create good conditions for assessing writers through the following elements I'll describe in this chapter:

- Teaching the content and craft distinctions in assessment

- Feedback on drafts

- Feedback in conference

- End notes and student self-evaluation

- Ongoing revision—the opportunity to improve

- Final portfolios

TEACHING CONTENT AND CRAFT DISTINCTIONS

Throughout a genre unit I teach students the elements of craft that contribute to the overall effect of the writing through studying mentor texts. As we create a list of understandings of how writing in that genre works, I relate those to the list of qualities I will use to assess the work. (These are on the DVD.) Our qualities for each genre are based on the six traits of writing that students in our district learn to define in elementary school.

I do not use rubrics in my class. Even before I read Maya Wilson's marvelous book *Rethinking Rubrics*, I struggled with the limitations of boxes and scores and had given them up in practice. Wilson's book helped me articulate my thinking for colleagues and administrators, and I am grateful. If you haven't read it, do.

I approach assessment the way I study all writing: I read for content and craft separately. I appreciate, encourage, listen, and respond personally to the content. I pick apart specifics of a piece and compare it to the qualities of writing well in that genre when I evaluate craft. It helps that we've used the terms *content* and *craft* throughout the study because students learn to appreciate the differences.

For example, following is a draft of a student narrative that we read in class. At the end of reading and annotating, each student was asked to quickly write a response to this question: *Which do you think was stronger in this piece: content or craft? Why?* After each student responded, he passed his paper to another student nearby who read his response and responded to the previous comment. One more pass and a response, and it was sent back to the first student. We then discussed our impressions in class, giving me the opportunity to clarify how the two terms are different and how they work in writing. Not all students are as articulate as the three in Figure 12.1, but gathering the collective impressions of the class helps students learn from each other.

"Well, let's start the Minton's," my mom interrupted, and pulled into the driveway of their peaches and cream colored house. Instinctively, I shot out the side door as soon as the car stopped and made a beeline for the front door. From behind me I could hear my mother clear her throat. I quickly slowed up and turned back towards Summer. <u>She held onto the door handle and pulled</u> *fl*(s) <u>herself out of the car, turning awkwardly to grab a T.J. Maxx shopping bag—her make shift trick-</u> *ing me* <u>or-treat bag.</u> The three steps leading to the front porch landing proved to be somewhat of a challenge, but a handful of Jolly Ranchers and ten minutes later, we were—*finally*—back on the road towards the next house.

Again, I dragged my feet towards the front door of the Jack-'O-Lantern clad house and waited for Summer. Again. And again. And again. But somehow, by the time 8:30 and the last house rolled around, my feet didn't feel so heavy. <u>She laughed every time we got to a house with</u> *determing* <u>a flight of stairs, but insisted that if I were going to get candy there, she wouldn't be left behind.</u> She painstakingly unbuckled and twisted lower body out of the car dozens of times that evening, pulling with all her weight to stand on her leg. Purposely walking at half speed, I walked next to her, as her stiff steps struggled to keep up. <u>I was patient; she was appreciative.</u> *Understanding*

"We don't have to keep going if you don't want to," she said, worried that she had bored me with the evening's events.

"No, no, this is fun," I replied, genuinely meaning it. I felt the empty hole in my heart from the past several years of nasty stares and deliberate secrets overflow. And she smiled, buck-teeth, goofy smile and all. I guess waiting for Summer didn't take so long after all.

I thought that the craft was much better than the content, as it needs to be. ~~A single~~

I thought that the detail was very good at painting pictures.

I don't think craft should be better then content. If the content isn't interesting I won't keep reading. I don't think you can compare them at all. Garrett.
I think Liz's craft was so good because it helped the reader (me) have a greater understanding of the content. This is how craft and content ought to interact.

Figure 12.1

Showing How to Evaluate Student Work

The next day I bring in an essay written the year before. The student's name is hidden, of course. I put a copy of the essay on the overhead and talk as I read the piece, evaluating the particulars as students watch. I want to take the mystery out of grading. I write comments on the essay and highlight errors I notice, just like I would at home on my couch. I talk to students about what I notice about the content of the piece as well as the craft of the writer. "I love this line!" I might say, "I can see the skin like tissue paper on her grandfather's hands. Here she needs to keep the comma inside the quotation marks, so I'll put a reminder next to the section on mechanics."

I talk aloud as I compare the essay to our qualities sheet and determine a final grade; I want every step to be as transparent as possible. I want my students to connect our list of qualities to the writing we read in class and to the evaluation process. When I have access to our writing lab and the Tablet PC, I insert the draft into a journal document and then highlight and write on the text while they watch. This is a neater way to save my thinking for a student who is absent; overheads tend to end up smeared and unreadable—you know, another dimension of my coffee-spilling, lunch-wearing personality.

This minilesson on how I will grade work is followed by student practice with their writing. As a part of creating end notes to explain the process used to create the piece of writing, a student has to evaluate his writing using our list of qualities. This puts the student and me on similar ground with evaluation. Because as much as I believe there is a bit of guidance counselor in me—the listener—as evidenced in the "High School" poem I wrote in class—"I return each fall with hands clasped around my notebook: bring me your stories, your lives, your spirits. Let us write these truths together"—there's also that English grammar teacher in me that notices every misplaced comma. The mechanics of writing are currency in the world. If you want folks to listen, respect them enough to offer clean, correct copy. I know I must teach, reinforce, and demand adherence to the writing code that educated people live by, even with our most challenging population.

FEEDBACK ON DRAFTS

Let me start with a story. Here's what happened: It was 7:00 on a Monday evening when I walked into Don Murray's house for writing class. I had driven almost two hours after working all day and was relieved to see his smile and a place near him as I came through the door. As I approached, Ellen said, "Oh, Penny! Here's some feedback on your writing," and handed me my stories with black ink all over them—words crossed out, arrows moving phrases here and there, and in large letters at the top of the page, "Try to use strong verbs instead of a lot of adjectives." She'd crossed out *sloppy, of those gathered, massive and slow,* and *swiftly* on just the first page of my piece.

I might have mumbled a thank you as I turned to sit by Don. I looked at the papers, stuck them in my journal and seethed. I could think of one response: Who gave you permission to put that on my work? I've been fumbling through these early drafts—trying to make sense of difficult memories—and you want to talk about adjectives? Are you really trying to help me?

As class started, I wrote in my notebook. *You smile as you hand it to me—so efficient and sure you're right, but your movements on my work are YOURS, not mine. Worse, they're insulting, distancing, shocking. I'm unable to look you in the eye.* And I have no relationship with this woman, nor a need for one, so I'm able to just vent and be done with it. This is infinitely safer for me as a writer than the typical student-teacher relationship. Her comments lie between us and I want nothing to do with her, but I don't have to depend on her for anything and can forget about it.

I soon scribbled in my notes, *every writing teacher ought to experience this feeling.* Even as my anger dissipated over the next hour I found myself distracted by her intrusion. I paid attention to how I felt so I wouldn't forget. *When she shares her ideas in class I don't want to listen to her—don't trust her—look for her faults. I don't like her haircut, her socks are all scrunched up—and yes, I realize this is a low point in my character and even though I know that, I can't stop it. I'm unwilling to accept what she's done to my work.* And yes, I did notice the parallel between my tantrum and the adolescents I teach every day. I was surprised and embarrassed at the intensity of my feelings, but they were real.

I talked to Don about the power and danger of written feedback later that week. I think it is a mistake to litter someone's writing with error correcting if there is no indication on the piece that the voice of the writer was heard and the message in the writing has been received. If Ellen had written anything to tell me she understood what I was writing and the purpose of my piece, I might have listened to her suggestions about particulars. You just can't develop a relationship with a writer by trying to fix everything. I think it is too easy to forget that a teacher has two roles as a reader of student work: one, to hear what the writer is communicating, to listen well, to consider and respond to the thinking in the piece; and two, to help the writer communicate it with as much grace as possible, which might mean to correct and suggest and model the conventions of the genre. I'm afraid in our rush to get that stack of papers off our desks, we sometimes jump to the second role without enough time spent on the first.

Another woman in class wrote this at the end of the same piece I turned in that night, "This is lovely, I'm not married so I have nothing to compare it to. But it seems like what I see: scary and lovely both at the same time. And this writing is, too. Thanks, Linda." With just a few words, I know Linda understands some of what I'm trying to say in the writing, and I want to go back to work on the piece and see where it is *scary and lovely at the same time.* She has given me a new vision for my story, which makes me want to work on it. She spoke to me with respect and offered me her impression, which is all I need to try a little harder on the next draft.

Ellen gave me two drafts back that night, both with the same kind of response. The first piece I had written was about the distance between my mother and me—it wasn't crafted well, but it was truly difficult to write. I tried to take a big feeling and put it into words and images. I needed a response to that move, not manipulation of the sentences themselves. Ellen was making a mistake Murray highlighted in a 1981 article on revision, "Unfortunately, many teachers—and, I have discovered recently, many newspaper editors—do not understand the logic of revision and, therefore, do not encourage or even allow revision. They pounce on first-draft writing and make corrections. . . . They work in ignorance of the writer's intention and take the writing away from the writer. When editors or teachers kidnap the first draft, they also remove responsibility for making meaning from the writer. Writing becomes trivialized, unchallenging, unauthoritative, impersonal, unimportant." For example, Ellen had written across the first sentence in my second piece, "Straight at the beginning and sentences are more active." My sentence read: "Across rows of maple-colored desks, a few messy towers rose." She changed it to, "A few messy towers rose across rows of maple-colored desks." I can imagine her thinking about the flow of that sentence and can appreciate that she is trying to help me, but I see it as an intrusion, because she hasn't established the right to do that to my work yet. Writers should be heard before they're corrected, and since she showed no indication that she heard what I was trying to explain, I rejected her feedback.

I knew it was a rough piece of writing, but I was looking for a reason to keep working with it. The feedback I wanted was motivation to keep trying to tell the story. Early in the work on a piece, a writer might be looking for meaning, crafting experience, considering how to represent personal truth. A writer can't fine-tune a sentence when the meaning is still a mystery. Teachers can't jump on grammar rules and expect that to motivate a student to revise. I hear teachers tell me, "I spend all of this time making corrections, but the kids today just don't care enough to fix their mistakes." I don't think that's it. My students are typical adolescents. They also write many, many drafts for most of their work and make huge leaps in revision. I really believe it is due to the response they get. I encourage and question and wonder as I read. The comments I make on drafts ask the writer to clarify or explain, but I also say, "I know just what you mean! And you say this so well. . . . I hope you'll continue to work with this piece." And they do.

Linda wrote at the bottom of that same piece of writing, "This is awesome. It takes a lot to understand that about people, especially when the family culture is to avoid problems, issues, difficulties, etc. It sounds familiar to me. I think you've nailed it head on. I don't have any other comments. Thanks, Linda." I was exhilarated. What is most important in my writing at this stage is to share what I can't quite make sense of . . . to communicate with another person about what I can't write well yet. This is a huge topic for me, but I'm trying to wrap my arms around it. The last thing I need at this point is the editing the other reader gave me. Hear me, then I'll let you tinker with my word choice and sentence structure. Yet, aren't we doing this exactly in our classrooms? We're offering the editing corrections and few comments about what the writer is saying. We're shaping a text instead of listening to voice. I know it is wrong for me; it must be wrong for my high school writers. My writing will not improve under Ellen's care. Those are her changes, not mine. With Linda, I am motivated to get back to work, and when I do I'll likely make lots of changes. What more does a teacher want?

And last, Terry, another writer in class, responds to that same piece about my mother like this. Not a mark on the text until the end where she has underlined this line: *I know she wants an intimacy between us; I try to believe it is she who makes it impossible. I still can't fix it, so I try to stand it.* Terry writes: "This is the line that hurts me. Penny, I've thought of this essay many times since I read it over the week we missed—saying the line 'I try to stand it.' So many things it serves better to stand them than to lose huge energy to fight. Thank you, Terry." And I told Terry, as I tell you, that I stole that line from Annie Proulx. The last line in the short story "Brokeback Mountain" from the collection *Close Range*, is: "There was some open space between what he knew and what he tried to believe, but nothing could be done about it, and if you can't fix it you've got to stand it." Sometimes another writer captures my thinking completely and I work with her words until I can find my own.

I wanted to spend time talking to Terry about the piece—searching deeper for what I was trying to capture that I'm sure she understands. I wanted to pull my chair beside hers and explain what I was trying to say—the best kind of writing conference when a writer tries to work through the issues out loud, and a listener can echo what was said and how the writer can put those thoughts on paper. Terry gave me an invitation to work through what is troubling me as a writer by first saying she understands the purpose of the piece. I can't make the piece better just by cleaning up the surface; I need to keep searching for the heart of the piece. That's what Linda and Terry nudge me to do—move to the center.

It is not insignificant to me that they both say, "thanks," at the end. I've offered a bit of my soul to them, and they are appreciative. I don't often write "thanks" on a paper a student hands me, but I will now. I could feel the power in that word: It says the piece mattered.

I know all about the short time teachers have to go deeply with writers in the busyness of high school life. My seniors move into our workshop and out again in eighty-three minutes each day. We have many things to accomplish in eighteen weeks, but I see writers make leaps when I limit my comments in early drafts to what I hear the writer trying to say. I see writers go back into the piece and craft with energy and vision and increased focus. In a later draft I often mark every editing error or suggest sentence fine-tuning that improves the piece—and yes, I read several drafts of each piece from almost every kid in class. I make the time. I can't confer with enough students each day, so I read and respond to drafts each night. I want better writers and that is how it happens—with respectful, regular feedback.

Figure 12.2 is an example of my notes on a student draft. Notice at the top of the page Sarah has written this: "I'm not sure I know what I want to do with

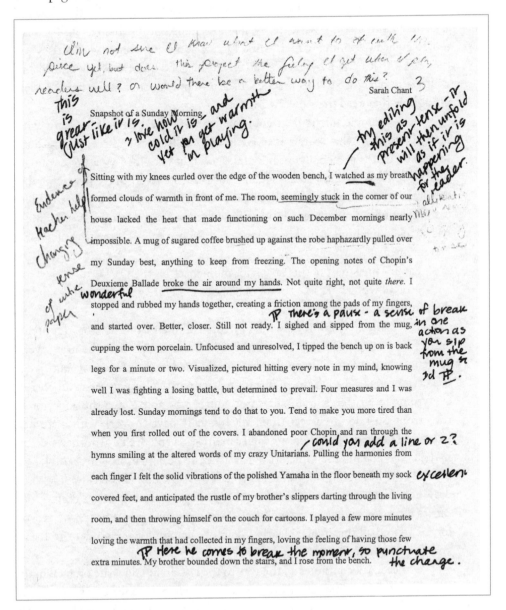

FIGURE 12.2

this piece yet, but does this project the feeling I get when I play to readers well? Or would there be a better way to do this?" I ask students to give me a direction for my reading. I teach them the kinds of comments or questions that help me read and provide feedback directed where they need it. "Is this good?" is useless. "Is my detail sufficient to put you in the moment?" is ideal. I have to help my students make increasingly effective evaluations of their work. I will be teaching them for only four months: I direct them toward tools they can use in the years beyond. And I also know that students need to know how much they know. I ask students to identify what they know to reinforce it for them as well act as a tool to guide my reading of their work. Notice in my conference with Kelsey (on the DVD) that I end by saying, "You ask really good questions on your drafts," which is in reference to this practice. I learn so much about my writers by looking at how they read their own work.

This example might help you, but I believe the best way to learn what kind of feedback helps writers is to circle a few colleagues and read and respond to writing that is personally meaningful to each of you. (See Writing Group on the DVD.) Write what you assign for your students to do, and then respond to the drafts of your colleagues and talk about what helps you as a writer. This is the professional development I've been involved in for the last eight years and it has changed me immeasurably. (More on this on the DVD under Professional Development.)

Sarah's final draft of this snapshot moment is on the DVD.

Not all writers are like Sarah, of course. In Figure 12.3 is another student draft from that class.

I sat with this draft for a while. I wrote comments on the story (content) and a few corrections to sentence structure. I drew a line after the first several sentences and wrote: *I stopped correcting the mechanics here and would like to work with you in class, please.* It doesn't matter what color pen I use; if I correct everything in Kristen's draft, she's not going to be able to see the good for all the errors. So I don't correct them all. I usually have to work with a student like this outside of workshop time over many days and drafts. Another student may just be making the same error (in dialogue punctuation, for example) repeatedly on a draft. Again, I don't correct every instance. I correct a few, then draw a line and write: *You are making the same error repeatedly in this draft. Please correct the rest according to my model here and see me in class.* There's no reason for me to find all the errors; clearly it is more helpful for the student to locate and correct them.

Feedback continues all the way to the last draft. I do write on final drafts and all over the qualities of writing sheet they turn in attached to a final piece of writing. I turn these final drafts around quickly, most within two to three days. I make this happen so that students can use feedback from one unit during the next. After all of the thinking that went into planning the curriculum for this course, it would be worthless if I held onto writing for weeks once we finish a unit. My students need to know what they know and what they don't so they can continue to improve as writers.

Kristen Hughes
Ms.Kittle
Writing Block 1

Growing up

First day of 6th grade my parents told me. It's a chance for you to start on the right foot; a new beginning my dad yells rushing out the door. SMILE as a turned my head to the right and saw this white flash come before my eyes. "Mom I wasn't ready." I yelled, "that's ok Kristen" have a nice day at school my mom said as she pushed me out the door. "Remember to listen to your teacher and DON'T GET INTO TROUBLE" that's was the last thing I herd as I was walking down to the bus. The bus arrived, the door opened and I steeped up onto the overly large steps. I got onto the bus and drifted to <u>MY</u> seat. As I walked to the back everyone was looking at me, but I didn't care because I knew I was different. I was not what you would call you're "average" girl. I was Unique. I would wear Sean John shorts that would go past my knees. I would wear a Phat farm shirt that was 2 sizes bigger then me and my Nike shoes that would fall off my feet when I would walk. I was a tough girl, I was myself. No one would want to sit with me but that does not matter because my friends had our own section. "Yo Kristen I've saved you a seat" said my friend Anthony. I stopped and gave him a nod...and after that I knew I had everyone's attention so I did that fly walk that looks like one leg is about 5in. smaller then the other one. I thought if people did not now who I was then they sure know who I am know. The bus pulled into our school; I looked up and saw a Welcome to C.D Hunking School. I knew just by looking at the school and the principal Mr. Marino that this was going to be a fun 3 years. I could tell that he was already judging me, I could already tell that we were not going to get along. I stepped off the bus and turned to Anthony and said "Welcome to Hell.

7th Grade
"KRISTEN HUGHES TO MR.MARINO'S OFFICE IMMEDITLY" said the security in the main office. Ohhh-Ohhh what did she do whispered my class. "Nothing" I said. I opened the cracked door with a plastic window and stepped outside the classroom. "Damn what did I do know" I said to myself. I took a deep breath and started to walk down the hall. I stopped mid-way and looked behind me. I slowly walked to the main office with my feet dragging and my head down counting the gum spots on the floor. "Mr. Marino Kristen has arrived, Do you want me to send her in" said the sectary in a your in deep shit kind of voice." Yes please send her in," he said. I wiped my sweaty palms on my blue jean shorts and got up." Kristen do you know why you are here." He said. "Umm no I have no idea" I said telling the truth." What happen to you" he said "Nothing why" There was a complaint by one of your teachers that you were being rude and talking back. "Is that true" he said "No I was not talking back to no teachers" I said to him in is that all voice. I'm going to let you go today because I am in a good mood, but the next time I hear a compliant from anyone a teacher or a student you will be in a lot of trouble. "Thank you" Kristen don't take advantage of this. "I wont I promise,"

FIGURE 12.3

FEEDBACK IN CONFERENCE

This is essential for helping writers, and after so many years in the classroom I am still, like Don Murray, "fascinated by this strange, exposed kind of teaching, one to one." Make it work; it makes a difference.

END NOTES AND STUDENT SELF-EVALUATION

Long ago I was given a real gift. I spent a day in Linda Rief's classroom in Durham, New Hampshire. As one class after another cycled through the day I read through student notebooks and portfolios and listened in on conferences. One thing that stuck with me was the evaluation sheet students filled out prior to submitting a final draft. It is available in *Seeking Diversity* (still one of my favorite books on teaching language arts), but it isn't necessary to have Linda's form to understand its power. Linda has students detail their writing process so she can better understand all the writing moves made that she might have missed. That thinking, plus Tom Romano's explanation of using process notes in multigenre, has helped me shape self-evaluation for each writing unit. (You may have noticed by now that there's a bit of kleptomania in this book, the grafting of bits and pieces from the smartest people I know.)

So, at the end of each unit my students respond to the following questions about their process. This list of question changes with focus areas in different units, but this is where I begin:

In end notes please answer these questions completely and thoughtfully:

- Tell me about your process—how did you get from beginning to end in writing this piece?

- Which mentor texts used in class had the biggest impact on your thinking and writing?

- What did you learn about narrative writing that is evident in this piece? Explain the annotations of your own work. (With this piece you will show where you used vivid details, where you can hear your authentic voice, and how sentence structure improved the music or rhythm of your work.)

- What did you learn from someone else in writing this piece: a student in class, a comment from another reader, something written on a rough draft, and so on?

- Where does this piece still fall short? If you had months ahead of you to work on the piece, what would you go after first?

- Grade the piece and explain your evaluation. Use the qualities of narrative that we have discussed in class and address each of these qualities in your evaluation.

I get a lot of "what to teach next" ideas from this writing. Students really surprise themselves with all they know. And I need to know that they know it. I learn which model texts are important and how they are important, and I have a good roadmap to refer to if a student decides to revise the piece. End notes have made grading easier. It is a rare, truly rare student who carefully measures his work against the qualities we've defined together and determines the piece is greater than it is. Most students are accurate in their assessment of the craft of their writing and determined to improve.

Here are the end notes from one student's argument. I write end notes for each unit and vary the questions slightly by genre.

1. About your process: how did writing the outline or organizer help you write the paper?

Since the beginning of time I have avoided organizers. The "brainstorm webs" of my elementary years always seemed to break up my story's flow. I just never really warmed up to them. That is, until now. Throughout high school I realized that if I knew what I was talking about and how I was going to say it, my paper would come out a thousand times better than it would have if I just sat down and spewed out paragraph after paragraph of unorganized, unsorted mess. I liked how this outline forced the writer to contain all the parts of a good argument without holding the writer to a specific format. It allowed for organization without interfering with the process. This made sure that I had an acknowledgment, a response, at least three pieces of evidence (supporting details), and a main claim. After I had all the main pieces it was just a matter of including them in the piece logically and skillfully. I tried to use evidence and make claims without bogging down the writing as a whole. I tried to keep it light without shirking away from the topic and continuing to make points.

2. Which argument model was most influential on your writing in this unit? Explain how the piece helped you as a writer.

I really loved the piece on Anna. I thought it made far more of an emotional pull than any of the other articles we read in class. I wanted to match the personality that spills out of that story, but found that with my topic, it was not the right approach. Thus, I loosely followed the style of the *Sports Illustrated* columnist Rick Reilly, but I didn't take it quite *that* far. I attempted, as I said before, to write my piece with humor and a light air, and I think I achieved that. I liked how Reilly could tackle a topic with a facetious tone and still make a point. He had the reader completely agreeing with him by the end, so naturally, it was incredibly effective. I tried to echo his voice in mine a little while I mixed it with a situation we are dealing with. His piece helped me to pull away from the standard persuasive essay we've been writing for the past few years and delve into something completely different, but arguably as effective.

3. In this unit we studied the claim, reason, evidence, acknowledgment, and response. Which of those are clear to you and which elements are still a bit muddy in your understanding?

I think after the many hours we have spent in class going over each of the essential elements of a good argument, I have come to understand each of them far better than when I first jumped into this unit. However, out of all of them I think my evidence is shakiest. It was not terrible, but I didn't have any absolutely solid pull. I didn't have that indestructible, hard fact that makes the reader sure that my view is the right one. I found examples of psychologists and education researchers all saying that homework is essential, but I couldn't seem to fit it right. I felt like they were echoing how I felt, and I couldn't place those quotes in without feeling incredibly repetitive. In conclusion, I think I should have spent more time getting indisputable evidence and meshing it into my piece.

4. Who was your audience for this writing piece? Who did you imagine you were writing to?

I wrote this piece like I was writing to the people who made this ridiculous rule in the first place. The voice sounds like it's talking to someone outside of Kennett High School, but it's sort of like speaking to someone behind their back and they find out. In the opening paragraph I faulted Kennett a few times, but I didn't directly say "you" like he or she reading the essay was at fault. However, I did write it like those who made the rule would be reading it. In that way it is kind of confusing to explain, but when you are reading I feel like it comes across.

5. Who read this piece besides you and me?

I didn't share this final piece with many. Elizabeth read it, but she was probably biased as both of us have been hanging on to the top of our class through homework in some of our particularly difficult classes. And naturally both of us were very unhappy when we were informed that doing our homework wasn't really going to count much anymore. My parents read my introduction. Being an attorney, my dad's job requires a lot of persuasive argument, so I valued his input on this piece. He thought it was "too flowery," but he says that about most of my work, so I didn't really change it much after he read it. My mom, a teacher, recognizes both sides of the homework battle, but she agrees that it should be weighted more. She taught high school for fifteen years and junior high for six and said she had never come across a number as low as 10 percent. So, I pretty much had too many readers who agreed with me. To further the piece I should have conversed with someone against my take on the issue.

6. How could you still improve this piece?

I could improve this piece with more time. Ideally, I would like to sit down and smooth out the rough transitions and increase the overall flow. I would like to fit in a solid fact, a number, or a quote that emphasizes my point and how much it matters. This piece hasn't been plowed through or critiqued as much as my others, and I think that shows. I would like to have it edited and read one or two more times.

Although students complain about writing end notes in addition to a last draft at the end of a writing unit, the process of self-evaluation will serve them well as writers in the world beyond school when they no longer have a writing teacher beside them. My work is to make students reflective, flexible thinkers, able to hear their writing like a reader and then to understand what might work to make it better.

ONGOING REVISION: THE OPPORTUNITY TO IMPROVE

This morning I was slow to get to writing. I had last night's dinner dishes still piled on the counters. I had email to read and respond to, laundry to start, and two dogs impatient to walk. I was thinking about writing while puttering, but not ready to sit down and do it. I was sliding into my day and my first mug of blueberry coffee, rehearsing and thinking about writing. It's part of my process, and it takes time. If this is true for me, then it must be true for my students, I know. The challenge is to make a busy high school writing workshop reflect that.

I know I have to push my students to produce, or they won't, but my deadlines can make writing more difficult and less elegant. There isn't any more time to find in my packed semester, so how could I keep us moving while also allowing more time?

Two years ago I tried something I expected would make my work harder, and that wasn't easy for me. I wish I were the Supreme Goddess of Good and could assure you that my students come first in my teaching world all of the time, but I have to admit sometimes it is only with effort. This is what I couldn't ignore, though: If I return to a piece of writing weeks or months later, I revise with greater power. Some ideas need to settle; some writing needs distance and living before it can come to be. And yet when I find new vision for a piece I thought I'd finished, it is powerful: My hands dance like twin spiders across the keyboard. There is intensity and energy and joy in writing that sings. I wanted that for my students.

How could I find the time?

I took a risk. I said, "I have a proposal. I care *most* that you write well, not *when* you write well, so you may continue to revise a piece of writing all semester. There is no last draft until you say so. The final grade for a unit will be on your best draft, even if it is months after our initial deadline." Now, I can hear all of your objections as you're reading this, you fellow teachers of dozens and dozens. Believe me, they were blaring in my ears. *I don't have time to grade the papers I have, let alone redrafted last drafts.* But stick with me here for a minute.

I accept the conditions of school—many that I disagree with—in order to do the work I love. But sometimes I have to question how I've adapted to those conditions. Adolescents resist being pushed and prodded toward an end when they've barely begun, and resistance can become refusal to try: playing the ho-hum game of school where nothing is risked and nothing is learned. I know long thinking creates better writing, which is motivating all on its own, and I need more motivated writers in my room.

I figured I could try it for one semester and if it buried me, I could go back to the march through the deadlines. I told my class, "You have a piece of writing due in two weeks and when you hand it to me it may not be the best you can do—for lots of reasons—so if you want to continue to improve it, you can. And I'll change your grade." Talk about shock and awe: I could feel the energy in the room change. Just in case someone misread this opportunity, I added, "But this isn't about procrastination: If you don't work to write the piece in two weeks, you don't get more time."

You see, I want my students to write about what matters to them—and I'm just not willing to accept less than that—and that takes time. I have to let students work to get to the heart of what they are trying to say. More time wouldn't make things easy, it would allow for deeper work. I remember what my job is—not to produce a bunch of products but to help my students write their way to clarity.

So writing pieces came in after two weeks of teaching and modeling and mentor texts and conferences and scribbled notes on drafts, and almost all of my students put them in their portfolios and moved on. A few kept working, even as we began our next genre study. They worked on two pieces at once. (Not a bad life lesson, actually.) And every once in a while a student handed me a new and improved draft stapled to the last one I graded, with end notes to explain how the piece had improved. I found that in a regular writing class of twenty-five to thirty seniors, about half of them took advantage of this at some point in the semester. Most took one piece and reworked it several times, a few rewrote almost every piece, some rewrote nothing. This did not result in a lot of extra grading as I feared, but it has produced some truly fine pieces of writing as well as students who realize all they're capable of when they set aside excuses and keep at it. They share this process in class and my workshop begins to feel real: writers pursuing their own purposes using a process that works for them to create something extraordinary to share with others.

THE FINAL PORTFOLIO

If I were in charge of the world—or my school—I'd leave all grades out of the picture until the final portfolio. I would have students writing and re-writing and doing many of the activities I direct in class, but they wouldn't be evaluated until it all came together at the end. Even though I can't do that, I devote the last week of our semester to assembling the final portfolio and writing for our class book (students submit a final piece and photo for a class book that I copy and distribute to all). These twin assignments create closure for our work.

I have modified the portfolio summary designed by Jim Mahoney in *Power and Portfolios* for the teaching in my course, but the thinking and the form are his. Students are asked to do two very important things with their work: one, to order their writing from best to worst and detail the reasons why; and two, to locate the skills taught throughout the semester in their final work. Although I ask students to show me how they've used what I've taught them on each of their final drafts, the final portfolio allows all of those skills to come together and is much more extensive than the work in individual units. A copy of a student's portfolio summary is included in Figure 12.4.

What you can't see is each essay Logan wrote with the skill highlighted and explained in his work. I've included an example of another student's work (Figure 12.5) to demonstrate what students are doing as they correlate skills taught with their writing.

Writing Final Portfolio Evaluation

Mrs. Kittle   2nd Semester   Date <u>June 2007</u> Name <u>Logan Dwight</u>

All answers should be completed thoughtfully and completely.

Listed below are the titles of pieces I've written this semester, ranked in order of their importance to me, followed by a reflection (history of the piece) on each one:

#1 Most effective piece of writing and why
Genre <u>Place Narrative</u> "Someone Once Told Me, 'It Couldn't Have Been That Bad'"

This piece taps into the most significant part of my life, my childhood. I really felt a strong connection to the piece as I wrote it. Many of the details come to life because they are so well engrained in my memory. Everyone who has read this piece told me it really affected them emotionally. I think I really got the feelings I had as a child through in my writing.

#2 Most effective piece of writing and why
Genre <u>Personal Narrative</u> "...And They Built Glass Walls For Their Concrete Castles"

This piece flows really well, and has a strong, concrete point. I really like the language I use in this piece. Many of my statements hit hard and fast, which makes nearly ever sentence have an impact. I also do a nice reversal at the end. I'm proud of how clearly my purpose comes through in this piece, and the heavy-hitting sentences that are my signature come through most strongly here.

#3 Most effective piece of writing and why
Genre <u>Commentary</u> "Whoa, is that a Magic Box?"

This piece does a good job of emulating the feel of a TV new reel. It also is successful in providing humor and sarcasm to make the point. I like the flow of it, and I feel its mocking attitude is effective in making my point.

#4 Most effective piece of writing and why
Genre <u>Fiction</u> "The Epic Tale of Jedediah Thunder"

This piece works well because it is more than just a funny story. I use a lot of jokes about society, and use the story as a vessel for commentary. I got a lot of laughs from this piece, so I think its purpose was served well.

#5 Most effective piece of writing and why
Genre <u>Snapshot</u> "Zach"

"Zach" is the story of my close friend who died in a car crash. It is short, but it also gets all my feelings across. A lot of my details are fresh and clear as well.

FIGURE 12.4

The conversations that occur in class as students talk about what they've learned and compare notes on good examples of particular skills teach me a lot in this last week. We play the radio; we relax. I get to float around the room and marvel at all they've accomplished. This June we were down to the last two days for seniors, and as we worked on portfolios, "School's Out for Summer" by Alice Cooper came on the radio. We broke briefly to crank it up. Final portfolio work should be a celebration: They've worked hard; it is time to take notice.

Choose a paper for each of the following categories and explain your choice.

Most Difficult to Write   <u>Argument</u>   **Why?**

I had no idea what I was going to argue, so it came off weak.

Most Enjoyable to Write   <u>Personal Narrative</u>   **Why?**

I really liked writing this piece, because I could bring my personal feelings to light. I enjoyed creating all the clever lines I use to make a hard point.

"The Piece I Would Like to Burn" (or work on more, or turn into a poem,)
<u>Argument</u>   **Why?**

My argument is weak. I didn't feel strongly enough on the subject, and it was too broad.

My pieces of writing in polished, final drafts, are numbered consecutively from most important to least important, and they are in the section of my portfolio marked "Essays." On each paper I have labeled in the margin and have highlighted some examples of what I've learned or can do. From all the papers, there are thirty areas indicating my skill/growth.

1. an effective title—creates an image
2. an effective lead moves the story forward
3. a major re"vision" (adding signif. details)
4. revising by cutting back (compression)
5. strong transitional sentence
6. my best example of "showing not telling"
7. strong verbs
8. visual, concrete nouns
9. my best sentence
10. evidence of a punctuation rule learned
11. establishing a clear, effective setting
12. evidence of effective use of semi-colon
13. a balance of sentence structure to improve rhythm
14. an effective ending using an echo
15. an ending line with punch
16. evidence of rehearsal or prewriting
17. effective use of rich, sensory detail
18. correct use of MLA citation
19. effective use of scene in narrative
20. correct use of possessive nouns

21. simile
22. metaphor
23. alliteration
24. taking a writing risk
25. figurative language
26. evidence of my voice
27. evidence of peer/teacher help
28. a line or a word that I got from someone else
29. clear evidence to support an argument
30. acknowledgement & response
31. evidence that reading has impacted your writing
32. evidence of expansion of an idea
33. effective of use of dialogue
34. identify area of needed revision
35. use of vivid, precise words

Where do you still need to grow as a writer? Explain in a few sentences.

I need to be able to maintain my voice and my interest for longer stretches of writing. I often only write short pieces, and lose my point if I go too long.

FIGURE 12.4 *continued*

Here are a few student notes on favorite pieces. Samantha wrote, "This essay gives me conflicting thoughts. I like it because I got all my anger out on a piece of paper. But I still hate reading it, and sometimes I wish I didn't write it. So it's hard to rate it. I placed it in my top five because of the truth within it."

Andy said, "The most difficult task in the writing process of my favorite essay, 'A Stone in Many Hearts,' was not included in the actual writing. For a

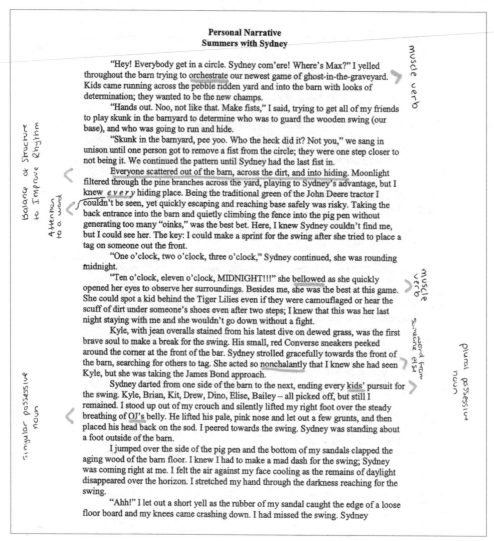

FIGURE 12.5

long time I had to dig deep into my mind and retrieve the memories that best define my life with Robby. Thinking about my friend and his impact on the community, I sat in front of my writer's notebook and created the first sentence now presented to the reader. I had hoped to bring a more direct meaning to this first phrase, yet as I finished the story I now believe that the story and introduction explain themselves without any further description. Once I had remembered the sound of Andy's laughter, remembered my days in school, baseball, and in the Mason, Ohio, neighborhood, words came easily. Though the story feels complete; I wish that I had brought more to the scene of the funeral. Looking ahead

"Are you okay?" she asked as she touched my shoulder.

"Yeah, but I just lost the game and you won," I couldn't help but laugh as I
grasped my knees in pain.

I grabbed Sydney's outstretched hand as we stood up and dusted the dirt from our
clothes. Intertwining our arms around one another, we slowly dragged our feet towards
the house, the rest of the kids following us in a dull hum.

The bottom of my pink, polka-dotted pajamas brushed the edge of the stairs with
each step down. I could smell my mom's chocolate chip pancakes and bacon; a farewell
breakfast I'm sure she made for Sydney. The dining room was flooded with new rays of
daylight that reflected off of every strand of Sydney's golden-blonde hair.

"Morning," I said, taking in a deep yawn to wake myself up.

"Morning," Sydney replied pouring herself one cup of orange juice and one of
water.

My mom walked in carrying a platter of steaming chocolate chip pancakes, crisp
bacon, and cheesy scrambled eggs. Sydney and I took a bit of each and ate our breakfast
in the silence that we were always accustomed to when she was about to leave; it was
especially perfect since the rest of the kids were still sleeping. We picked up our syrup-
covered plates and fingerprint-covered glasses as my mom cleared the rest of the table.

The black Toyota Camry pulled around the corner and up to the door; Sydney's
parents were here. Carrying her Adidas duffel bag in one hand and Harry Potter
pillowcase in the other, I trailed behind Sydney out to the car. Her parents took her things
and made their way to the trunk.

"Have a good trip home. Hopefully the Reds will start to get as good as the Sox,"
I said, jokingly trying to ease the pain I was feeling.

Sydney laughed "Oh, I'm sure they will. Don't be surprised if you see them in the
World Series."

So don't forget to email me and you have my screen name right?" I double-
checked even though we always had the same email and screen name at the end of every
summer.

"Of course," she replied, glancing down at the dirt.

We reached our arms around each other for the last farewell hug of the year. Tears
started to run down my cheeks and onto her hair. Her arms gave me a short squeeze, the
last I would ever feel, and then we let go. I wiped the tears form my face with the back of
my hand as I watched her get into the car. The car started moving, but Sydney managed
to roll down the window, stick out her head, and put out one arm for one last wave. And
like that she was gone.

It has been four years since the last summer I spent with Sydney, and the last time
I actually saw her. After she left that summer I kept sending emails, at least once a
month, but no response. Around a year later, I stopped writing. It was like she had cut me
off from her life completely and I didn't understand why – and I still haven't. Maybe her

major revision - added a lot since 1st draft

Evidence of a punctuation rule learned

FIGURE 12.5 *continued*

in the story as I wrote, I had imagined the funeral as a major and significant part
of the story. I was wrong. To anyone, life is far more important than death."

Kristen (speaking of the narrative draft in Figure 12.3, which she continued to work with most of the semester) said, "The best piece of writing that I did
would have to be my narrative. The reason I chose my narrative was because I
believe it was the piece that I showed the most voice in. I put my voice into that
story really well. At first it was hard for me to write about my life because I was

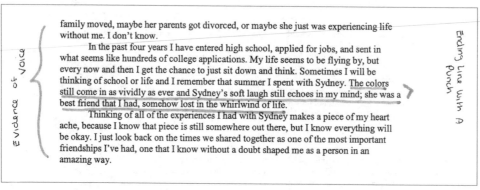

family moved, maybe her parents got divorced, or maybe she just was experiencing life without me. I don't know.

In the past four years I have entered high school, applied for jobs, and sent in what seems like hundreds of college applications. My life seems to be flying by, but every now and then I get the chance to just sit down and think. Sometimes I will be thinking of school or life and I remember that summer I spent with Sydney. The colors still come in as vividly as ever and Sydney's soft laugh still echoes in my mind; she was a best friend that I had, somehow lost in the whirlwind of life.

Thinking of all of the experiences I had with Sydney makes a piece of my heart ache, because I know that piece is still somewhere out there, but I know everything will be okay. I just look back on the times we shared together as one of the most important friendships I've had, one that I know without a doubt shaped me as a person in an amazing way.

FIGURE 12.5 *continued from previous page*

not sure how I was going to make it sound like me, but after a couple of drafts I finally got the hang of it. I figured that if I was going to write a piece about me, then I was going to have to put my language into the writing. So I did just that. I basically wrote like I talk. This narrative took me the longest to write because I was trying to capture four different years into one story. That was definitely a challenge for me. I wanted to add my four years of middle school all in one story, but I was not sure if I was able to make it go all together. But I did it and it turned out good."

Students also list the books read over the course of the semester and review their top three. The reviews are for students in future classes who are looking for a good read. They rank their favorites from our daily poetry and these rankings help me know which poems to definitely repeat with new classes. And last, they write an introductory letter to the portfolio that invites readers in and summarizes what they take from the course. These portfolios do not take long to grade. This is definitely a time when the students work harder than I do. I read for interest, and I notice how they evaluate their writing, but my teaching time is finished with this group so my feedback is minimal. I am most interested in the collective impact of the work: where did they start and where did they finish. I hope the final portfolio can capture some of that.

WEIGHTING THE COURSE GRADE

In Chapter 6, Figure 6.2 shows a copy of the course outline for parents and students that I use in class. The weighting of work in this course is important to me. There are three categories that encompass everything we do in my class, and they are weighted as follows: writing: 70 percent; homework: 15 percent; and class work: 15 percent.

I tell my students that no one *should* pass a course devoted to writing if they haven't demonstrated the ability to write well. And in fact, no one can pass my course without demonstrating effective writing. That means that I will work with some students before and after school and during lunch. I will have some students rewrite their papers over and over. I believe, as Deborah Meier said so well in her book *The Power of Their Ideas,* "The question is not, can we educate all children? The question is, do we want to do it badly enough?" I do. All of the individual writing pieces and portfolio work go into the writing category. Drafts do not. Sometimes those are part of a classwork grade, but more often they are only part of the process of developing thinking and are not graded at all. All of the reading and annotating of texts done at home (see sample texts on the DVD) goes into homework, and all of the work we do in class from group work to minilessons on mechanics to vocabulary development to annotation of texts goes into the category of classwork. In the end the class is mostly about writing, and I expect every one of my students to make marked improvement there.

Shaina

Writing stories has given me the power to change things
I could not change as a child.
I can make boys into doctors.
I can make fathers stop drinking.
I can make mothers stay.

—CYNTHIA RYLANT

She said, "Mrs. Kittle, you're a mom. Could you feel my head and tell me if I have a fever?" There's a faint line of sweat across her upper lip and she's pale. I know it before I reach out to put my fingers across her forehead, but a little bit of me breaks inside as I touch her. I've read Shaina's notebook entries on losing her mom to cancer. What if this were my daughter a few years from now? So yes, let me feel your head and send you to the nurse. I wish you'd go home, but you've written that piece too: Your new stepmom has changed your house so much that you don't recognize it—can't be there—can't quit looking at the empty chair on the porch where Mom used to watch the sunset. It's easier to be at school.

This mothering of Shaina began early, but I would never have believed it when she burst into my room all smiles in her jeans and boots: all that was fashionable, confident, and brilliant. The head of the Prom Committee, the student most likely to charm a teacher out of detention—Shaina was a powerful force. As always, on the first day I shared my "Where I'm From" poem that seems to lay a particular kind of ground rule in my classroom: The truth matters. And later that day when I sat on my couch surrounded by writing notebooks, there was Shaina's tight life summary: *My mom had ovarian cancer when I was entering the seventh grade at Kennett. My mom passed away in 2001. Her death made me mature a lot quicker than other kids.* But of course there was much beneath. No teenager I've known escapes the intensity of a loss like this. Sometimes it surfaces all at once at the end—like our last day of class one year when Christine sobbed as she read her final writing piece and recounted losing her dad at eight years old. Sometimes it seeps out like a slow drip from a faucet you thought was tightly fixed. Writing reaches for the center of who we are: there's no use hiding. Sure we can stay antiseptic and rule bound and write nothing except what is furthest from our emotional lives, but the real investment in making meaning—in making writing work—often comes when the words are just beyond our reach and the experience so important that we have to keep seeking the right way to show what we know. Certainly I'd come to expect divorced families and children living with one parent, but to find this girl alone in her grief felt like an old Yankee quilt pinning me down to a place I didn't want to be. I wondered if we had been drawn together for a reason.

Later that week when Shaina wrote *I am what I am a teenager without a mother, a father as a best friend and his girlfriend as my enemy. . .* I felt a hollowness inside. My husband asked me once, "What are you most afraid of?" and I said immediately, "Me dying." He wrinkled his forehead and looked at me. "I thought you would have said one of the kids."

"Well," I sighed, "that is beyond fear—but that would hurt *me*, not them. Right now while they're still just growing up, I fear leaving them alone and how hard it would be for them day after day. I fear not being able to mother them: to protect them and love them and tell them they're precious beyond measure."

I remembered when a routine foot X-ray revealed something mysterious and the doctor said, "I don't *think* it's cancer." I'd gone home in a daze to wait for results and burst into tears when I saw a photo of our twelve-year-old son: so innocent, so young. I thought, who's going to tell him he's handsome and some girl is going to just fall over for him? Who's going to be able to convince him of that besides his mother?

And yet Shaina's mom went home from her appointment with a doctor to a precious little daughter just twelve and, gripped with that same fear, had to begin a fight that would consume her a year later. When Shaina created a heart map of songs during quick writing, she wrote:

"*Ain't No Mountain High Enough*"

This song means a lot to me and reminds me of my mom. Her and I watched the movie Stepmom. *I can remember the night perfectly, we were having a mother daughter bonding because my dad wasn't home. At this time she already knew she had cancer and was going through kimotherapy. It was hard to watch this movie together but when "Ain't No Mountain High Enough" came on we stopped crying and started singing together.*

Ah, life: so lovely and so wrenching in the same breath.

So I didn't want to be close to this thing called cancer—this topic called losing a parent. But I also wanted to support this girl, on the brink of leaving childhood behind and stepping forward into her next life. So every time she bobbed near this topic in her notebook I encouraged her. "Write this for yourself, or for your sister: It seems like such a rich topic for you."

And she did. From quick write to draft, from genre to genre, from "I Remember" list poetry to research on ovarian cancer, to her letter to her mother catching her up on what she'd missed, shown in Figure 1.

FIGURE 1

Shaina wrote to her mother and for her mother and for herself. She could analyze all the particulars in her writing, and she could share it with her peers, even as her voice broke and the tears started. She also knew what mattered: as I chastised her to clean up the punctuation in her letter, she told me her mother wouldn't care. She was right, of course.

When Mitch's father finally succumbed to pancreatic cancer and the assistant principal came to retrieve Mitch from our class, Shaina was on her feet—and somehow suddenly we all were—as if standing to bear witness as he went out the door, his chin sunk against his chest. We knew a little of the pain he'd be facing because Shaina had taught us that the haunting went on long after everyone else moved on. In the following weeks we all took care of Mitch—in little and big ways—and we took care of each other.

Shaina's off to the University of Hawaii, to a land where she had to watch her mother die, where her half-sister almost two decades older waits to welcome her, where she won't see her mother's empty chair on the porch as she pulls out of the driveway each day, or hear the voice of her father's new girlfriend in her mother's kitchen. And I told her I'd come to visit. I told her to stay in touch, but you know how those things go. It is rare when you turn down the hall at school and come face to face with a student from the past, so much older and so much the same all at once. They move on, as they should, and leave their teachers behind.

I'm grateful for these fragments of Shaina preserved in my notebook. I have a few pieces of her writing to read to new students who might be afraid to speak of what they experienced or what they fear. I'll miss this girl. Shaina's work will remind me that students can be stuck on one topic all semester because it is so big that it blocks out everything else—and still learn all the moves in different genres. And still say when all is done, as Shaina wrote in her final portfolio evaluation, "I want to add more writing pieces to my final project on my mom. Add more good memories to the piece along with more pics."

Shaina says after all that writing, *I want to write more.*

That's *my* final evaluation: if I've brought a student to a place where writing answers something inside and brings solace to a wound so deep, I've done my work.

I think I'll sleep well tonight.

 Shaina's place narrative "14 Black Birch Lane" is on the DVD.

CHAPTER THIRTEEN
In the End, What Writing Is For . . .

Your absence has gone through me like thread through a needle.
Everything I do is stitched with its color.

—W. S. MERWIN

We began class in silence that day. Marianna was sniffling behind a tissue while the others looked like they were just wobbling to a stand after a punch. Every one of my students knew well what had happened and there were stories to share—*How did you hear? Where were you?*

Sophie told of an energy in their dance performance that night that no one could explain, but they were "on" and filled with joy, imagining Mr. Millen out in the audience watching as he did every spring. Instead the news of his death passed from student to student, was whispered across the rows and text-messaged from one end of the auditorium to the other while the girls tapped and twirled on stage.

No, it can't be.

OMG.

I just saw him.

We talked in the hall—what—two hours ago?

Not Mr. Millen. He was so alive with joyful energy and purpose, still joking in the halls with students, still marking kids tardy and keeping them after school, still volunteering for everything, not one of those almost-retired teachers that slink from classroom to car, barely noticing the kids who pass by. Not Mr. Millen. This football season had been uninspiring and everyone looked to the next, but not without the head coach of the last twenty-eight years. Sons of fathers who had played for Coach Millen waited to take the field in September. How could he not be there?

And as spring rounded the corner and burst into a brilliant May that Monday, my students sat before me waiting. How would we write of this? The plans for research remained in my office, and as we talked and cried and tried to get through that first hour of school, I passed out our writer's notebooks. I explained our Memory Book project that would be delivered to his family. "Just moments," I said, "like we've written all year. Capture a few that show what Mr. Millen meant to you, so that his wife and daughter can see how much we loved him." And I doodled in the margin of my notebook to stop the tears forming behind my eyes again. I wouldn't be writing this with my class, not while I could still hear his voice in the halls, still see his smile and white shirt and tie: my friend, my mentor, my colleague. Words couldn't even come close, but they were all we had.

Johnny wrote of gratitude and regret—appreciation for being chosen as a varsity captain that fall, but never telling Mr. Millen how much it meant to him. I read over his back as he sat, head in hands, searching for words. I squeezed his shoulder, but I couldn't comfort him: His coach was gone.

Grant and Kim wrote of the YMCA program Youth and Government and their trips to Concord, how his passion for history and civic life had inspired them to reach higher each year, campaigning to lead a state delegation of their peers. These seniors had shared their college plans and expected to be returning during vacations to visit him in his cramped office on the third floor as they'd seen former students do for years. This death brought a premature close to four years of high school; Mr. Millen *was* Kennett—for thirty years—and what would we be without him?

Memorials appeared in the halls. A bulletin board in the main lobby soon held photos and football jerseys. Someone cut out small squares of colored paper and left pens so students could add a personal message. On the school's front lawn cardboard signs curled and weathered, "R.I.P. Mr. Millen," "Fly Like an Eagle," and everywhere there was silence—a hush over passing time between classes, an eerie lunchroom, teachers huddled near doorways talking in whispers. Flowers arrived from schools nearby and those across the state, "We share in your loss of a great man." Gary Millen was fifty-three years old and disappeared without warning—a heart attack he couldn't recover from one Friday afternoon just home from school. And all we had were words, a few pictures, the spirit of a man we adored and were determined to record.

By Tuesday former students began arriving home from college for the memorial service, stopping by to share their sadness and walk our quiet halls. Kyle met me at my office door in his military uniform with a few handwritten notes in one hand. "Mrs. Kittle, can you help me with this? I want to speak at the service or write it and leave it for the family and I thought you could help me with punctuation and stuff,"

Writing Matters.

Of the twenty speakers asked to address a crowd estimated at 1,500 that day, each labored over words. I watched a former football captain and class president, pages in hand, scribbling and rereading, as our seniors passed out programs and filled the rows of seats in our gymnasium. Each speaker shared moments of Gary's life, from high school and college days to raising children, early teaching, and glimpses of glory and heartbreak on the football field. We laughed and wept and squeezed hands nearby. It was a celebration almost worthy of him.

What is writing for? What do we teach and why? It can't only be for next year—or college—or the April test. Sometimes it is for now: a path through dark days. We teach life writing, not school writing, life writing in all its complexities: the tools for the tasks we can't anticipate. It is about this day—this lesson—what students can reach for that will matter—for the lives stretched out before them peppered with joy and loss.

What power—what importance—lies in the blank lines of an open notebook.

Go and fill yours.

Then share.

Alexie, Sherman. 1993. *The Lone Ranger and Tonto Fistfight in Heaven.* New York: Grove Press.

Anderson, Carl. 2000. *How's It Going?: A Practical Guide to Conferring with Student Writers.* Portsmouth, NH: Heinemann.

Atwell, Nancie. 1998. *Inthe Middle: New Understandings About Writing, Reading, and Learning,* Second Edition. Portsmouth, NH: Heinemann.

————. 2002. *Lessons That Change Writers.* Portsmouth, NH: Heinemann.

————. 2007. *The Reading Zone: How to Help Kids Become Skilled, Passionate, Habitual, Critical Readers.* New York: Scholastic Teaching Resources.

Bales, David, and Ted Orland. 2001. *Art & Fear: Observations of the Perils (and Rewards) of Artmaking.* Santa Barbara, CA: Image Continuum Press.

Bomer, Randy. 1995. *Time for Meaning.* Portsmouth, NH: Heinemann.

Brownstein, Michael, Joe DiMartino, and Sherri Miles. 2007. *Principal's Research Review,* National Association of Secondary School Principals, Vol. 2, Issue 3. May.

Burke, Jim. 2007. *Tools & Texts for 50 Essential Lessons.* Portsmouth, NH: Firsthand.

Calkins, Lucy with Shelley Harwayne. 1991. *Living Between the Lines.* Portsmouth, NH: Heinemann.

————. 2003. *Units of Study for Teaching Writing Grades K–2: The Conferring Handbook.* Portsmouth, NH: Firsthand.

————. 2006. *Units of Study for Teaching Writing Grades 3–5: A Guide to the Writing Workshop.* Portsmouth, NH: Firsthand.

Clark, Roy Peter. 2006. *Writing Tools: Fifty Essential Strategies for Every Writer.* Boston: Little, Brown and Co..

College Entrance and Examination Board. 2003. *The Neglected "R": The Need for a Writing Revolution.* Found online at: http://www.writingcommission.org/prod_downloads/writingcom/neglectedr.pdf.

Collins, Billy. 2001. "Days." In *Sailing Alone Around the Room: New and Selected Poems*. New York: Random House.

Culham, Ruth. 2003. *6 + 1 Traits of Writing: the Complete Guide*. New York: Scholastic Teaching Resources.

Deci, E. L., and R. M. Ryan. 1995. "Human Autonomy: The Basis for True Self-esteem." In M. Kernis (Ed.), *Efficacy, Agency, and Self-esteem* (pp. 31–49). New York: Plenum.

Edwards, Kim. 2006. *The Memory Keeper's Daughter*. New York: Penguin.

Elbow, Peter, and Pat Belanoff. 2000. *A Community of Writers: A Workshop Course in Writing*. Boston: McGraw-Hill.

Ernst, Karen. 1997. *A Teacher's Sketch Journal: Observations on Learning and Teaching*. Portsmouth, NH: Heinemann.

Essley, Roger. 2005. "The Odd Fish Story." *Voices from the Middle*, Vol. 12, No. 4, Urbana, IL: National Council of Teachers of English.

Fletcher, Ralph. 1993. *What a Writer Needs*. Portsmouth, NH: Heinemann, 1993.

——————. 1996. *Breathing In, Breathing Out: Keeping a Writer's Notebook*. Portsmouth, NH: Heinemann.

——————. 2006. *Boy Writers: Reclaiming Their Voices*. Portland, ME: Stenhouse.

Fried, Robert L. 1995. *The Passionate Teacher: A Practical Guide*. Boston: Beacon Press.

Graham, Steve, and Dolores Perin. 2006. Alliance for Excellent Education. *Writing Next: Effective Strategies to Improve Writing of Adolescents in Middle and High School*. New York: Carnegie Corporation of New York.

Graves, Donald H. 1983. *Writing: Teachers and Children at Work*. Portsmouth, NH: Heinemann.

Graves, Donald H., and Penny Kittle. 2005. *Inside Writing: How to Teach the Details of Craft*. Portsmouth, NH: Heinemann.

Heard, Georgia. 1995. *Awakening the Heart*. Portsmouth, NH: Heinemann.

Houston, Pam. 1999. *A Little More About Me*. New York: Washington Square Press.

Jago, Carol. 2002. *Cohesive Writing: Why Concept Is Not Enough*. Portsmouth, NH: Heinemann.

——————. 2005. *Papers, Papers, Papers: An English Teacher's Survival Guide*. Portsmouth, NH: Heinemann.

Jerome, John. 1992. *The Writing Trade: A Year in the Life*. New York: Viking Penguin.

Kittle, Penny. 2001. "Writing Giants, Columbine, and the Queen of Route 16." *Voices from the Middle*, Vol. 9, No. 1.

——————. 2003. *Public Teaching: one kid at a time*. Portsmouth, NH: Heinemann.

——————. 2005. *The Greatest Catch: a life in teaching*. Portsmouth, NH: Heinemann.

Lamott, Anne. 1994. *Bird by Bird: Some Instructions on Writing and Life*. New York: Random House.

Lane, Barry. 1992. *After the End: Teaching and Learning Creative Revision*. Portsmouth, NH: Heinemann.

Lyon, George Ella. 1999. *Where I'm From: Where Poems Come From*. Spring, TX: Absey & Co.

Mahoney, Jim. 2002. *Power and Portfolios: Best Practices for High School Classrooms*. Portsmouth, NH: Heinemann.

Meier, Deborah. 2002. *The Power of Their Ideas: Lessons for America from a Small School in Harlem*. Boston: Beacon Press.

Moyers, Bill. 1995. *The Language of Life: A Festival of Poets*. New York: Broadway Books.

Murray, Donald M. 1982. *Learning by Teaching: Selected Articles on Writing and Teaching*. Portsmouth, NH: Heinemann.

——————. 2004. *A Writer Teaches Writing Revised Second Edition*. Boston: Heinle.

——————. 2006. "Now and Then." *The Boston Globe*, Feb. 14.

Newkirk, Thomas. 1994. "A View from the Mountains: A Morning with Donald Graves." In *Workshop 5: The Writing Process Revisited*. Portsmouth, NH: Heinemann.

——————. 2005. "Boys and Literacy." Durham, NH :The University of New Hampshire Summer Institute.

Pilkey, Dav. 1999. *The Paperboy*. New York: Orchard Paperbacks.

Pirie, Bruce. 1997. *Reshaping High School English*. Urbana, IL: National Council of Teachers of English.

Probst, Robert E. 1987. *Response and Analysis: Teaching Literature in Junior and Senior High School*. Portsmouth, NH: Boynton-Cook.

Proulx, Annie. 1999. *Close Range: Wyoming Stories*. New York: Scribner.

Ray, Katie Wood with Lisa B. Cleaveland. 1999. *Wondrous Words: Writers and Writing in the Elementary Classroom*. Urbana, IL: National Council of Teachers of English.

——————. 2004. *About the Authors: Writing Workshop with Our Youngest Writers*. Portsmouth, NH: Heinemann.

——————. 2006. *Units of Study: A Framework for Planning Units of Study in the Writing Workshop*. Portsmouth, NH: Heinemann.

Rief, Linda. 1992. *Seeking Diversity: Language Arts with Adolescents*. Portsmouth, NH: Heinemann.

——————. 2003. *100 Quickwrites*. New York: Scholastic.

Robinson, Marilyn. 2006. *Gilead*. New York: Picador.

Romano, Tom. 1995. *Writing with Passion: Life Stories, Multiple Genres.* Portsmouth, NH: Boynton/Cook.

—————. 2000. *Blending Genre, Alternating Style: Writing Multigenre Papers.* Portsmouth, NH: Boynton/Cook.

—————. 2004. *Crafting Authentic Voice.* Portsmouth, NH: Heinemann.

—————. 2008. *Zigzag: Essays on Teaching and Learning.* Portsmouth, NH: Heinemann.

Rule, Rebecca, and Wheeler, Susan. 2000. *True Stories: Guides for Writing from Your Life.* Portsmouth, NH: Heinemann.

Rylant, Cynthia, and Lauren Stringer. 2001. *Scarecrow.* New York: Voyager Books.

Spandel, Vicki. 2005. *The Nine Rights of Every Writer: A Guide for Teachers.* Portsmouth, NH: Heinemann.

Stafford, Kim. 2003. *The Muses Among Us: Eloquent Listening and Other Pleasures of the Writer's Craft.* Athens, GA: University of Georgia Press.

Truss, Lynne. 2006. *Eats, Shoots and Leaves: The Zero Tolerance Approach to Punctuation.* New York: Gotham.

Wilson, Mariah. 2006. *Rethinking Rubrics in Writing Assessment.* Portsmouth, NH: Heinemann.

Zinsser, William. 1998. *Inventing the Truth: The Art and Craft of Memoir.* New York: Houghton-Miffflin Co., Mariner Books.